PENN & TELLER'S CRUEL TRICKS *for* DEAR FRIENDS

PENN & TELLER'S CRUEL TRICKS *for* DEAR FRIENDS

THE RED LETTER EDITION

by

PENN JILLETTE AND TELLER

VILLARD BOOKS / NEW YORK / 1989

NOTE: This book contains three mistakes for Paul MacCready.

Grateful acknowledgment is made to Edwin H. Morris & Company for permission
to reprint lyrics from "You've Been Taking Lessons in Love (from Somebody New)"
by Winston Tharp and Grady Watts. Copyright 1935 by Edwin H. Morris & Company,
a division of MPL Communications, Inc. Copyright renewed 1963 by Edwin H. Morris & Company,
a division of MPL Communications, Inc. International Copyright secured.
All Rights Reserved. Used by permission.

Library of Congress Cataloging-in-Publication Data

Jillette.
Penn and teller's cruel tricks for dear friends.

1. Tricks.   I. Teller.   II. Title.
GV1547.P42   1989   793.8   88-40148
ISBN 0-394-75351-8

Manufactured in the United States of America

9 8 7 6 5 4 3 2

First Edition

Design by Robert Bull Design

CONTENTS

PENN & TELLER'S CRUEL TRICKS

for

DEAR FRIENDS

THE NO-WORK, HIGH-YIELD, ALL-ELECTRONIC COMPUTERIZED CARD TRICK

We owe you something for buying this book. You've put your hard-earned cash into our pocket, and we think you deserve a real return on your investment, something *more* than your money's worth: the chance to *make a profit.*

Write this phone number down, and carry it with you at all times:

212-572-6016

This vital piece of information is your secret key to winning big in casual bets. Guard it carefully. Only people who have paid the price of this book deserve to be able to take advantage of it.

3

This telephone number is hooked into a computer system which enables the tones of your Touch-Tone telephone to control a digitally recorded random-access compact disk.* This permits you to do the ultimate card trick, in which virtually all the work of the magician is done with an electronic off-on flow-chart. To be sure you understand how to do the trick, do a dry run (without betting) on a trusted friend.

You will need:

1. A standard deck of fifty-two playing cards.
2. A partner.
3. A Touch-Tone telephone.

Procedure:

1. Remove the jokers and all instructional or advertising cards.
2. Shuffle the cards thoroughly, and cut the deck once.
3. Begin to deal the cards one at a time onto a table. Instruct your partner to say "Stop!" at any time.
4. Without looking at it, hand your partner the last card dealt.
5. Ask your partner to turn his/her back and to look at the card in private.
6. While your partner is turned away, count the number of cards that you dealt on the table. Have that number ready *before* you move on to Step 7. In Step 7, you will be asked to enter this number by pressing the numbered keyboard on your Touch-Tone telephone.
7. Call the Penn & Teller computer at: 212-572-6016.

Successful? Now, what about the profit we mentioned?

Next time set this up as a bet. Follow the procedure to Step 4. Ask your "partner" whether there is any way at all you could possibly know the card. He will, of course, say no. Act smug. Get on his or her nerves. Bet twenty bucks that you can identify the card. If the sucker hesitates, cast aspersions on his or her family or private life. Rage adds spice to a bet like this, and

* Sorry, this won't work with rotary-dialed phones.

makes your success a more meaningful triumph. When the bet has been confirmed (it is best to have the money held by an impartial third party), continue from Step 5 and finish the trick.

Collect what you deserve.

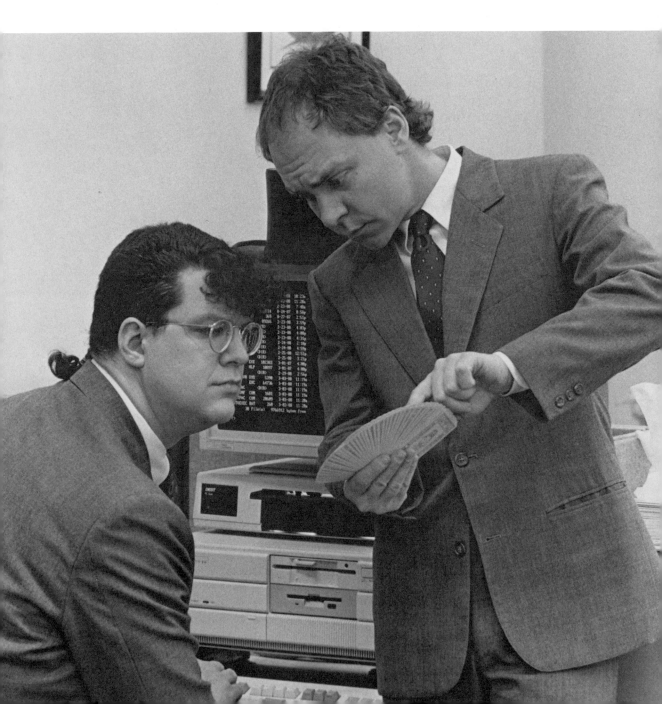

THE BEST MAGIC TRICK I EVER SAW

by

PENN JILLETTE

I've only been to one Society of American Magicians convention. We performed at the opening-night show of the 1978 get-together in New York, and we sucked. But we had a suite at the Waldorf Astoria for a few days and our meals were free, so we decided to have fun. The morning after our show, Teller decided to have fun by staying in his room asleep. I was up at ten o'clock and looking for magical entertainment.

I walked into the Waldorf ballroom with my diet-cola breakfast and joined the audience for the Junior Magic Competition. The crowd was all middle-aged men talking about monofilament, coin shells, and thumb tips. The feeling was an ungodly marriage of a Midwestern grain and feed meeting and a *Star Trek* convention. These men performed magic exclusively for captive nephews.

On stage was a kid about sixteen and his assistant, a girl about fifteen. It had to be his sister; no one who does magic in high school has ever gotten a girlfriend. They were both blond and their costumes fit badly. There was an up side to the ill-fitting clothes and the up side was Sis. I guess Mom had made their costumes a while ago and they had outgrown them. On her, the bad fit was very attractive. While my fellow audience members were talking to each other and munching on doughnuts, I was watching a girl become a woman under sequins.

Her brother had learned that timing to music was critical to a magic act. He was bouncing self-consciously to a *Star Wars* disco tape that he had edited. He was doing a dove routine and dancing while his sister handed him props and went through puberty. His act, at first, was nothing special, little cages painted like pagodas that vanished doves, piles of silk handkerchiefs that produced doves, a scared-shitless smile, and that constant little bounce to the music. Music was very important to this kid.

6

It was right after he had produced a dove out of a popped balloon that he went into The Best Magic Trick I Ever Saw. It was a Dove Pan. A lot of magicians have accused Penn & Teller of giving away secrets. See if you can figure out this one by yourself.

continued on p. 10

Where could you hide a dove in this apparatus?

PENN & TELLER GET KILLED By PENN Jillette and Teller September 27, 1987 OPEN ON: BLACK SCREEN. DEAD SILENT. MAIN TITLES start to flash against the black as we hear The HARSH SCRAPING SOUND of a Lavaliere microphone being clipped in place. We hear VOICES VERY LOUD with close-microphone presence. CONTROL-ROOM VOICE Sixty seconds. TECHNICIAN'S VOICE (urgently) Try it again! PENN'S VOICE One. Two. Three. Four. TECHNICIAN'S VOICE Keep going! PENN'S VOICE (reciting, very rapidly) "Johnny's in the basement, Mixing up the medicine. I'm on the pavement, Thinking 'bout the government. Man in a..." TECHNICIAN'S VOICE (interrupting sharply) That's a go! Get in place! PENN'S VOICE Aren't you going to tape up the wire? TECHNICIAN'S VOICE There's not much time. Get up there first! PENN'S VOICE How much time is "not much time"? TECHNICIAN'S VOICE Forty seconds! Get the hell up there! PENN'S VOICE You just want my head to explode. Tape the goddam wire now. LOUD CRACKLING AND SCRATCHING. PENN'S VOICE The coat okay? WOMAN'S VOICE (DISTANT) It's done! CONTROL-ROOM VOICE Thirty seconds. PENN'S VOICE You got that thing taped out of sight or what? TECHNICIAN'S VOICE It's done! Get up there, you moron! PENN'S VOICE Yeah, I got your "moron"... INTERIOR – TELEVISION STUDIO – LIVE TELEVISION BROADCAST SOUNDS OF STUDIO AUDIENCE MURMURING and CREW PREPARING during the last few seconds of the commercial break on a weekly comedy-variety show, WEEKEND LIVE. PENN's head, upside down, drops into the picture from above. He has a long forelock of hair which is hanging straight down. WOMAN (O.S.) Let me get that! It's sticking straight up. A WOMAN'S HAND reaches in, puts a piece of toupee tape on PENN's forehead, and presses the hair up against it. WOMAN (O.S.) There you go! PENN Thank you. Make sure Teller's okay. PAN OVER to TELLER's inverted face. It looks a bit swollen and there's a red blotch on his forehead. The WOMAN'S HAND reaches in with a makeup sponge. WOMAN (O.S.) Teller! TELLER turns quickly towards the WOMAN'S HAND and gets the sponge in his eye. He recoils, and, in doing so, starts to swing uncontrollably. WOMAN (O.S.) Sorry! Here, let me... PULL BACK TO REVEAL PENN and TELLER, hooked by inversion boots to a horizontal pipe. Their clothing is all attached in place, so that nothing looks disheveled or reflects the fact that they are upside down. At their waist level is a demonstration counter, also inverted, with an inverted sign, PENN & TELLER, tacked to the front. The WOMAN, A MAKEUP ARTIST, is wiping TELLER's eye with a tissue while a STAGEHAND steadies him. PENN sees TELLER's discomfort. PENN (snidely, to TELLER) "What, and get out of show business?" FLOOR DIRECTOR (O.S.) Fifteen seconds. Quiet, please! The STUDIO AUDIENCE quiets. PENN (suddenly panicked) There's no cup! Where's the cup? PROP PERSON hands PENN a styrofoam cup. PENN places it on the table in front of him. Even though it is upside down, it does not fall. FLOOR DIRECTOR (O.S.) Okay, Bob. Ten seconds. Nine. Eight. TELLER's feet in their inversion boots edge an inch closer to PENN. STAGE MANAGER (O.S.) Seven. Six. PENN's hand gropes under the demonstration counter and feels a wrench, tied to a string. STAGE MANAGER (O.S.) Five. During the ensuing five seconds of silence, we PAN DOWN to a TV MONITOR. We come in close on it until it fills the screen. We see the logo of a show, WEEKEND LIVE, and simultaneously hear the AUDIENCE BURST INTO APPLAUSE, and the BAND kick in with the show's THEME MUSIC. The logo wipes away and we see BOB, the show's host. There is a ripple of laughter from the STUDIO AUDIENCE. BOB, THE HOST Okay. We're back. You hear a little bit of laughter in the studio...because my next guests are comedians PENN and Teller. BOB starts a round of applause. The MONITOR shot cuts to PENN and TELLER. The picture has been electronically inverted, however, so that they appear to be standing upright behind a counter. PENN addresses the home viewer. PENN Good evening. My name is Penn Jillette and this is my partner Teller. We'd like to be serious for a moment, and say that we think being funny is not enough. Entertainers should try to have some real skills. The real skill we've chosen is magic. We will be performing the best magic you've ever seen, so amazing that we're afraid you may think it's some sort of hi-tech electronic trick. We see the STUDIO AUDIENCE watching PENN and TELLER hanging upside down. VARIOUS AUDIENCE MEMBERS point to the MONITOR and laugh as they realize that a scam is about to be perpetrated on the home viewer. Some people are craning their necks to see what the live action on stage looks like upside down. Again, we watch PENN and TELLER in the MONITOR. PENN So, to prove to you that you at home will be seeing exactly what the audience here in the studio is seeing, I'll be asking the studio audience, "Are we live?"And, if there are no camera edits, blue screen, or special video effects, I'll ask the audience to answer "Yeah!" Let's try it once.(to STUDIO AUDIENCE) Everything they're seeing at home is what's really happening in the studio. Right? Are we live? STUDIO AUDIENCE (O.S.) (with gusto) Yeah! The STUDIO AUDIENCE LAUGHS. We continue to watch PENN and TELLER on the MONITOR. They appear to be right side up. PENN My partner Teller in his spare time is the world's greatest card magician. Teller's amazing Rising Card! On the MONITOR we see TELLER holding a pack of cards. One card seems to jump up into his waiting hand. Along with the studio audience we are aware of the fact that the picture is upside down, and that he's just dropping the card. The STUDIO AUDIENCE LAUGHS, then APPLAUDS. PENN And now, Teller's Rising Cards! TELLER releases the cards rapidly one after the other, and they float "up" into his waiting hand. MORE APPLAUSE. PENN Are we live? STUDIO AUDIENCE Yeah! Once again we see the STUDIO AUDIENCE laughing and pointing out to each other the difference between the way the action looks on the studio MONITORS (where it looks amazing) and on stage (where it looks silly). Conspicuously seated in the studio audience is PENN and TELLER's manager (and PENN's girlfriend) CARLOTTA. She is enjoying the STUDIO AUDIENCE's reaction. INTERIOR – TV ROOM IN A FRATERNITY HOUSE – CONTINUOUS ACTION A GROUP OF FRAT BOYS, surrounded by junk food and soft drinks, is gathered in front of the TV set, watching the show. We watch with them. PENN (ON TV) Now watch closely. See if you can see any strings or wires, as I perform The Amazing Bouncing Muffin. On TV we see PENN takes out a blueberry muffin and throw it at the table top. It appears to bounce like a rubber ball. PENN (ON TV) Bounces like rubber and tastes like Mom used to make. PENN takes a bite out of the muffin. PENN (ON TV) (his mouth full) Are we live? STUDIO AUDIENCE (HEARD ON TV) Yeah! FRAT BOY #1 So how are they doing this one, smartass? On TV we see PENN reach to the counter, pick up his styrofoam cup and apparently sip water from it, and replaces it. We hear a BIG LAUGH from the STUDIO AUDIENCE. FRAT BOY #2 (O.S.) What's everyone laughing at? FRAT BOY #3 Look at the way it's being shot. Tight twoshots and closeups. Nothing below the counter. They're just not wearing pants. That's all. That keeps the studio audience laughing. And they're just using a jet fan to blow the stuff up in the air. PENN (ON TV) Okay! And now Teller's Amazing Bouncing Bagel... INTERIOR – TELEVISION STUDIO – CONTINUOUS ACTION We watch with the STUDIO AUDIENCE as TELLER throws a bagel against the counter surface and then catches it before it has a chance to fall to the floor. In the MONITORS there is the illusion that the bagel is bouncing. STUDIO AUDIENCE applauds and laughs. PENN (ON STAGE) And now for some sleight of hand. Would you bring the camera in close on this one? We watch with the STUDIO AUDIENCE as TELLER places a small billiard ball in his fist. On the MONITORS, we see that the CAMERA HAS ZOOMED IN for a close-up, so close that the edge of TELLER's fist just touches the frame of the shot. On stage, we see what the audience at home cannot see: that TELLER is dropping the ball to a stagehand crouched below. The STUDIO AUDIENCE laughs. In the MONITOR we see TELLER making a rubbing gesture with his fist and then opening his fingers. On the MONITOR it looks as though the ball has vanished. The STUDIO AUDIENCE, in on the scam, LAUGHS. PENN Now you see it. Now you don't. The STUDIO AUDIENCE applauds. INTERIOR – THE SAME FRAT HOUSE – CONTINUOUS ACTION The BOYS are still watching the show. FRAT BOY #1 Oh, yeah. One of those new jet fans that makes everything invisible. PENN (ON TV) No camera edits, no blue screen, no video animation. Just good old fashioned sleight of hand done live here in the studio. Are we live? STUDIO AUDIENCE (HEARD ON TV) Yeah! PENN (ON TV) No magic show would be complete without the levitation of a beautiful young woman. We unfortunately could not afford a beautiful young woman, but we do have our beautiful magician's assistant, Rainbow Brite! ON TV we watch as TELLER brings out a large doll dressed in rainbow colors. FRAT BOY #2 Hey look, Brian! That's your girlfriend from back home. I always knew her fashionable clothing would get her somewhere. She's on TV. PENN (ON TV) Watch closely: you're not going to believe your eyes. How does she do it? TELLER holds the doll by the hand and releases the body. The body seems to float. TELLER twirls the doll, and the BOYS can see up her dress. FRAT BOY #1 (BRIAN)(O.S.) Jeez! I never got her dress up that far. Showbiz has turned even Debbie into a slut. INTERIOR – TELEVISION STUDIO – CONTINUOUS ACTION We watch with the STUDIO AUDIENCE. TELLER is dangling the doll by one arm, but in the MONITOR, of course, she seems to float like a helium balloon. The STUDIO AUDIENCE LAUGHS, then APPLAUDS. PENN Are we live? STUDIO AUDIENCE (O.S.) Yeah! PENN Thank you Ms. Brite. We'll call you. In the MONITOR we can see TELLER stand the doll upright, hold a hoop over her head, and release the doll. She rises straight through the hoop and out of frame. The STUDIO AUDIENCE can see the doll hit the floor head first. They LAUGH and APPLAUD. INTERIOR – THE SAME FRAT HOUSE – CONTINUOUS ACTION We continue to watch TV with the BOYS. ON TV PENN picks up the pack of cards, and starts releasing them one by one. They seem to rise up into the air and fly away. TELLER pulls out the muffin and bagel, releases them, and they disappear off the top of the screen. FRAT BOY #2 (O.S.) Look at these guys! PENN (ON TV) My name is Penn Jillette, and this is my partner, Teller. We are Penn & Teller, comedians, and the best magicians in the world. Are we live? STUDIO AUDIENCE (O.S. ON TV) Yeah! ON TV PENN pulls out a wrench on a string tacked to the counter. The wrench seems to float like a helium balloon. But now the TELEVISION CAMERA pulls away, and we can see clearly in the MONITOR that PENN and TELLER's feet are hooked onto the bar. We now see the STUDIO AUDIENCE, upside down in the top of the picture. PENN (ON TV) Thank you. Good night! By this time the full stage picture is visible on the TV. Slowly and deliberately the video image rotates 180 degrees, so that a home viewer can now see what the STUDIO AUDIENCE could see all along, the fact that all the action was upside down. FRAT BOY #1 (BRIAN) pokes his face in next to the TV, and points to the screen with mock seriousness. FRAT BOY #1 (BRIAN) Okay, Paul. Now let me get this straight. The jet fans that make things invisible have now become invisible. And they're now above Penn and Teller, held in place by a skyhook? The other FRAT BOYS laugh derisively. FRAT BOY #3 (PAUL)(O.S.) Fuck you! ON TV we see PENN and TELLER unhook their feet, land on the stage and take a bow, breathing hard, with the blood pulsing in their temples. INTERIOR – TELEVISION STUDIO – CONTINUOUS BOB, THE HOST walks over to join PENN and TELLER. BOB, THE HOST (applauding) Penn and Teller! That was something! You guys look just awful. PENN And that's an ugly tie. BOB, THE HOST I'm sorry, I meant you look like you were awfully uncomfortable. You were up there a lot longer than the people at home knew. PENN We hate it, but it's our job. BOB, THE HOST Well. Now that you're right side up, let's go over here and have a seat. BOB, THE HOST, leads them to the interview set. BOB, THE HOST How about you, Teller? Were you uncomfortable? TELLER raises his fists in front of his eyes. Twin squirts of blood spurt out. BOB, THE HOST Is he okay? PENN Who cares? TELLER puts the two squeeze-bulbs that were in his fists down on BOB, THE HOST's desk. BOB, THE HOST You have these business suits and you look like fairly normal guys... BOB looks at TELLER cleaning up the blood. BOB, THE HOST ...but I've go a couple of questions I have to ask you. First of all, Penn, I won't even ask you about the hair. But what's with the one red fingernail? PENN's left ring finger is beautifully manicured red. PENN It means I shot a man for asking personal questions. BOB, THE HOST Okay. He turns to TELLER picks up his left hand and examines his ring finger nail. It is not painted. He feels safe asking TELLER questions. BOB, THE HOST So, why don't you ever talk? TELLER smiles and says nothing. BOB realizes he's hit a dead end. He consults his notes. BOB, THE HOST You have been involved lately in a much more serious issue. You've said publicly that psychic surgeons and faith healers are all phony. PENN First of all: we don't believe in anything. It just so happens that lately the psychic surgery racket has been getting out of hand. It also happens that it is very easy to explain how these so-called "healers" do their tricks. Save those little plastic squeeze-bulbs and next time we're on, we'll show you how to pull tumors out of your band leader's stomach. BOB, THE HOST Is that okay with you, Steve? The TV camera shows STEVE, THE BAND LEADER. He's smiling. STEVE, THE BAND LEADER That's swingin' with me, Bob. You know I love these Penn & Teller cats. BOB, THE HOST Okay, so you hang upside down for a living. And as a hobby you chase around those that you think are charlatans... PENN Oh, we know they're charlatans. BOB, THE HOST Okay, so you chase charlatans. What kind of personal life do you two have? I somehow don't picture Teller enrolled in an aerobics class. What do you guys do for fun? PENN We don't have fun. We just work. BOB, THE HOST That's awful! You've got to find something to put some pizzazz in your personal life. PENN You know what I'd like? You know what would be great? I wish...somebody were trying to kill me. The FLOOR DIRECTOR looks up from his clipboard. He thinks PENN is a jerk. CARLOTTA, PENN's girlfriend in the audience shakes her head and laughs. PENN Wouldn't that be great? It would give focus to your life? Excitement! You'd be like James Bond or something, all that secret agent stuff: (in a "Secret agent" voice) "I'd love to go see that new French film tonight, Dear. But, someone is trying to kill me. And I shouldn't really do the dishes because there's that window over the sink and there could be snipers." TELLER is listening with intense interest. PENN All I'm saying is, I wish someone were trying to kill me so I wouldn't sweat the small stuff... PENN That'd be great. I wish somebody were trying to kill me. TELLER whips out a switchblade, reaches over and slits PENN's throat. Blood pours out and splatters BOB. BOB, THE HOST Geez. Next time you guys come on, I'm wearing an apron. We'll break for a commercial now. PENN is still slumped down in his seat, gurgling. TELLER is breathing hard, and wiping the blade of the knife with his hanky. BOB, THE HOST But, Penn, sit up and let them know you're okay. PENN (big showbizzy grin) Oh, just kidding! And don't forget, we'll be at one of Trump's Casinos in Atlantic City for two weeks starting this Friday. Thanks, Bob. PENN and TELLER, blood all over their hands, shake hands with BOB, THE HOST, who does the appropriate "takes", shakes his head... BOB, THE HOST (starting the applause) Penn and Teller! Thank you, guys. We'll be back after this with a man who's teaching Man's Best Friend to run computers. EXTERIOR – AIRPORT

HEAT

The Fire Triangle
Oxygen + Heat + Fuel = Fire

The lid looks like nothing on this planet. Every audience member knows, the second the dove appears, where it came from. But every *magician* knows that the dove is sitting tortured in the lid before the trick even happens. This is the crux of The Best Magic Trick I Ever Saw. The magicians saw the lid out of the corner of their eyes and knew a dove was hiding.

To make the dove appear, the magician needs some motive for slamming a lid down on an empty pan. This motive has always been the breaking of the fire triangle. The magician squirts a little lighter fluid into the pan, touches a match to it, and acts surprised by the fire. (Only a magician could be surprised when a petroleum product, touched with a match, starts to burn, and only a magician, who just seconds ago didn't know that fuel + sufficient heat

10

The Dove Triangle
Load Compartment + Pan + Fire = Dove

+ oxygen = fire, would now pretend to know that fire minus oxygen goes out.) With his newfound knowledge, he slams the lid down, cutting off the oxygen and putting out the fire he intentionally started just moments ago. To convince the viewer that these are normal human actions is the acting job of the magician performing the Dove Pan.

The kid had mistimed his music. Sis handed him the Ronson lighter fluid, its yellow-and-blue container disguised in a little glitter sleeve made out of the same material as Sis's stage bra, and he began squirting the can to the disco beat into the bottom of the dove pan. BOM BUM BABABA BOM BUM BABABA BOM BUM BA BA BA BAAAAAA. But then it went again BOM BUM BABABA BOM BUM BABABA BOM BUM BA BA BA BAAAAAA. Well, he kept swaying back and forth and his sister kept wiggling back and forth and he kept squirting and squirting in rhythm. And even though he was having to go three times as long as he was supposed to, with every BOM BUM BABABA BOM BUM BABABA BOM BUM BA BA BA BAAAAAA he kept squirting. He squirted on every beat and his sister wiggled on every beat and they had damn nearly filled the bottom of the dove pan with the highly volatile liquid. Finally, the music was in the right place and our hero, the kid that did The Best Magic Trick I Ever Saw, lit the match, and as I screamed in slow motion "NO!" he touched the match to the fluid and a very big fire started. For a moment he did the expression that he had rehearsed, but the mock surprise melted off his face in the heat and turned into a real goddam fire-in-a-crowded-theater panic! He didn't know what the hell to do. But his sister, functioning on auto-pilot, handed him the lid. BOM BUM BABABA BOM BUM BABABA BOM BUM BA BA BA BAAAAAA. As he put the lid on the fire the audience of magicians, awakened by the fire, joined me in yelling, "The DOVE! The DOVE! SAVE THE DOVE!"

He slammed the lid. The lighter fluid sloshed out and spilled, burning, all over his little fringe prop table. BOM BUM BABABA BOM BUM BABABA BOM BUM BA BA BA BAAAAAA, as the inferno grew. There was a burning ring of fire on stage with a dove hiding in the middle of it. The audience, led by yours truly, was still screaming, "The DOVE! THE DOVE! SAVE THE DOVE!" He looked at the audience, looked at the flaming table, and bravely reached in. Ouch! He drew back. It was too hot. As we hit our sixth BOM BUM BABABA BOM BUM BABABA BOM BUM BA BA BA BAAAAAA the flames had died down. He tried to reach in again, but the metal of the dove pan was still too hot. He pulled his tux sleeve down over his hand and gingerly pulled the lid off the pan.

12

There was a moment of silence (I'm sure BOM BUM BABABA BOM BUM BABABA BOM BUM BA BA BA BAAAAAA was still dragging on but I remember it as silence) and, ever so slowly, a little bird poked its head over the edge of the pan. It looked with dazed but victorious eyes at the audience. BOM BUM BABABA BOM BUM—THE FIREPROOF DOVE! The dove shook its head and fluttered its wings, our feathered friend's reaction to smoke inhalation. It would have looked like death throes except for the bird's clear, determined eyes. The dove took all its strength, hopped up on the edge of the pan, shook its head violently, and pulled itself together to accept, graciously, the thunderous applause. It was deafening. I was on my feet. It was The Best Magic Trick I Ever Saw.

The dove tumbled onto the floor and staggered around, but I enjoyed it because Sis, in her too-small bra top, bent over to pick it up. She patted the dove on the head and smiled, assuring us, with only a little doubt in her smile, that the bird was all right.

13

It was the only magic trick I saw at that convention that didn't insult the audience. It took it for granted that everyone knew the dove was in the lid. It was funny, exciting, amazing, and, thanks to Sis, sexy. It was everything entertainment should be. It even had us all yelling together (audience participation). And still, and I've talked to Teller about this, I have not figured out how it was done. How was that dove not turned into a squab frite?

It might have been an accident, but great art is always an accident. It was The Best Magic Trick I Ever Saw.

TERMINAL – THE NEXT MORNING PENN and TELLER (wearing duplicates of the gray business suits we saw on Weekend Live) and CARLOTTA are checking their luggage with the curbside porter. They have a huge trunk with them. PORTER I ain't lifting that. PENN It's empty. PORTER Why do you carry empty luggage. PENN (indicating TELLER) We're going to put him in it. CARLOTTA plucks the receipt from the porter, tips him, and leads the way. INTERIOR – AIRPORT – TWO MINUTES LATER PENN and TELLER and CARLOTTA are walking toward the "Departing Flight" gates. A JESUS FREAK approaches. JESUS FREAK May I talk to you about my religion? PENN Interesting you should mention that. We have a religion too. How long do you figure it will take for you to talk about jesus? JESUS FREAK Just ten minutes of your time, sir. PENN Great. My partner, Teller, would like to demonstrate his religion with a few card tricks. JESUS FREAK Does his religion have anything to do with jesus? PENN I'm sorry. I can't answer that question. You'll have to wait through the card trick and find out. JESUS FREAK I'm sorry. I haven't got time for that. JESUS FREAK starts to walk away, then turns back... JESUS FREAK You said Teller, is that right? Like Penn & Teller. And you got that haircut and that finger nail. So you're Penn. Right? PENN Yes, I am. JESUS FREAK opens up one of his bibles, which is hollowed out, and pulls out a gun, sticks it into PENN's stomach and yells in PENN's face... JESUS FREAK Bang! Bang! Bang! Pretty exciting, huh? Does that make your empty, godless life more worth living? JESUS FREAK runs away, leaving PENN, TELLER and CARLOTTA a little stunned. PENN (to CARLOTTA) What are the exact demographics of Weekend Live? TELLER gives a "go-ahead" nod to CARLOTTA. CARLOTTA looks down at the tickets. CARLOTTA Uh-oh! The flight's not twelve-fifty, boys. It's twelve fifteen. We're missing our plane. PENN starts to glance up at the monitor. CARLOTTA grabs him. CARLOTTA It's gate 12-H! Let's go! As she is speaking, TELLER is slipping something into PENN's pocket. PENN jesus! That's the other end of the terminal! PENN takes off at a dead run. TELLER and CARLOTTA, exchanging knowing glances, follow at a jog. PENN We can make it! Come on! INTERIOR – CORRIDOR APPROACHING SECURITY CHECKPOINT – A MINUTE LATER. PENN is rushing. TELLER and CARLOTTA are following at a fast but not frantic pace. PENN Move! Put a wiggle on! CARLOTTA Take it easy, Penn. We've got two minutes! PENN Go! He pushes her ahead of him through the metal-detector gate. Meanwhile, TELLER slips something into PENN's other jacket pocket. PENN walks through the gate. The alarm goes off, and the GUARD stops him. CARLOTTA turns to wait for him. PENN (to CARLOTTA) Go! Go! Get your carry-on stowed. PENN goes back through the gate and feels his pockets. He pulls out a big Swiss army knife, and a large set of keys, leans to drop them in the GUARD's box. Meanwhile, TELLER slips something else in PENN's pocket. PENN I never carry this with me. I leave it backstage. PENN goes through the gate again. The alarms go off again. The GUARD sends him back. While PENN checks one pocket, TELLER pulls a metal ball out of his other pocket. PENN finds nothing. PENN There's something wrong with your fascist machine! GUARD Maybe it's your belt. PENN It's never set it off before. PENN takes his belt off and gives it to the guard. TELLER drops the ball back in. PENN goes through the gate. The alarm sounds. The GUARD stops him. PENN Your machine is shorting out! It's like HAL. It's out of control. Unplug it. PENN comes back through. TELLER pulls the ball out again. GUARD Do you have a plate in your head? PENN No! Do you want one in yours? GUARD Is there a metal buckle on the back of your vest? PENN I don't know!! PENN rips off his coat and vest, and throws them down. He goes through the gate again. TELLER rolls the ball through the gate by his feet, just as he steps through, setting off the alarm. PENN (yelling) I hate that sound! The GUARD stops him. He comes back. PENN You're machine is haywire. We got a plane to catch! You try it, Teller. TELLER walks through with no trouble. PENN Go! Go! Tell them to hold the plane for me. We follow TELLER as he walks over to the ball which has come to rest by the wall. He looks back with quiet satisfaction at PENN arguing with the GUARD. PENN (O.S.) So does my shirt look like it's made out of metal? Here, take the goddam shirt! Okay, now! TELLER rolls the ball out of frame, back towards the metal detector gate. He rounds the corner into the gate-side snack shop. We hear the ALARM go off again, and PENN shouting. Waiting in the snack shop, with three cups of tea on the table is CARLOTTA. She smiles at TELLER. CARLOTTA Did he take his shirt off? TELLER nods proudly. They dunk their tea bags. In the background we see a MOTHER and LITTLE BOY. The LITTLE BOY is in a complete cowboy outfit, with chaps, hat, and gun in holster. PENN comes rushing by. His shirt is barely tucked in. He is carrying his jacket and vest in one hand with his computer bag slung over the other shoulder. He rushes up to the gate. CARLOTTA Penn! PENN turns. He sees CARLOTTA and TELLER. He realizes what has been going on. He takes it really well. This kind of practical joke is an everyday activity with these people. PENN Were you dropping stuff in my pocket and then pulling it out? While I was yelling at the guard? And I didn't notice, because I was yelling at an innocent man. That's great! When is the flight? CARLOTTA You've got a half an hour. We got tea here for you. PENN I'm gonna go put my tie on, get straightened up, and apologize to the guard. Should I tip him? CARLOTTA I don't know. PENN I was yelling right in his face. I'll buy him a magazine from the gift shop. That was great. TELLER looks up inquiringly, and extends his hand. PENN smiles. PENN No hard feelings. They shake hands. INTERIOR – THE WAITING AREA – TWENTY-EIGHT MINUTES LATER PENN, TELLER, and CARLOTTA are sitting in the waiting seats. LOUDSPEAKER ANNOUNCEMENT This will be your final boarding call for Flight 78 to Philadelphia. PENN Do we have a minute? CARLOTTA We have two minutes, exactly. I'm going to get some gum. I'll see you on the plane. She hands tickets to PENN and TELLER. PENN Teller, you know that thing we're doing with the thumb cuffs for the tv thing? TELLER nods. PENN Well, your elbows are giving away that you're picking the lock. You're doing kind of a... PENN reaches into his carry-on bag and pulls out a pair of thumb-cuffs. PENN Let me show you. TELLER cuffs one thumb. As he reaches up to cuff the other, PENN pulls a realistic toy gun out of his suit coat, slips it into the other bracelet of the cuff, and locks it. PENN I know how fast you can pick those. But I think you should learn to do it with the keyholes full of glue. Just in case we get some psycho some night. I'll see you on the plane. Don't let Security see the fake gun. No hard feelings? PENN shakes TELLER's hand and puts the toy gun in it. TELLER looks at him with incredulous admiration and frantically scrambles with the cuffs. PENN steps to the end of the line of waiting seats, and taps a waiting TRAVELER on the shoulder, and points to TELLER, fumbling with the toy gun. The TRAVELER is alarmed. TRAVELER (pointing to TELLER and shouting) He's got a gun! PENN heads merrily towards the airplane. Ahead of him in line is the MOTHER and LITTLE BOY dressed as a cowboy. The BOY is crying and carrying his empty holster. MOTHER Don't cry, honey. We'll get you a new one when we get to Grandma's. As PENN enters the gangway, we hear... SECURITY GUARD (O.C.) Slowly raise your hands up over your head. Very slowly. We see TELLER raising his hands, with the gun cuffed between his thumbs. EXTERIOR – PHILADELPHIA INTERNATIONAL AIRPORT – LATER THAT DAY At the baggage claim area. PENN and CARLOTTA look bedraggled and irritated. PENN How can you get delayed 45 minutes after you land? And we don't even have Teller to carry the luggage. CARLOTTA We can just swing the car around. But if he misses the show tomorrow night, it's your ass. PENN There are plenty of ways to get into Philadelphia. CARLOTTA With thumb cuffs and a gun? PENN The gun is plastic. He can talk his way out of it. PENN checks his pockets. PENN Do you have the keys? CARLOTTA No. Teller took them to drop in your pocket. PENN (peeved) I must have left them at the metal detector! PENN suddenly brightens. PENN (smiling) That joke worked even better than he thought. We lost the keys to the car. Give me a coat hanger. CARLOTTA reaches into the carry-on garment bag that PENN is carrying, takes out a coat hanger. PENN hands her the garment bag, and holds up the coat hanger with enthusiasm. PENN I defy the Ranchwagons of the world to hold me! CARLOTTA (parentally) It was your joke. You break in and bring the car around. I'll have a cup of tea. INTERIOR – PARKING GARAGE – TEN MINUTES LATER PENN has slid the coat hanger, now bent into a hook, in through the rubber insulation of the PENN and TELLER-mobile, a podunk, cherry 1961 Ford Ranchwagon. He is fishing to engage the lock button. PENN Come on...come on... Just as he almost has it, a hand comes into view from inside the car below the window. The hand guides the makeshift hook over the lock button. TELLER pokes his head up from the floor of the car where he has been hiding. He proudly shows the unlocked thumb cuffs and the plastic gun. PENN grins with happy amazement. TELLER points to a "Jr. Helicopter Pilot" lapel pin. PENN You got to take the chopper? TELLER beams and nods. PENN I'll pay for half. No hard feelings? They shake hands. EXTERIOR – HIGHWAY – THE NEXT AFTERNOON We start close on a sign, "BUGGS & RUDY TRAVELLING REPTILE SHOW – FEATURING MOFO, THE GREEN MAMBA, WORLD'S DEADLIEST REPTILE." PULL BACK to reveal this sign on the side of a moving car, the Ranchwagon. INTERIOR – THE RANCHWAGON – MEANWHILE PENN is driving. TELLER is in the back seat, writing a script on a Zenith lap-top computer with a lighted screen. CARLOTTA is seated in the front passenger seat. PENN's arm is around her. She is in the midst of a business call on her mobile telephone CARLOTTA ...But remember, "Weekend Live" is a youthoriented show. So there Penn and Teller do material with shock appeal...and they do use a little blood. But they would never do that at your dinner theatre. (listens, then reassuringly) No no no. The "bad attitude" was just for that one show.(listens) That's in addition to the guarantee. You pick up the expenses. And...if there happens a fridge backstage they like cola and Yoohoos... (listens) Thanks. Oh, by the way, how is little Joshua? Teller was just telling me how he can't wait to teach him some new card tricks. (listens) Yup. See you next month. B'bye. She hangs up. She addresses PENN and TELLER. CARLOTTA The "I-wish-someone-were-trying-to-kill-me" bit is not playing in the midwest. PENN You think you got trouble now. Wait 'til Teller gouges little Joshua's eyes out and staples them to the proscenium. EXTERIOR – TOLL BOOTH, 'EXACT CHANGE LANE' – CONTINUOUS TELLER sticks his arm out the rear passenger-side window and hooks a quarter for the toll over the roof of the car into the funnel of the machine. The car barely slows down. EXTERIOR – HIGHWAY ON THE WAY INTO ATLANTIC CITY – LATER The car pulls into a toll booth. PENN gives an extra quarter to the toll-booth operator. PENN (to TOLL-COLLECTOR) Here's for the guy behind us, too. Tell him, "Penn says hi. Work for world peace." The car pulls away from the toll booth. EXTERIOR – ATLANTIC CITY – STREET – LATER The ranchwagon is pulling into a parking spot by a meter. PENN and TELLER and CARLOTTA get out. CARLOTTA Lock it? PENN No. Teller's got it. PENN and CARLOTTA start away along the sidewalk. TELLER pulls the magnetic sign ("Travelling Reptile Show") off the side of the car and replaces it with one reading, "Atlanta Center for Disease Control, Specimen Transfer Unit." He runs to catch up with PENN and CARLOTTA. They are standing outside the entrance of a large casino hotel. On the lighted marquee we can read: TRUMP PLAZA HOTEL AND CASINO PRESENTS PENN & TELLER THRU JULY 15TH. Underneath is a sign advertising a Million Dollar Slot Festival. CARLOTTA I don't need you to be around while I check us in. Here's twenty dollars. Go to the casino and throw it away. They head into the hotel. INTERIOR – CASINO FLOOR BY THE SLOT MACHINES – A LITTLE LATER A large, middle-aged SERIOUS GAMBLER is playing a slot machine. His machine's receiving tray is loaded with quarters. He puts five coins in the slot. He pulls the handle. He watches the little windows in his machine. According to the windows, no payoff. But as he goes to put a few more coins in, all of a sudden, he hears five quarters land in the receiving tray. He looks down, puzzled. He returns to his play. He inserts his coins. Again no payoff is indicated, but he hears coins land in the tray. He looks around. TELLER is standing behind him, staring at him. TELLER is holding a plastic coin bucket full of quarters. The GAMBLER turns back to his machine, and hears two coins drop into the tray. Then another three. He turns and sees that TELLER is just throwing money into his tray. TELLER sits down at the machine next to the GAMBLER's machine. The GAMBLER puts a few more quarters in. As he pulls the handle, he watches TELLER carefully. TELLER looks blankly back and tosses a few more coins into the GAMBLER's tray. The GAMBLER is peeved, but is having trouble justifying slugging TELLER for giving him money. PENN (O.S.) You gonna put up with that? GAMBLER No. I mean yes. I mean, I can't clock him for giving me money. The GAMBLER puts in a few more quarters. He pulls the handle. TELLER heaves in a few more coins. We now see that PENN is playing his slot machine. His suit jacket is off, and he has only a few coins in his hand. PENN Yes, you can. I would. It's just another example of the pig power structure throwing worthless trinkets to the proletariat. PENN starts to play his machine. He pulls the handle. Coins crash into PENN's tray. TELLER has tossed them. PENN throws his handful of coins at TELLER. PENN Commie bastard! I'll show you distribution of wealth. The GAMBLER gives TELLER a long look of warning, then plays again. Defiantly TELLER tosses a big handful of coins into the GAMBLER's tray. PENN That's it! The GAMBLER, responding to PENN's exclamation, picks up a handful of coins from his tray and throws them at TELLER. PENN scoops up all the coins in his own tray and throws them. PENN grabs a handful of the GAMBLER's coins and also throws them at TELLER. TELLER throws back. GAMBLER and PENN keep throwing the GAMBLER's coins. TELLER picks up coins and throws them back, but each time he throws, he retains a few and slips them into his bucket. He is making money. A CROWD begins to gather, people picking up coins. Coins are flying everywhere. SECURITY GUARDS arrive and grab PENN and the GAMBLER. PENN (screaming) Ah! The Revolution! Starting in the most unlikely of places! Trump Casino, Atlantic City! We've been downtrodden long enough! We will take no more money from the pigs. (singing) "A working class hero is something to be!" Security guards carry off PENN (singing, "We shall overcome!") and the GAMBLER (trying to explain), as TELLER continues to scoop the profits. INTERIOR – FRONT ENTRANCE OF A MEXICAN RESTAURANT IN ATLANTIC CITY – THAT EVENING It is a homey place with year-round Christmas decor. PENN and CARLOTTA, his girlfriend, are waiting for the Maitre D'. PENN, of course, is in his usual gray suit. PENN ...if you'd been there, you wouldn't be mad. It was great. Teller got people throwing money at each other. He made four dollars and seventy five cents, you know. CARLOTTA Yes. And you got thrown out of the casino. It was a stupid idea. PENN It was Teller's idea. The MAITRE D' approaches. MAITRE D' Table for two? PENN Yeah. MAITRE D' (yelling to the cook) Oye, Marcitos, no crees que el parece como el gran gringo hijo de puta que pidio por television que la gente le matara? Mirale! The COOK, looks out through the window between the kitchen and the dining room. He nods, smiles, and brandishes

THE CREATION OF LIFE

by

TELLER

I never hear Penn's dove story without thinking of my own guilty past.

When I was at college, I persuaded a drama professor to let me do an independent study course in which I would work on my magic act. I was to spend the year preparing an original theatrical magic show that would also serve as my final exam. To get our academically dubious project past the authorities, we entitled it "The Figure of the Magician in Dramatic Literature."

I was lazy and disorganized and a dreamer. Instead of practicing, I filled notebooks with ideas for tricks inspired by other courses I was taking.

In my psychology course I was reading Freud. So before long I was making notes on a trick in which there would be a black box (the Id) with something inside, straining to escape. I (the Ego) would imprudently unfasten the lock (the Superego) on the box, then raise a piece of cloth in front it. A vague form would push against the cloth and leap around, as though the Id had escaped. I would push the cloth (even I couldn't figure out the symbolism of the cloth) from behind with a hinged stick with a pillow tied on the end). I would wrestle around the stage with it (the Struggle of Passion and Reason) and finally duck my head under the cloth, where I would slip over my face a translucent mask covered with bloody wounds. I would lower the cloth, revealing my mutilated visage (the Scars of Sublimation), and the light would fade out on my tragic pose.

This would be Art. I would become the Shakespeare of magic, raising the form from nightclub sensationalism to Theater. But I needed a denouement for my show: something that would depict my role as Creative Artist. That's what gave me the idea for "The Experiment; or, The Creation of Life."

In this one I modestly played the role of the Life Force toying with the Fabric of Nature (a piece of brown, tweedy cloth), which I would fold and pin into a crude dummy of a rabbit. I would then try to induce the effigy to behave as if alive, offering it a carrot.

The dummy would sit there. Brokenhearted at my failure, I would wrap the corpse of my failed creation in a little white quilted shroud and cradle it lovingly in my arms, weeping. Suddenly I would feel the dummy stir with life of its own, generated by the touch of my tears, and open the blanket to disclose a live rabbit, which I would set on the stage, and allow to walk around at my feet as it nibbled at the carrot I offered.

I was especially proud of two technical features of the trick: first, that I had found an oddly colored rabbit, a tweedy brown to match my fabric, thus avoiding the cliché of the white rabbit; and second, that I had devised an ingenious way to keep the rabbit hidden and comfortable throughout my show. This was no small trick; all my plain black, timeless furniture was bare, with nary a cushion to conceal anything in. My coarse black, timeless peasant's wool tunic had no room for anything as bulky as an animal. None of my austere, geometrically plain props was preset on stage to afford a hiding place for the bunny; at the beginning of the show I brought on everything I needed in a black, timeless valise (evoking, I thought, wandering *jongleurs* of the Middle Ages).

So where was the rabbit?

In the valise. In a secret compartment constructed out of cardboard at one end. When the valise was set on the timeless black stool, the end hung over, and there was a trapdoor in the bottom which I would release, dropping the animal into the quilted blanket when the audience was distracted by a particularly poignant moment of the Life Force's despair. So confident was I in the ingenuity of my arrangements, and so ill organized in my rehearsal schedule, that it was not until the morning before the final examination performance (it was to happen at eight that evening) that I actually tried it out.

I loaded the rabbit into his little chamber, and began my final dress rehearsal.

Almost immediately I realized I was in trouble. The rabbit, a wild breed, would not stand for it. He hated his cramped quarters, and expressed his hatred first by kicking, then by gnawing at the valise, behaving more or less like the Id in the Freudian trick. When I finally released him, he clawed my wrist, then jumped to the floor and lodged under the supports of the stage platform. I knew now why magicians used trite white rabbits. They were tame.

I finally cornered the little bastard in the dirt and splinters under the stage and, despite his screaming protests, thrust him back in his cage. Have you ever heard an anguished rabbit scream? It's an awful, pained, wild sound that they only utter in moments of extreme panic or discomfort. It's the sound I wanted to make when I realized how desperate my situation was.

And then I got an inspiration. I went to my friend the Med Student. I explained my problem to him. After a full ten seconds of ethical reflection, he proposed a plan. He would smuggle a syringe of sedative (he would find out the proper dosage) out of the biology lab. At the appropriate time before the show, he would inject the bunny in the large muscle tissue, and all would be well. He said, reasonably, that we should not try it out before the show, lest we overwhelm the poor thing with too much relaxation in the same day.

I gave thanks for modern science, and, skipping lunch and dinner, practiced other tricks all afternoon. I set my props one final time, and then at seven forty-five, as I held the tweedy brown bunny down, the Med Student injected the sedative in his left hind leg. I watched with growing relief as he became quieter and quieter, and finally allowed me to place him in his apartment in the valise.

My advertising, homemade signs posted in dormitory entrance halls, had worked pretty well. By eight o'clock, twenty-five people curious to see what I was up to were sitting in the dorm basement theater. My professor was seated at the rear of the audience with a clipboard.

All went as smoothly as I could have hoped, considering how much more interested I was in the inner meaning of tricks than in their competent execution. A coin-producing routine in which I played the Beggar who falls asleep and dreams of endless wealth, but wakens to find his "insubstantial pageant" melted into thin air, might have seemed more magical if I had not dropped any of the half-dollars, but people applauded at the end. The Id trick came off pretty well, considering that the thread that lifted the lid broke, and my light man (whom, I must confess, I had never given a chance to rehearse) missed his cue and left me dramatically posed in my mutilation mask much too long, waiting in vain for him to fade out the light at the end. But overall, I was getting through it, and the audience was not leaving.

And then it was time to create life. I gave it my all, acting it with restrained passion. As the Life Force I was a naive Prometheus.

The first hint I had that all was not well was when I was loading the rabbit from the suitcase into the cloth. It seemed

21

heavier than I remembered it. It was not kicking, as it had done in rehearsal. In fact, it was not moving. So at the climactic moment when it was to come to life, my acting job became harder. I had to move the blanket, puppetlike, *and* react to the movement with awe. I opened the blanket.

It wasn't dead, I was pleased to find, only stupefied. I set it on the floor. It rolled over onto its side. I held the carrot inches from its nose. Not a twitch. Finally, in an endeavor to make it show some sign of life, I poked it gently with the carrot. The audience laughed. They thought I had it trained.

I set the rabbit upright and poked it again with the carrot, and it started to walk. Mild applause. Then I noticed that it was dragging its left hind leg. My creation, like Nature's, was flawed.

Immediately I picked it up, took a Russian Ballet bow and exited. As the audience left, I stood in the boiler room, lifting and dropping the rabbit's leg. It was as limp as a piece of raw liver. There was a knock at the door. It was my professor. He was very kind. He told me my concepts were strong, and carried the show over the technical problems. He did not ask about the limping rabbit.

Later that night the veterinarian said the rabbit would live, but that we had severed the nerves that controlled movement in the left hind leg. He assured us that the rabbit would always limp.

Against the vet's recommendations, I did not have the rabbit put to sleep. I named it Hephaestus, after the crippled blacksmith of the Greek gods (I was studying the *Odyssey* in another class), and gave it to the local first-grade class, where it was a popular pet, lived and was loved, and helped teach mythology.

So, when Penn tells his story about the dove, I laugh with the rest, but always have a flash of guilt and bitterness. The guilt is for what I did to Hephaestus. The bitterness is because I only got a B in the course.

On October 16, 1985, Penn & Teller produced five hundred live cockroaches on national television. Here's how you can, too.

HOW TO PRODUCE
FIVE HUNDRED COCKROACHES
ON DAVID LETTERMAN'S DESK

continued on p. 27

his carving knife as a little joke to the MAITRE D'. CARLOTTA Simplemente no "parece" como el gran gringo hijo de puta. El es el gran gringo hijo de puta. PENN You know when people are talking a foreign language you always think they're talking about you. MAITRE D' Perdoneme. No quise llamarasu esposo un gringo hijo de puta. CARLOTTA Esta bien. No es mi esposo, pero si es un gringo hijo de puta. MAITRE D' Right this way. MAITRE D' leads them towards a table. PENN What were you talking about? CARLOTTA He wanted to know if you were the big Yankee son-of-a-hooker that went on TV last week and asked people to kill him. MAITRE D' is uncomfortable that CARLOTTA has translated so literally. PENN (to MAITRE D') Yes, I am that big Yankee son-of-a-hooker. And the big Yankee son-of-a-hooker and his girlfriend would like a couple of colas. MAITRE D' Certainly, sir. He hands them each a menu. PENN hands his menu to CARLOTTA. PENN Order me something exotic that is not made with any part of a cow's stomach. CARLOTTA begins to look over the menu. PENN That was great. Penn and Teller are finally starting to break into the Hispanic community. CARLOTTA They only recognized you as the crazy sonofabitch that went on TV and asked people to kill him. PENN Hey, there's no such thing as bad press. CARLOTTA Wasn't it Lee Harvey Oswald that said that? The WAITRESS approaches. WAITRESS What would you like? CARLOTTA Yo quiero el plato de combinacion – numero tres. El quiere cualquier plato que puedes recomendar que es hecho de tripa. WAITRESS Very good. PENN Gracias. CARLOTTA (to PENN) Very good, and how do you say "son-of-ahooker"? PENN (mispronouncing) Hijo de puta? CARLOTTA (correcting his pronunciation) Hijo de puta. PENN Hijo de puta. That's great now I can say, "thank you", "son of a bitch" and, "The dog is big and black." I'm becoming a world citizen. What's up with your uncle? CARLOTTA He's real sick. He has an abdominal tumor. PENN Jeez. Is he going to be okay? CARLOTTA Well he would be. They can cure it with surgery and radiation. But he is refusing to go into the hospital. He wants to spend his life savings to go to the Philippines and have one of those psychic-surgeon quacks work on him. PENN Goddamn, he really is gullible. CARLOTTA I want you to tell him that they're fake. PENN Why don't you tell him? He's your goddam uncle. Give him articles to read. CARLOTTA He's a very, very wealthy man. And I'd hate to see him lose all his money to charlatans. I'm also his closest relative. PENN Well, you know, if we can save just one human life... Ernesto hasn't met Teller has he? CARLOTTA No. The WAITRESS brings the food. PENN Good. Tell him I got a tumor too. And tell him I got an even better psychic surgeon right here in Atlantic City: Dr. Tellero. CARLOTTA (smiling, correcting PENN's pronunciation) Tiero. CARLOTTA leans across the table and gives PENN a little kiss. PENN looks at his food. PENN What is this? CARLOTTA Un tripa con achoa y alga marina—caliente. PENN (looking at his food, adventurously) Looks good! It doesn't, really. EXTERIOR – THE PATIO OF CARLOTTA'S UNCLE'S HANDSOME SEASIDE HOME –A FEW DAYS LATER On a garden patio by a swimming pool TELLER, costumed for the role with white tropical suit and Panama hat with a large cross hanging from a beaded necklace, is beginning to perform psychic surgery on PENN, who is lying on an air mattress from the swimming pool. PENN's tie is off, and his dress shirt is open exposing his abdomen. PENN looks around. PENN Nice day for an operation. CARLOTTA and ERNESTO, her dignified old uncle seated in a wheelchair, a nurse, and several serious SPECTATORS are grouped closely around PENN's body. TELLER pokes around on PENN's stomach. Where he pokes, PENN reacts. PENN Ow. Ow. OWWWW! TELLER places the hands of the volunteers on various pressure points. He wipes PENN's abdomen with a wet sponge, getting it plenty wet, concentrates deeply, and presses on PENN's abdomen with his hands. As he presses, blood flows in a stream down onto ERNESTO's hand. ERNESTO holds his position firmly, although he is clearly shaken. TELLER reaches into a fold of flesh and extracts a disgusting piece of tumor-like material. He raises it triumphantly very close to ERNESTO's face. ERNESTO is shocked, revolted, but riveted and impressed. TELLER tosses the tumor into the swimming pool and wipes the blood away from PENN's skin. There is no trace of a wound. PENN is completely healed. PENN Whoa, doc! What a relief. Thanks. He sits up and pokes himself in the stomach in various places, cheerfully. PENN See? All better! PENN gets dressed. TELLER wipes his hands, rolls down his sleeves, and prepares to leave. One of the spectators approaches TELLER. SPECTATOR Exactly what type of tumor was that? TELLER shrugs. PENN A very bad one. He doesn't speak English. PENN looks at CARLOTTA and ERNESTO. PENN Or Spanish. He only speaks Tagalog. ERNESTO(trying to express himself to TELLER with explanatory gestures) You have a very remarkable gift. PENN No. ERNESTO (to PENN) What? You're just a patient, Penn. PENN I'm not just a patient, I'm the patient. It's just a scam, Ernesto. This is Teller. TELLER takes off his hat and shakes hands. ERNESTO Teller? Is this a joke? I can't believe you would joke about this. PENN It's not a joke, Ernesto. We wanted to prove to you that psychic surgeons are fakes. Let me show you how it's done, so you can check out your guy. Let's start by looking at the doctor's hands. See his finger? No, this finger right here. TELLER has an extra long finger on his left hand. It is made of hollow, flesh-colored plastic. PENN You aren't born with a finger like that: you gotta buy it. It's full of chicken blood and guts. TELLER slips the finger into a fold of skin on PENN's abdomen. The goop flows out, as from a wound. PENN If that doesn't seem like enough blood to you, use one of these sponges. They're full of water, and when you squeeze 'em, they make it look like there's a lot more blood. ERNESTO So that's how he does it! I'll tell that bastard where where he can stick his plastic finger. EXTERIOR – ON THE BEACH – A FEW DAYS LATER – AFTERNOON PENN, TELLER, and CARLOTTA have set up a beach umbrella, a few chairs, and a card table far from other bathers. The furniture is arranged like the set of a late night TV talk show: CARLOTTA is seated behind the table as host. She is wearing a preppie sport coat and tie and is playing with a pencil. Side-by-side next to the table sit PENN and TELLER, as usual wearing their gray suits. They are rehearsing. PENN spoons Drano onto a piece of raw chicken, which foams as it is eaten away. PENN So, Dave, you've seen what one teaspoon of Drano does to a piece of raw chicken. Now imagine... TELLER grabs the spoon, takes a spoonful of Drano and eats it. PENN Teller! Stop that. Now Dave, hold out your hand and think about the last time you went skiing. (breaking character) I think we can count on Dave to be a little freaked and we can also figure he'll say something funny. (back to "Dave") A hip guy like you must ski. TELLER makes a little mountain of Drano. CARLOTTA (as Letterman) Yeah, I ski. (breaking character) ...or funny words to that effect. PENN (breaking character) Teller, Teller. Nope. It ain't working. I can see the little tab of the cellophane sticking out of the side of your mouth. TELLER feels around. PENN No, the right side. TELLER pulls a combination of Drano, dental dam and cellophane very carefully out of his mouth. PENN You gonna be OK on this? TELLER isn't quite sure, but he starts to make the necessary changes. PENN (to Carlotta) Would you notice the plastic in his mouth? CARLOTTA No, I'd be too busy looking at the Drano eating away at the chicken. But the camera might see it. PENN Okay, let's keep going. PENN notices somebody approaching. PENN Wait a minute. TELLER replaces the bag of Drano in his mouth, as we see three the approaching strangers, third-world types, swarthy, fat, and muscular, respectively. This is JUAN and his two brothers. PENN (to the STRANGERS at a little distance) Hi. We're a little busy right now. The strangers keep coming. PENN What's up? JUAN (To PENN) So, you must be the big one with the hair. And is he the little one that doesn't talk? And who's she? PENN Yes, I'm the big one. And he doesn't talk right now because he has a mouth full of Drano. And this is Carlotta, who is pretending to be David Letterman. She is Hispanic, and she is our friend. Now it's my turn. You're the one who speaks with an accent. He's the fat one. And who is this gentleman? JUAN My name is Juan, and these are my brothers. Are you the ones who convinced Ernesto Garcia to cancel his psychic surgery in Manilla? PENN Yes, but some of the credit goes to the fact that he had a brain in his head. JUAN My brother is the leading psychic surgeon in Manilla. We can't have smart-assed scum like you defaming the name of a great healer. The visitors take out their guns. PENN (to TELLER) Better take the Drano out of your mouth. This is getting serious.(to JUAN) Okay. We are smart-assed scum. I'm sorry for any inconvenience we may have caused your family. PENN reaches into a cooler and brings out three cans of soda. PENN Would you like a beverage before you run along? JUAN Spineless. Repulsive. Slimy creatures. They are weak. They are of no consequence to us. PENN is nodding in agreement. TELLER and CARLOTTA look uneasy. The visitors start to put their guns away. TELLER jumps up with a can of Drano in one hand, flings Drano in the air, kicks the guns out of their hands, and is decked with one punch by the muscular brother. They pick up their guns and look back at PENN. PENN Jesus christ! Did you see that? Who is that asshole? Don't you be troubled by him. Just leave him here. Me and the girl will beat him up for you.(to CARLOTTA) After they leave, I'll hold him and you hit him. (to VISITORS) So long, guys. JUAN (to his BROTHERS) They're trouble. We'd better bring them back to the doctor. PENN Do what you want to the girl, but leave me alone. The VISITORS point their guns. JUAN Come with us. CARLOTTA looks at PENN. PENN (to CARLOTTA) I was gonna come and rescue you later. JUAN (to the FAT ONE) The boss isn't interested in the girl. THE FAT ONE No, but I am. JUANJust make sure she talks to no one. JUAN tosses a gun to THE FAT ONE, who starts to drag CARLOTTA away. JUAN and his brother turn to lead PENN and TELLER to a waiting car. CARLOTTA catches PENN's eye and nods, significantly. PENN nods back, knowingly. PENN (whispering to TELLER) What does that mean? I mean she just nodded and I nodded back. And I have no idea what she meant. Does she think she can overpower the guy, get away, and talk to the police? What's going on? What are we supposed to do? TELLER nods, significantly. INTERIOR – DARK, OMINOUS CORRIDOR – A FEW HOURS LATER PENN and TELLER are strapped on wheeled hospital tables, being pushed down a corridor side by side. PENN is blindfolded. TELLER is not, and is watching and listening to PENN with intense attention. PENN Teller! Are you there, Teller? Now, what she probably meant when she nodded is that we shouldn't do anything. We should just cooperate and do what they want us to. That must be what she meant. TELLER listens, but says nothing. PENN Are you even here, Teller? I trust that in this desperate and important situation, with me blindfolded like this, you would say something, right? Like some appropriate warning if I was in immediate danger. I mean, you know I'm blindfolded. And you know we're talking life or death here. So to yell a couple of words wouldn't hurt your image at all. TELLER watches and listens, but does not answer. INTERIOR – CORRIDOR – A FEW MINUTES LATER Deadly surgical instruments are being wheeled along on a second cart behind PENN and TELLER. PENN I just think that we should be comparing notes, getting some sort of unified strategy. You know, your "not talking" thing, when I can see you is tiresome and irritating, but now with me blindfolded, it's exasperating. I mean if I were you, and blindfolded with no idea what's going on, I'd just be chattering a blue streak. Okay, let's try this: You whistle once for yes and twice for no. Teller: Are you here with me? Are you blindfolded too? I know you can whistle. I've heard you whistle. Are there other people here? Are you gagged? No reply. PENN You do know that I'm blindfolded, right? If you're gagged, just tap your fingers or bang your feet or something. Once again: once for yes and twice for no. Large doors have swung open, PENN and TELLER are wheeled through. There is the clang of the closing doors behind them. PENN Teller? Did you make that clanging sound? It was once. That means "yes". Now is that "yes, you're here with me?" Or "yes, you're blindfolded?" Or "yes, you're gagged?" The DOCTOR's hand cuts the blindfold off PENN, who sees that TELLER is there beside him, neither blindfolded nor gagged. PENN (to TELLER) I hate you. PENN catches sight of one of TELLER's hands. He has a scalpel and is sawing away at his strap. PENN (seeing that TELLER is going about a plan) Oh! I see. DOCTOR So, you two wiseacres... PENN "Wiseacres"? DOCTOR...do not believe that I know anything about medicine and anatomy. Well I will now give you proof that you can see with your own eyes by removing Teller's liver. PENN sees that TELLER is sawing furiously. PENN realizes that TELLER needs more time. PENN Um...Uh... DOCTOR is approaching TELLER with the knife. PENN gropes for some way to stall him. PENN Uh...Uh... PENN suddenly gets an idea. PENN Hijo de puta! DOCTOR looks at him. PENN So, Mr. hijo de puta, what are you going to do? Slip some pig's liver under Teller's smock? Any two-bit Filipino cruise magician with a fake finger full of pig guts could do that. DOCTOR I think you'll find my demonstration quite convincing. TELLER is sawing desperately. DOCTOR returns to him with the knife. PENN Oh, yeah? Hijo de puta! DOCTOR Shut your mouth. DOCTOR returns to TELLER with the knife. TELLER continues to saw. PENN Hijo de puta! DOCTOR If you don't shut your mouth, I may demonstrate to your little friend how to remove a living larynx with a pair of rusty pliers. DOCTOR turns again to TELLER. PENN (waiting till the last possible moment before the knife touches TELLER) Hijo de puta! DOCTOR (turning furiously) That's it! DOCTOR turns his attention to PENN. TELLER has almost sawn through the strap. PENN needs to give him just a little more time. PENN (making conversation) So, are you originally from the Philippines? DOCTOR What? PENN Your English is very very good. But you seem to have a little trouble with your "b"s and "v"s. I'm a native speaker of the American language. Now listen to me: "And I can't remember if I cried, when I read about his widowed bride, but something touched me deep inside, the day the music died. Listen to these "b"s carefully: "Bye. Bye. Miss American Pie. Drove my Chevy to the Levy." Doctor, your gift, psychic surgery, is done with the mind and uses no instruments and makes no incisions, right? "Chevy to the Levy." Now hear those "v"s: Not "Cheby to the Leby" but "Chevy to the Levy, but the Levy..." There it is again: levy! "... was dry. Okay! Now, with me... The assistants are cutting off PENN's shirt and the DOCTOR has selected a knife which he is bringing towards PENN's throat. PENN ..."Bye. Bye. Miss American Pie." Now, I want you to keep in mind, this is a New England American accent. A lot of our foreign friends want to learn that BBCEngland English, and, frankly I think it sounds a little bit pretentious on a secondlanguage speaker...Now, if you don't want to do this along with me, just listen to me a little bit: "The jester sang for the king and queen, in a coat he borrowed from James Dean, and a voice that came from you and me." Now listen to these "j"s: "Now Jack be nimble, Jack be quick, Jack Flash sat on the candlestick, 'cause fire is the Devil's only friend. TELLER just has a few threads to go, but the DOCTOR is about to make an incision in PENN's throat. PENN You know, everybody knows, of course, Doc, that Jack Flash refers to Mick Jagger. You know, "Jumping Jack Flash – Sympathy for the Devil". It's all there. But I figure the Jester in the James Dean coat is Bob Dylan. TELLER is free. He quickly unstraps his other hand, neck, and feet and, unnoticed by the DOCTOR and his assistants, sneaks up to the DOCTOR's instrument table. The

1. Get five hundred cockroaches. This is harder than you think. Don't try to use the ones from under your stove. They move too fast and will drive you nuts. Find yourself a bug expert, and have him recommend a breed or blend of breeds that looks unpleasant but is easy to wrangle.

Dave Brody, Bug Wrangler.

2. Let them crawl all over your hands. Pick them up and play with them. Make them your friends.

3. Make a secret box to hide your roaches in.* Don't worry about putting air holes in it. Bugs don't need much air, and, frankly, nobody will notice if they are out of breath.

* If you make your box out of foamcore (the sheet Styrofoam with paper facing, obtainable at art supply stores) the roaches will slide right out when you release them, and make an impressive entrance. Try as they might, they just can't dig their little toes into the smooth surface to get a grip.

4. Mount your secret box in a top hat. We made it removable with Velcro tape, so that if we wanted to wear the hat afterward, to formal weddings and such, we could.

continued on p. 34

DOCTOR is holding the knife against PENN's throat. PENN Wait! Wait! Wait! Wait! "The outlook wasn't brilliant for the Mudville Nine that day. The score stood four to two with but one inning left to play...." You're going to want to listen to this one, Doc. It has a surprise ending. TELLER has picked up a large scalpel from the table, and is ready to stab the DOCTOR. Just as he's about to stab, he changes his mind and goes for a different weapon. PENN Hey, Doc: Knock Knock. It's a great one, Doc. Knock Knock. TELLER by this time has selected a cleaver, and is poised behind the DOCTOR. PENN You know, Doc: I never believe those letters to "Penthouse". But just last week I was flying into New York, and there were these identical-twin blonde blue-eyed stewardesses, and we got to talking, y'know. So I invited them out to dinner. TELLER, about to strike, changes his mind. He returns to the table, and picks up the knife he originally had, and holds it up in one hand and the cleaver up in the other, inquiringly, to PENN, to ask his opinion about which weapon would be the better choice. PENN (screaming) Either one!!! Just go! Go! Do it! So they're both naked on my bed, and they're fondling each other's breasts, and one of them had all the hair on her body shaved off, and all of a sudden they tell me where they've hidden millions of dollars worth of gold and priceless art. And I could tell you where all of it is hidden. TELLER unable to decide between the weapons, sets down both weapons and throws his hands in the air. PENN (screaming) AAAAAAAAAAAAAAAH! DOCTOR plunges knife into PENN. Nothing happens. PENN is puzzled. Suddenly everybody in the operating room yells in unison: EVERYBODY Surprise! They all pull off their surgical masks and don party hats. TELLER approaches and stands, beaming with pride, beside Penn. PENN (to TELLER) This is a great joke. I said on TV, "I wish someone were trying to kill me," and my little buddy staged this whole thing for me. What a sweetheart. Someone release me now. I'd like to shake his hand. The DOCTOR pulls off some additional fake eyebrows, and we recognize UNCLE ERNESTO. ERNESTO Just a few fake eyebrows and you don't recognize Uncle Ernesto. You're gullible. I like that. PENN You aren't even sick? ERNESTO Of course not. It was a joke, Penn. Carlotta said you love these jokes. I'm not sick, I feel great. No hard feelings? ERNESTO shakes PENN's hand, without releasing his strapped arm. CARLOTTA removes her surgical mask and nurse's cap and climbs up on the gurney that PENN is strapped to. She has a paper plate of cake and she sits on PENN's chest. PENN (to CARLOTTA) You were in on this too? Why don't you untie me. I'd like to give you a hug and a big kiss. You know, I wasn't just lying: I had those twin flight attendants and they were terrific. CARLOTTA takes a fork full of cake and delicately shoves it into PENN's mouth. CARLOTTA Yum! INTERIOR – TRUMP PLAZA THEATRE – TWO WEEKS LATER TELLER is tied spread-eagle to a rectangular wooden table. His wrists, ankles, and neck are each tied with a hemp rope. The ends of the ropes run through the table top, and are held taut by MEN from the audience. TELLER is trying to untie the knots. It is the middle of the final trick in PENN and TELLER's show. Suspended over TELLER is a wooden board, the full size of the table, through which fifty household electric drills with 24" bits are affixed. The drill bits are pointed straight downward at TELLER. Each drill is plugged into a power strip, affixed to a cable which runs to a variac next to PENN. There is a cloth bag over PENN's head. The board that supports the drills is held up by hemp ropes running up over a system of pulleys and down into PENN's hand. A WOMAN from the audience is standing nearby. She can clearly see TELLER struggling to free himself. He is not doing very well. The WOMAN is reading a stop watch and speaking uncomfortably into a microphone. WOMAN Twenty-five... Throughout the following, the WOMAN continues to count down, second by second. At regular intervals, PENN turns the knob on the variac and increases the speed at which the drills are turning. PENN Having released his left arm, he immediately goes to free his neck so he can discover what kind of knots the audience members have freely tied around his ankles, and the best way to liberate himself. WOMAN Ten, nine... TELLER has not got even one knot completely open yet. PENN is oblivious. PENN Having looked at the knots on the ankles, he frees his right arm, sits up, left ankle, right ankle... A translucent screen drops into place, concealing the struggling TELLER. A bright light turns on from behind and we can see the silhouette of the struggling body. WOMAN two, one... PENN ...and rolls off the table. PENN releases the rope. The board of drills falls. The drills are stopped momentarily by the flesh below, then gradually drill their way all the way through the body and the table. The translucent screen is splattered with blood. The points of the drills protrude from the underside of the table. The audience members on stage and in the theatre are shocked and/or laughing and applauding. PENN whips off the hood, steps to the center of the stage with a big smile, and prepares to take his bow side by side with TELLER. PENN notices TELLER isn't there. PENN Hmmm. He looks behind him. A hand bursts through the blood-soaked screen in a death spasm. PENN Oooh. He turns to the WOMAN timekeeper and speaks in a quiet, depressed tone. PENN You could hear me tell you where he was supposed to be. Why didn't you tell me that he was stuck? WOMAN I...I was just supposed to count off numbers. PENN (to the men holding the ropes) Why didn't you guys say anything? Where'd he get stuck? How close was he? The MEN laugh uncomfortably. FIRST MAN I don't think he got out of anything, really. SECOND MAN He didn't even loosen it. PENN What kind of knots did you tie? SECOND MAN You told us to tie him up tightly. So we did. PENN Yeah. I guess. It is a little stupid to be holding the ropes now, isn't it? Why don't you guys sit down. (to the WOMAN) You too. Sit down. Thank you. WOMAN Sorry. The audience members leave the stage. The audience applauds for them. HECKLER FROM THE AUDIENCE I thought you were the one that wanted to die. PENN Hey, you win some, you lose some. That's our show for this evening. My name is Penn Jillette, and this was my partner, Teller. We're Penn & Teller. Good night. PENN leaves, wheeling off the torture table. Applause. ANNOUNCER (O.S) Penn and Teller! Audience applauds. PENN runs back on stage to take a bow. PENN My partner, Teller! The torture table zips out from the wing with amazing speed, and stops next to PENN in the perfect, choreographed curtain call. PENN takes hold of the limp, dead hand and bows. PENN exits, pushing off the torture table. ANNOUNCER (O.S) Penn and Teller! Audience applauds. INTERIOR – BACKSTAGE – CONTINUOUS PENN has been met backstage by a bush-league television crew. It is an on-the-spot interview for local news. PENN ...We've been here for three weeks and we'll be here 'til the fifteenth, so come on down! INTERVIEWER Now what do you and Teller really hate about magic? PENN Teller can answer that much better than I can. INTERVIEWER I thought Teller was dead. PENN Don't patronize me. I've got to go let him out. INTERVIEWER Can we come along with you? It'd be good TV. PENN I'm sorry. I can't let you do that. If you see Teller getting out of the trick, you'll know how it's done. And I know we're the "Bad Boys of Magic", but we would never expose an actual magic principle. I'm sorry. You stay here, and Teller will be out in a moment. PENN goes over to the spiked table. PENN (to table) The local TV station wants to know why we hate magic. He releases a latch on the front section of the spike plate, and pulls all the front spikes up out of the way. The "dead" hand clenches and unclenches. PENN reaches under the table. As he sticks his hand in, we see it reflected in several angled mirrors. He releases another catch, and the mirrored doors spring open. In the compartment formerly masked by the mirrors we see TELLER is crouched under the rear section of spikes. He twists to pull his arm from above, and crawls out. His jacket sleeve is a little torn and slightly bloodstained where a few of the spikes have caught it. PENN Chinese okay? TELLER nods as he removes his torn jacket and tosses it into a laundry basket. He does not notice that his sleeve is slightly torn and bloody where the spikes have scraped him. He takes another identical jacket from a coat hanger hanging on the wall and puts it on. PENN I'll go clean this up. You go show the tv what we hate about magic. TELLER nods, takes some items down from a shelf, stuffing them into his pockets and sleeves and walks away. PENN throws open two large doors and wheels the spike table out into the alley. INTERIOR – BACKSTAGE WITH THE TELEVISION CREW – MEANWHILE INTERVIEWER Penn said you'd tell us why you two hate magic. TELLER does a soft-shoe step, a rhythmic slapping of the thighs and produces a string of silk handkerchiefs, a bouquet of paper flowers, and a cane. He walks away twirling the cane with a vapid smile. EXTERIOR – IN THE ALLEY – MEANWHILE PENN is hosing down the bloody spike table. CARLOTTA joins him. CARLOTTA You guys about set to eat? PENN Teller's finishing up an interview. Then he wants to eat Chinese food. CARLOTTA (looking at her watch) Perfect. EXTERIOR – WHERE THE ALLEY MEETS THE PARKING LOT – FIVE MINUTES LATER PENN, TELLER, and CARLOTTA are walking out of the alley. TELLER is folding up his vanishing cane and sticking the silks back up his sleeve. PENN (to CARLOTTA) We've got to stay for Dean's show some night. Teller saw it last night, and Dean does this thing on Shirley McLaine, where he's talking about what a nut she is, and how she has these uncanny, creepy feelings before something awful happens. SOUND OF GUNSHOT. PENN grabs his arm. PENN, TELLER, and CARLOTTA stand shocked and stunned for a moment. TELLER looks in the direction of the shot. It has come from the top of a huge billboard showing the giant faces of PENN and TELLER. From TELLER's P.O.V. we see the billboard looming over the parking lot from just outside a tall chain link fence topped with barbed wire. A very sharp eye (sharper than TELLER's or a first-time viewer's) could discern the shadowy figure of a MAN, THE FAN, hanging upside down from the bottom of the catwalk. TELLER, not noticing, turns back to PENN, and reaches up to try to examine the wound. PENN Ow! What are you trying to do? Stick your finger in to see how deep it is? Shouldn't we be ducking or something, or running away? TELLER is frantically trying to help. PENN Hey, you want to help? The shot came from up there. PENN points toward the billboard. We see the billboard from TELLER's P.O.V. NOTE: Sharp-eyed viewers and second-time viewers will actually be able to see the shadowy, hanging figure, and have the fun of pointing it out to their friends who are so deceived by the optical distraction (big bright picture on the billboard) that the figure of the FAN will be invisible to them. It is still very hard to notice the hanging FAN, and TELLER doesn't. PENN You go get the bad guy. I'll stay down here screaming and cowering. Go be a hero. TELLER runs towards the billboard. CARLOTTA is still stunned. A MAN, a passer-by, having heard the gun shot runs up. MAN He got you in the arm, huh? At that range you were lucky. PENN No, I'm not lucky! I got shot! I don't consider getting shot to be lucky. Lucky is winning the lottery. MAN Wait a minute. With that hair and the red fingernail, aren't you that guy that goes on TV and asks people to try to kill him? PENN No! I didn't ask people to try to kill me. I said I wished someone were trying to kill me. MAN And you said that on national TV? There are a lot of nuts out there, pal. What an asshole! Jesus, I'd like to blow your fucking brains out. You're lucky I don't have a gun. PENN Yup, I'm the luckiest man in the world. Mr. Lucky just got shot in the arm. MAN Well, it's probably all for the best. Maybe you'll think twice from now on before you say stupid shit on TV. If I had a gun I'd blow your ass off right now. EXTERIOR – THE PARKING LOT – BY THE FENCE IN FRONT OF THE BILLBOARD – CONTINUOUS TELLER is staring through the chain-link fence just in front of the huge supports of the billboard at a car parked in the street behind. It is a ranchwagon, a duplicate of the PENN and TELLER-mobile. TELLER looks back around the billboard at PENN, surrounded by the crowd, and clearly too busy to help. He decides to investigate by himself. He looks up at the fence, thinks, then does a soft-shoe step, a rhythmic slapping of the thighs and produces the string of silk handkerchiefs, a bouquet of paper flowers, and cane that he produced for the TV crew. He throws down the flowers, ties the string of hankies to the cane, and tosses the cane up so that it intertwines with the barbed wire at the top of the fence. He climbs the makeshift rope. From a distance we now see the scene. TELLER is climbing the fence. Directly above him the shadowy hard-to-notice figure of the FAN moves, and we now notice him. He is wearing a stocking mask, holding a rifle, and he is moving to point his rifle at TELLER. Still from a distance we see TELLER reach the top of the fence, look around, look up, freeze, and quietly climb down the fence again. With a set of amazing, gymnastic gyrations the FAN reverses himself and climbs quickly down from the sign. TELLER is scared, but also impressed. As the FAN reaches the bottom, he comes close to the fence, and grasps it with his fingers. TELLER sees that his left ring fingernail is painted red, just like PENN's. TELLER looks up at the FAN's stocking-masked face. Through the mask he looks back, and through the mask we can tell he is smiling at TELLER. It is not sinister, but warm, benign, almost friendly. The FAN turns, walks to the ranchwagon and drives away. TELLER, very excited, turns, then runs back across the parking lot. EXTERIOR – IN THE PARKING LOT – CONTINUOUS ACTION PENN and CARLOTTA are seated in the PENN and TELLER ranchwagon about to pull out of their parking spot. TELLER runs to catch up to them to tell them what he's seen. The back door is locked and the window is rolled up. PENN rolls down the window. TELLER is out of breath but wants to talk. PENN yells in this face out the window. PENN SHUT UP! Don't you say a word. Did you pay off your slimy, sick friend with the gun? It's dawning on TELLER that he's being blamed for shooting PENN. PENN Do you know where you blew it? Eh? You were just a little too anxious to run after a guy with a gun. I know you, you're not that brave. You're a coward. And that's where your little joke fell apart. You weren't even... CARLOTTA (interrupting, angry) Penn, Shut up! TELLER is ready to talk again. CARLOTTA (to TELLER) And you shut up too! You've gone too far. (to PENN & TELLER) This in not ringing a doorbell and running. This is serious. One of you has been shot. You have crossed from pleasant eccentrics to dangerous psychopaths. (to PENN) I'm taking you on a romantic ride to the hospital. (to TELLER) And you and go laugh alone at your last practical joke. PENN and CARLOTTA drive away in the ranchwagon. TELLER stands watching their car drive away. Poignant moment. WE PULL BACK from OVERHEAD, as TELLER stands alone. Still in the long overhead shot, we see the DUPLICATE RANCHWAGON pull into the parking lot from another driveway. It glides past TELLER, just out of his reach. TELLER watches it, knowing he could never catch it on foot. The DUPLICATE RANCHWAGON, drives out of the parking lot, through the parking lot of the adjacent casino, and halfway through the parking lot (of, say, Caesar's), beyond. It parks and TELLER realizes he can catch the driver. TELLER takes off in a dead run towards the RANCHWAGON. As he runs, he sees the driver get out, peel off his sniper jumpsuit, revealing underneath a gray suit that matches PENN and TELLER's, and walk with leisurely strides out the far driveway into the alley between two casinos. TELLER follows, running as fast as he can. There is nothing romanticized about the way TELLER runs; he is a normal guy, very out of breath. TELLER turns the corner and sees a ramp, leading to the boardwalk.

5. Get booked on *Late Night with David Letterman.*

6. Hide your hat full of cockroaches on the set. You don't have to be too clever about this. Remember, David doesn't know what you are going to do. If he did you never would have gotten past Step 5.

7. Show David another top hat. Pull a rabbit out. Ask him what he thinks of your trick. He will ridicule it. Good. This is his nature. It will keep him occupied while you switch the hat you pulled the rabbit out of for the hat full of bugs. Put the hat on his desk.

8. Egg him into complaining that the trick was lacking in surprise. Then say, "Surprise, David? You want surprise?"

9. Release the bugs all over everything. Pick them up and wave them at the camera. Dance them around on the desk.
10. During the commercial break, pick up as many as you can and give them back to your bug wrangler, but be sure to leave a few behind so Dave will remember your visit.

Penn Jillette with Albert Camus (right).
Café Rive Gauche, 1939.

KAMUS
KING OF CARDS

A Reminiscence by

PENN JILLETTE

Albert Camus is known to most as an existential writer and philosopher. But to me, he was much more. To me, Camus was the best damn table magician that ever lived. When I watched Albert handle a deck of cards, roll a franc across his fingers, or vanish a Gauloise, it didn't bother me that we were living in a random, godless universe. As a matter of fact, I liked it.

It was 1939, Paris amid the French and European disaster. I was struggling in Paris doing any odd job that came along. Not many came along, and there were more than a few days I went without a solid meal. I was poor, but in poverty there is clarity. I kept my dignity. Even if I went to bed hungry every night, I would not do mime. I had spent the last few days house-painting for a heavyset matron on rue des Fleurs and was celebrating my relative affluence over a couple of double espressos. I had settled in for an evening of free-form poetry in the café when a man in a beret came over to my table and asked if I would like to see some magic tricks. He had the sad pensive eyes of a philosopher and the aggressive, toothy grin of a magician.

I told him thanks but no thanks. I told him I was waiting for an old friend and I wanted to have some time alone with my thoughts. I told him we'd had a death in my family. I told him I would rather eat crêpes with the Boches than see a magic trick. I begged him to go to another table, but Albert was a pro. He smiled and ran through a few fancy shuffles and flourishes. He handled a deck competently, but what really knocked me out was his patter. I still remember every word.

"What does life mean in such a universe? Nothing else for the moment but indifference to the future and a desire to use up

continued on p. 42

39

From TELLER's POV we see the mysterious FAN in the gray suit at the top of the ramp. He turns to walk along the boardwalk. TELLER runs up the ramp after him, stubbing his toe on the way. EXTERIOR – THE BOARDWALK – CONTINUOUS TELLER is painfully exhausted. He looks down the boardwalk and sees the FAN walking away at a brisk pace. Too weary to follow on foot, TELLER spots a vacant wicker strolling chair passing, and hops in, points to the FAN, and says something to the chair pusher, and gives him money. The strolling chair starts to follow the FAN at the leisurely pace of the boardwalk. EXTERIOR – TRUMP'S PARKING LOT – SOME TIME LATER PENN and CARLOTTA have just gotten out of the RANCHWAGON. PENN's jacket is off. His arm is bandaged and in a arm sling. He takes a rotating emergency road light from the back of the RANCHWAGON. PENN & CARLOTTA walk to the back of the car and PENN opens the rear door. CARLOTTA You came down pretty hard on Teller. PENN What about you? CARLOTTA I just didn't want him to feel that this was just another practical joke. PENN My arm look okay? CARLOTTA It looks awful. How does it feel? PENN Well I can move it well enough to get at... PENN open his suitcoat and brings an envelope out of his inner breast pocket. PENN ...my five hundred dollars which is my per diem for the week, or more accurately my per weekem, and we're going to go out tonight and find out what it's like to be big winners. We deserve to unwind a little. We've had a tough day. Besides, tonight's our night – the guy said so. I was lucky to get shot in the arm. PENN puts his arm around CARLOTTA, they head into the casino. EXTERIOR – ON THE BOARDWALK – MEANWHILE The chase continues. The FAN stops, looks in a shop window, looks around casually. He hails a strolling chair of his own. TELLER hands a $20 bill to his taxi pusher. TAXI PUSHER (Pocketing the money) Follow that cab? Sure. TELLER's taxi moves out after the FAN'S taxi. INTERIOR – CASINO – CONTINUOUS PENN and CARLOTTA walk up to a change booth on the casino floor. PENN (to WOMAN IN CHANGE BOOTH) I'd like 500 silver dollars. He gets a giant bucket of 500 coins and walks over to a slot machine in the middle of a row. PENN puts the ghetto blaster on top of the slot machine. PENN (to CARLOTTA) Would you stand over there by that pillar, please? CARLOTTA crosses the floor, and stands by a pillar. PENN puts a silver dollar into the slot machine. PENN (yelling, to CARLOTTA, in a dumb voice) Hey, honey! I got a good feeling about this here silver dollar. He pulls the handle. While the machine spins, he turns on the ghetto blaster, which plays the sounds of jackpot alarms. Meanwhile, PENN noisily pours all the coins from his bucket into the receiving tray of the machine, then tries to catch them in the bucket again as the tray overflows. PENN Yeee Haw! (yelling, to CARLOTTA) Come over here, honey. Help me pick up all this loot. PENN starts to scoop up the money. CARLOTTA joins him. PENN puts his arm around CARLOTTA. PENN Feels great to be with a winner, doesn't it, baby? He gives her a big kiss. PENN Yeeee Haw! He picks up CARLOTTA, spins her around and kisses her again. PENN and CARLOTTA go back to picking up the loot. EXTERIOR – THE END OF THE BOARDWALK – A LITTLE LATER TELLER's taxi is still following the FAN's taxi. TELLER pulls a blanket up over his knees like grandma. We see the TAXI PUSHER, quite weary, pushing from behind. TAXI PUSHER How long we gonna follow this guy? TELLER's hand comes around the side of the cart with a $20 bill. As the FAN's taxi reaches the end of the boardwalk, it turns around. The FAN's taxi passes within a yard of TELLER's taxi, and TELLER looks in. In the darkness of the taxi, TELLER can just make out the shadowy figure of a man with a haircut with a long forelock like PENN's. Although we don't see his face clearly, we can tell that he is looking at TELLER. As the taxi passes, TELLER sees the FAN's fingers. One of the nails is painted red, just like PENN's. TELLER is more excited and mystified than ever. TELLER's taxi reaches the end of the boardwalk and turns around. From TELLER's P.O.V. we see the FAN's hand come around his taxi and hand a $20 bill to the driver. The driver begins to jog. TELLER digs out a $20 bill and hands it to his driver. His driver starts jogging also. The FAN's hand passes a $100 bill to his driver. His driver starts to run. Taking up the challenge, TELLER whips out his wallet plucks a $100 bill and flicks it to his driver. INTERIOR – CASINO – A CHANGE BOOTH BY THE BOARDWALK ENTRANCE – CONTINUOUS PENN puts his bucket of dollars on the cashier's counter. PENN 'Scuse me, pretty lady, could I trade in my winnin's for four hundred and ninety-nine crisp, new bills please? And why don't you keep five for yourself? The cashier makes the exchange. PENN takes the cash, puts his arm around CARLOTTA, and walks with her towards the boardwalk door. PENN Come on, little lady. I'm going to buy you the thickest steak in town. They go out the door and step onto the boardwalk. We watch from inside. As they stand there, a boardwalk taxi, pushed by a panting, running man whizzes by. PENN and CARLOTTA watch it. Four seconds later a second taxi zooms by. PENN and CARLOTTA watch it too, then head off to dinner. INTERIOR – BACKSTAGE AT THE CASINO – IN THE SHOP – THE NEXT MORNING Sunlight streams into a stainless steel sink. A drop of blood falls into the water collected at the bottom by the drain. Then another drop. PAN UP to disclose TELLER with an eyedropper of stage blood, testing its viscosity. He is satisfied. He picks up a gallon Clorox bottle, labeled, BLOOD – THICK, and goes to put it away. Suddenly, from on stage, he hears PENN's voice. PENN (O.S.) Teller! (pause, in different inflection) Teller? TELLER puts down the test tube and, still carrying the large bottle of stage blood, pokes his head out of the curtained prop area. He hears the voice again. PENN (O.S.) (as if announcing the act) Teller! As PENN's voice repeats TELLER's name again and again, each time with a different inflection, as if tape recorded on numerous previous occasions, TELLER follows the sound. Now he sees PENN, standing in silhouette in the middle of the empty stage. He starts to walk towards PENN. At about the middle of the chest, a flame begins to eat through the form, and the fire discloses that the silhouette of PENN is in reality a life-size rifle practice target, altered with paper and paint to resemble PENN. A gray suit coat has been drawn on him. String has been colored with magic marker and glued on to resemble hair. It is on cardboard stilts to make it the right height. The fingernail is beautifully painted in with bright red nail polish. TELLER stares, fascinated, mystified. PENN's voice is coming from a small tape recorder, attached with masking tape to the form. TAPE RECORDING (in PENN's voice) Teller! (tape edit) I wish somebody were trying to kill me. This message repeats twice, and the fire continues to burn a larger and large hole in "PENN"'s chest, as TELLER watches. TAPE RECORDING (Johnny Cash singing) I fell into a burning ring of fire. I went down, down, down, and the flames kept coming higher... The burning form begins to crumble. TAPE RECORDING (PENN's voice, laughing) Hey! It was just a joke! The voice continues, the burning form collapses next to a curtain. The base of the curtain starts to catch fire. TELLER spots the danger, and quickly quenches the flames with the handiest available extinguisher, his bottle of blood. INTERIOR – OUTSIDE THE BACKSTAGE DOOR – CONTINUOUS PENN is arriving. He has a note from TELLER in his hand. He is about to enter the backstage area. A SHOWGIRL sees his bandaged arm, and runs up to him. SHOWGIRL I heard about what you guys did. I think it's so brave of you to challenge anybody in the world to kill you. PENN (macho) Well, a man's gotta do what a man's gotta do. CARLOTTA walks up to PENN. CARLOTTA (dryly) Yuh. Did you find Teller yet? PENN He must be backstage. PENN and CARLOTTA enter backstage door. They see TELLER pouring blood on the talking, burning cut-out of PENN. TELLER's hands are covered with blood. It's a weird scene they are watching. PENN begins to laugh. TELLER is startled. CARLOTTA is just a little freaked out. CARLOTTA This is a little too weird. PENN You don't get it, honey. It's a great joke. The comedy stylings of Teller. This is another joke you're preparing right? This one's great. You send us a note saying you spent all night chasing my doppelganger in a strolling chair, and meanwhile you got your little Penn/Mrs. Bates talking doll that you're lighting on fire and dousing with stage blood. You're such a witty guy. I think we all should go to the dressing room and sit to talk. I think you should be resting. C'mon Mr. Funny, let's talk. CARLOTTA No. I think you two should talk. And I think you should alone. And I think you should talk seriously. I have only one thing to say, and that is: Please keep in mind that one of you was actually shot. (smiling quizzically) I don't really understand this male-bonding thing. Practical jokes are your life. I know that. I don't want to steal your fun. But why don't you have a little heart-to-heart, and find out how you can have your fun and still keep our health insurance at a reasonable rate. When you've worked it out, give me a call. I'll be at my uncle's. CARLOTTA starts to exit, then turns back, gives PENN a little kiss. CARLOTTA You talk to him. I can't help you with everything. A man's gotta do what a man's gotta do. PENN and TELLER exit towards dressing room. INTERIOR – PENN and TELLER'S DRESSING ROOM – FIFTEEN MINUTES LATER It's a very spacious, plush, comfy place. TELLER is sitting at the dressing table, putting finishing touches on a plaster head of PENN. As the conversation progresses, TELLER adds torn flesh to the neck, puts a wig on it, and completes it with prop glasses to match PENN's. PENN You tied me to an operating table. Forced Uncle Ernesto to go at my throat with a scalpel. That was funny. We all had a good laugh. But now I've been shot in the arm. And only a very, very sick individual would think that's funny. And forget about the burning dummy gag. I don't like it. I don't think it's funny. Carlotta is right. You have turned into a goddamn psycho. You know her. She's really mad at you. And I bet she won't even talk to you until you calm down and apologize. A window is open just a tiny bit at the far end of the dressing room. There is the sound of a gunshot, and the dressing room mirror shatters, throwing shards of glass all over PENN and TELLER. Neither PENN nor TELLER reacts at all to the explosion. PENN Let me tell you something, my little friend. That better have been a blank powder charge over by the window and a squib behind the mirror. Because if you hired someone to shoot a real gun off between us, I don't think that's funny. Actually, even the blank and the squib is only mildly funny. This is not a knee-slapper. This is the end of the joke. Since my arm is sore, why don't you sweep up all the glass, oh, Comedy King. I'll tell Carlotta about the squib. She'll be anxious to talk to you when it's chilly in hell. You know how she's enjoying your jokes. PENN grabs the dummy head and exits. TELLER reaches behind the mirror and pulls out a squib (small explosive special-effects device). He is amazed. From the hallway we hear a loud GUNSHOT, and SCREAMS OF SHOWGIRLS. TELLER looks to the door. PENN enters, holding his plaster head, of which a large portion has been blasted away. PENN is covered with a film of plaster, and looks pale and shaken. PENN slams the door behind him and locks it. PENN (quietly) It isn't you, is it? TELLER shakes his head "no". PENN heaves the remains of the plaster head onto the floor. The wig with the forelock and the glasses fall prominently at PENN's feet. PENN takes his glasses off, and tosses them on the floor. He removes his gray suit jacket, tie and unbuttons his shirt. He walks into the bathroom of the dressing room, takes scissors and fingernail polish remover and brings them back into the room. PENN hands the scissors to TELLER, and sits down. TELLER knows what to do; he begins cutting PENN's hair, as PENN starts to remove his red nail polish. PENN So, how 'bout those Mets? EXTERIOR – SEEDY MOTEL – A FEW HOURS LATER Film noir. Pan over Atlantic City, away from the boardwalk, to a the land of seedy, fleabag motels. We swing in on one. INTERIOR – THE SEEDY MOTEL – CONTINUOUS We are looking at a yellow legal pad and an ash tray overflowing with unfiltered cigarettes, a dirty hotel-room glass, half full of a dark liquid. We WIDEN to include a 2 liter bottle of cola. We continue to WIDEN to include PENN sitting at the desk. His hair is cut severely short. His glasses are gone. His fingernail polish is gone. The motel room has been converted into a fortress, a B-movie gangster hideout. PENN is smoking a cigarette, and writing on a legal pad. He reads the passage he has written. PENN "Memoirs of the Hunted, page 3. Soon, a hundred and fifty pushups a day. Every stranger a potential assassin. I'm smoking too much and drinking much too much cola. I must stay alert." ONE SIGNAL KNOCK ON THE DOOR. PENN looks sharply up, walks to the door. He taps once on the door. ANOTHER KNOCK ON THE DOOR. THIS TIME IT IS THE MIDDLE OF THE DRUM SOLO OF INNAGODDADAVITA. PENN swings open the door very quickly. TELLER, wearing a full Ninja outfit complete with mask is carrying a shopping bag. He slams the door behind him. PENN puts his ear to the door as TELLER puts the shopping bag down on the counter. PENN Were you followed? TELLER shakes his head "no". TELLER nods and takes a box of cocoa puffs off the top of the grocery bag. PENN takes the Cocoa Puffs and eats them by the handful, while TELLER begins unloading the bag. He next takes out a stack of audio cassettes, including "Johnny Rivers' Greatest Hits". He puts one cassette into the tape deck and plays it. TELLER pulls out of the bag a roll of surgical tape. He pulls out a utility knife, and tapes it in the back under his shirt. He pulls out a hatchet and puts it under his belt in the back of his pants. He backs away a few paces from PENN, reaches behind his back to grab the utility knife he just taped in place, whips it out and slits his left pants-leg. He pulls out a gravity-knife and slides it in the top of his boot, pulls out a blackjack and tapes it to his leg. He pulls out a package of razor blades, and tapes one in the instep of each boot. He puts a set of brass knuckles on his right hand, and reaches to take the box of Cocoa Puffs from PENN, holds the box between his legs, takes out a set of nunchaks and hefts them while he munches the cereal. The music plays from the cassette player: Martial arts movie music, alternating with film noir sax. TELLER looks at PENN and smiles paternally. PENN turns back to his writing. INTERIOR – THE MOTEL ROOM – LATER We see the ghetto blaster. Next to it is a stack of opened tapes, including the sound tracks to "Taxi Driver", all the James Bond movies, "The Silencers" (starring Dean Martin as Matt Helm), "Left-Handed Gun", "Films of Violence" by Moraconi, "To Live and Die in LA", etc. He selects one of the cassettes on which no royalties are due and plays it. PENN is still writing. PENN "Memoirs of the Hunted, page 117. I'm running a fever all the time. Every cell in my body longs to live its final moments to the fullest. I'd never noticed how beautiful the blue on a yellow legal pad is. I haven't slept in so long that I'm...really tired." TELLER is drawing a medical textbook heart with blue veins, etc. on the wall of the motel room with crayola crayons. PENN "I have entered a different world: a world of junkies, buggers, prostitutes, hunters, and me—the hunted. Shuffling off the mortal coil is lonely. I will die alone, even though Fats is here with me." (to TELLER) I'm just calling you Fats so they won't know it's you. I don't want to get you stiffed too. TELLER has placed himself at the far side of the room and is throwing ninja stars at the heart drawn on the wall. PENN (returning to his manuscript) "Death row, Main Street, it's all the same to me now. I can see the future, reflected in puddles of my own blood, on the dirty concrete. I need another cigarette." PENN takes the last cigarette out of a pack. He throws the pack into a waste basket, which contains nothing but used cellophane cassette-wrappers, crushed packs of cigarettes, and Cocoa Puffs boxes. He lights a cigarette and looks over at TELLER. PENN We gotta call the police again. I hate this. They get paid to protect people like us. PENN everything that is given. Belief in the meaning of life always implies a scale of values, a choice, our preferences. Belief in the absurd, according to our definitions, teaches the contrary. But this is worth examining. Pick a card."

He offered me a fan of cards. I pulled out one card and listened to his directions.

"If one could only say just once: 'This is clear,' all would be saved. But these men vie with one another in proclaiming that nothing is clear, all is chaos, that all man has is his lucidity and his definite knowledge of the walls surrounding him. All these experiences agree and confirm one another. The mind, when it reaches its limits, must make a judgment and choose its conclusions. Look at your card and remember it."

I looked at the card. I *still* remember it: it was the three of clubs.

"Conscious men have been seen to fulfill their task amid the most stupid of wars without considering themselves in contradiction. This is because it was essential to elude nothing. There is thus a metaphysical honor in enduring the world's absurdity. Conquest or play-acting, multiple loves, absurd revolt, are tributes that man pays to his dignity in a campaign in which he is defeated in advance. Return the card to the pack."

He did a perfect one-handed fan, I slid the card in, he snapped the fan closed and began shuffling feverishly but without passion. He continued talking about card tricks.

"Hence I can choose as illustration a work comprising everything that denotes awareness of the absurd, having a clear starting point and a lucid climate. Its consequences will enlighten us. If the absurd is not respected in it, we shall know by what expedient illusion enters in."

He stopped and took a deep drag on his unfiltered cigarette. As the smoke curled out of his mouth he inhaled it into his nose —a French inhale for effect as the French magician continued. It was building nicely.

"There have always been men to defend the rights of the irrational. The tradition of what may be called humiliated thought has never ceased to exist. The criticism of rationalism has been made so often that it seems unnecessary to begin again. Yet our epoch is marked by the rebirth of those paradoxical systems that strive to trip up the reason as if truly it had always forged ahead. But that is not so much a proof of the efficacy of the reason as of the intensity of its hopes. On the plane of history, such a constancy of two attitudes illustrates the essential passion of man torn between his urge toward unity and the clear vision he may have of the walls enclosing him."

On this Camus gestured wildly toward the "walls enclosing him" in the café. He stood up on my table and with empty, unmotivated violence he threw the entire deck into the air. He shook his head, shrugged, and while the cards were fluttering to the floor, reached in and snatched out a single card. He was thrilled at the commotion he had caused to the other beret-wearing espresso sippers. With a flick of the wrist he showed me the face of the card he had just grabbed. It was the queen of hearts.

"Is *this* your card?"

I shook my head. He grinned and said, "You see? To the absurd man, it means nothing."

He handed me his business card:

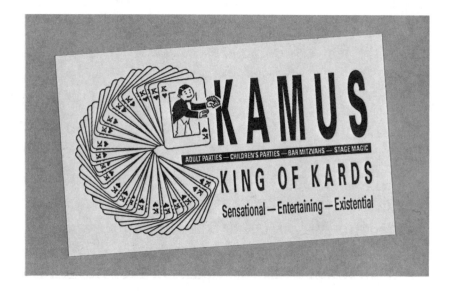

"It's an old card," he said. "Lately, I do a lot more with cigarettes. I also have a great act for bachelor parties."

I kept the card.

PSI TV

Traditionally people who claim to be psychic have looked like jerks. They have surrounded their work with superstitious window dressing: crystal balls, astrological charts, tarot decks. Or they have used drugs or hypnosis to help them do what any healthy person can do naturally.

James ("the Amazing") Randi, a Canadian magician (who now claims to be a U.S. citizen), is perhaps the world's foremost investigator of the paranormal and debunker of psychic fraud. He says:

> When it comes to the occult, most of us are suckers. People believe anything in print, however it contradicts common sense and experience. It is comparatively easy to fool people with trick rhetoric, and lead them to asinine behavior.

But, ironically, this asinine behavior can provide the scientific observer with important clues to the conditions which promote the appearance of genuine PSI phenomena. A recent study (Knapp & McCarthy, 1987) examined the practices of occultists and found striking patterns:

1. Most of the people who claim telepathic powers are not too bright. It seems that *knowledge and education interfere with PSI experiences.* There is no doubt that drug-damaged old hippies looking at tea leaves often say startling things. If we want to exercise our full psychic potential, *we must be prepared to suppress our intelligence* and go with the flow.
2. Psychics are not afraid to look silly. Goofy garments, mantras, rituals have no physical function, but a very important psychological effect. They symbolize freedom from inhibition. And *eliminating* inhibition is absolutely essential to the experience of PSI phenomena.

45

3. It is no accident that religious fanatics tend to have PSI experiences more often than others. The ability to *believe* in things that often contradict experience and defy logic is essential. To be a psychic, *you must be willing to accept as truth the first thing that comes to mind.*

Thus, to gain access to all your telepathic abilities* you must adopt three simple attitude adjustments: Set aside all knowledge, eliminate inhibition, and accept whatever happens with uncritical belief. These things are not hard to do. They take, in fact, much less effort than you use in rational life. It's as easy as watching TV.

In fact, TV is a useful concept in learning to do simple tricks of mind reading. The passive state of the television viewer bears marked similarities to the trance condition, and shares with it an effortless, disconnected, sensual, visual orientation.

Which brings us to our trick, PSI TV. This is an easy, good, impressive stunt for parties.

Here's how it works:

1. Choose a partner. Any cooperative person will do. Remember, intelligence is not a plus in PSI experiments.
2. Have your partner select an image to concentrate on: Tell him or her to take a random magazine or book, flip open to a random page, read the top line and make a mental picture of it. Tell him to make sure he's chosen a vivid visual image, like "house," "airplane," or even something slightly more complex, like "flat tire," "broken violin." Avoid things like "schizophrenia," "noblesse oblige," "the laws of the Iroquois nation" and so forth. It is also important *not* to allow your partner to select any image that comes to mind. You don't want to get involved in his or her personal life. As soon as your partner has chosen an image, ask him to close the book.

---

* Telepathy, the projection of pictorial data from one mind to the other, is the only proven form of PSI experience. Telekinesis, poltergeists, precognition, and astral projection appear from all current studies to be sheer bunk.

3. Now, on a piece of paper draw a TV set such as the sample
we have drawn here:

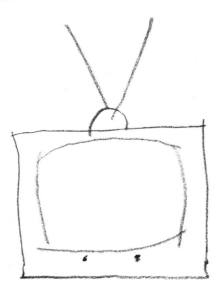

Yes, it looks silly, but you *must* take it seriously and cast
your inhibitions aside. Hold it up in front of your eyes, and
move it back and forth toward and away from your face.

4. Ask your partner to picture his image, drawn in black lines
on a white television screen.

5. Keep moving the paper toward and away from your eyes.
Breathe deeply. You will find yourself beginning to day-
dream. Good. Let your eyes close. Slowly a simple image in
white lines, like chalk on a blackboard, will appear. Open
your eyes and look at the picture of the TV. Imagine your
mental image on the screen of the TV, then take a pencil
and draw it in. What you have drawn should be identifiable
as a simplified representation of what your friend is pictur-
ing. Compare notes with your friend.

6. With increased practice you will find yourself able to make
more and more complex drawings. This is especially enjoy-
able with new friends, as it will help you to establish a rap-
port easily. Try it on a first date; you'll be amazed the effect
it can have on somebody you want to get close to.

reaches for the telephone and dials the police. PENN Hello, Police? My name is Penn Jillette. I reported the attempted homicide about five hours ago. P. E. N. N...... TELLER is a little disappointed that the fun may end soon. INTERIOR – THE MOTEL ROOM – LATER PENN is still waiting for the police to arrive. TELLER saws off two three-inch pieces from a dowel. He meticulously drills tiny holes in them. He threads the ends of an 18-inch loop of piano-wire through them, and twists them in place. He walks up behind a chair in which he has stacked pillows as a makeshift practice dummy. He loops his homemade garrote around the dummy's neck and strangles it. PENN "I'm beginning to know my murderer like I know myself. And I don't hate him. I feel hate, but the hate I feel is for the dogooders, like the do-gooder that called in the cops. We don't need some flatfoot. Why can't they leave Fats and me alone to vanquish the dragon of our vanished dreams...?" (to TELLER) Are there any more Cocoa Puffs? Where are the goddam police? We could have been killed three times over. (PENN returns to his writing) "Yeah, the cop was a goody-two-shoes all right. He had one of those faces like the inside of a pork sausage, after you inject it with water from a hypodermic needle. All full of bourgeois loyalty. He was gonna be a big help." A KNOCK ON THE DOOR. PENN (relieved) It's about time. TELLER with all his weapons sneaks up to the door and motions to PENN to stay back where it's safe. He peeks through the peephole in the door. He looks out and sees a woman in street clothes. She has red hair and a pony tail. He catches just a glimpse as she slides a gun into her purse. TELLER stands behind the door with his nunchaks ready, and releases the lock. The woman pushes the door open. She steps into the room. WOMAN Are you Penn? TELLER slams the door behind her, and brandishes his nunchaks. The WOMAN turns. In swift, professional combat, she takes the nunchaks from him, incapacitates him, and deftly removes all his concealed weapons one by one as if checking off a mental list of all the places amateurs typically hide weapons. She is sitting on TELLER, her gun to his head. PENN (to TELLER) You shouldn't have done that, Penn. Now you're really in trouble. Excuse me. PENN rises and heads towards the door. THE WOMAN barks an order at PENN. WOMAN Call the police station! Have them send a patrol car. PENN What? You want me to call the police? So that's what's going to do in my arch-nemesis! Her own desire to be punished. WOMAN What? I'm officer Mac Namara. 37th Precinct. She shows her badge. OFFICER MAC NAMARA You fit the description of the big asshole who asked people to kill him. And this wimp under my knees fits the description of some pathetic psycho trying to carry out your wish. PENN That's close to right. But the pathetic psycho is my partner Teller, and he wasn't trying to kill me. He was trying to protect me. OFFICER MAC NAMARA gets off TELLER's chest. TELLER pulls a ninja star from his breast pocket (where it had been sticking into his chest while she sat), and glares resentfully at MAC NAMARA. PENN, on the other hand, looks admiringly at MAC NAMARA. PENN This is great. I thought they'd send some fat guy who ate donuts. EXTERIOR – ALLEY BETWEEN OMINOUS, TALL BUILDINGS – TEN MINUTES LATER OFFICER MAC NAMARA is leading PENN and TELLER. She is very calm. They are very nervous. PENN is grabbing OFFICER MAC NAMARA's hand and sticking it in under her coat. PENN Keep your hand on your goddam gun. If anybody comes near me, BAM! They're history. You're supposed to be a professional at this law-enforcement stuff. Why are we walking? Don't you have a parking space at the police station? TELLER looks up at a building nervously. Suddenly he sees the barrel of a gun emerge from a window. He tackles PENN, knocking him down, just as... GUN SHOT. OFFICER MAC NAMARA stands, pistol out, pointing at the building, her body between the unseen assailant and PENN. We see the gun and the vague form of the assailant withdraw from the window. OFFICER MAC NAMARA (yelling) Let's go! OFFICER MAC NAMARA jumps onto a trash can, pulls down the fire escape, and scampers up onto it. OFFICER MAC NAMARA I got the fire escape. You two get in the building, and make sure he can't get out. TELLER dashes towards the building. PENN jogs behind him with less enthusiasm. PENN Yo! With all due respect, I think we should be running the other way. If a man has a gun, you run away from him. We should be running the other way. TELLER gestures to PENN to follow. PENN No. PENN does not run into the building. He runs back into the alley, looking for a safe place to hide. As PENN stands there cowering, we see a back door of the building open. The FAN who has been following PENN and TELLER comes out. He is close to PENN's height and has a haircut that copies PENN's. He is built very strongly, like a giant gymnast. FAN Penn! OFFICER MAC NAMARA on the fire escape hears the voice, pivots, and points her gun at the FAN. PENN glances up and sees OFFICER MAC NAMARA. By now TELLER has reached the room from which the gun originally emerged. He looks out on the scene. Throughout the remainder of this scene, TELLER watches, as if a spectator at a movie. FAN Penn. He reaches into his inner jacket pocket as if for a gun. OFFICER MAC NAMARA is ready to fire. PENN sees the corner of a notebook coming out of the FAN's jacket. He realizes it is not a gun. PENN throws himself between the FAN and OFFICER MAC NAMARA, protectively, and looks up at OFFICER MAC NAMARA with a smile. PENN It's just an autograph book. We're okay. We're cool. We're cool. He takes the notebook from the FAN, pulls out his pen. PENN (to the FAN) Who do you want it made out to? FAN Penn. PENN Now, that's a remarkable coincidence. It's not that common a name. The FAN reaches into his jacket pocket, pulls out a gun, and sticks it against PENN's throat. We notice he has a red fingernail. PENN Damn. OFFICER MAC NAMARA tries in vain to get a clear shot at the FAN, but PENN's body is blocking her trajectory. PENN Could I just turn a little bit? The sun's right in my eyes. The FAN sticks the gun harder into PENN's throat. PENN Hey, piece of cake! My pupils will adjust. No problem. OFFICER MAC NAMARA (O.S.) (herself) C'mon, Penn. I can't shoot him through your head. Damn it! OFFICER MAC NAMARA, on the fire escape below lowers her gun. PENN (to the FAN) So, I guess you've seen us on TV, eh? You know, a lot of the stuff I say on TV I don't mean. You know, I just kid around. I make jokes and stuff. FAN Penn. PENN That's right. So I guess, sitting at home in your little apartment, doing pushups and shaving your head, stuff on TV seems pretty real to you, eh? FAN Penn. PENN I was just saying to Teller, my partner, the other day, I was saying, there's a certain kind of bond that we have with the people that watch us on television. I mean they come up to us and ask us for an autograph and we just give it to them, because we like them and we trust them. So when they ask for something, we give it to them. By the way, that's a really neat gun. Could I see it? The FAN pushes the barrel of the gun directly against PENN's eye. PENN Thanks. It is a nice gun. Is it heavy? FAN Penn. PENN You know my partner, Teller... PENN points up to TELLER. OFFICER MAC NAMARA crouches out of view. The FAN points his gun at TELLER. PENN No. That's not what I had in mind. That gun sure looks like fun. Could I hold it? I'll hold it on Teller. I think I have a better angle. Wouldn't it be fun to have Penn holding a gun on Teller? We are close on PENN and the FAN again. FAN Penn. PENN That's right. You can trust me. Just give me the gun. The FAN hands over the gun to PENN. PENN accepts the gun and relaxes. FAN Penn. PENN You don't care about me at all. What you told me was the same kind of lie you always tell on TV. Except there you do it for money, and here you were doing it because you thought I was going to shoot you. You lied, because you didn't trust me not to shoot you. PENN I...I trust you. It's just you had a gun in my neck. FAN No. You don't trust me. You don't trust anybody that watches you on TV. It's just your job. You don't trust me at all. PENN I do too. FAN You do not. PENN No...I, I really do. I'll prove it. FAN No, it's too late for that. PENN gives the gun back to the FAN. OFFICER MAC NAMARA and TELLER watch incredulously. The FAN, receiving the gun back, is touched. Then suddenly he grabs PENN by the hair and shoves the gun against his neck. PENN So you don't really trust me. FAN No, I don't. PENN What do you mean, you don't? FAN I don't trust you. PENN If you really trusted me, you'd give me the gun back. FAN We already established that I don't trust you. OFFICER MAC NAMARA quietly withdraws from the fire escape. PENN All those nights you were sitting alone in your little psycho apartment. And Teller and I came on TV and amused you. What do you think we did that for? FAN Money. Power. Fame. PENN Okay. Yeah. But we also did it for you. This trust thing is a two-way street. FAN I agree with that. I gave you the gun. You gave it back. Two way street. PENN Okay. Maybe trust is a three-way street. Just give me the gun. FAN I already gave you the gun. PENN And I gave it back. Just give it to me once more, and I promise you I'll give it back to you and you can stick it into my neck, just the way you like it. FAN Well, you did give me the gun back once. PENN Yes, come on, my brother-in-trust. Just give me the goddam gun. The FAN backs away from PENN, stares into his eyes. PENN stares back. There's a moment of understanding. The FAN hands the gun to PENN. He turns and walks away, a deliberate few steps, then jogs out of sight. MAC NAMARA and TELLER run back into the building. PENN stands, holding the gun, as the FAN disappears around a corner. TELLER and OFFICER MAC NAMARA arrive at street level. OFFICER MAC NAMARA (gun drawn, urgent) Where'd he go? PENN (still dazed) It's okay. He gave me the gun back. He's all right. Around the corner that the FAN retreated around roars the FAN's ranchwagon, at top speed, heading straight for PENN. TELLER pushes OFFICER MAC NAMARA and PENN safely into a doorway, and dives on top of them. As the ranchwagon passes, OFFICER MAC NAMARA steps out behind it and fires shots at it. The car gets away. INTERIOR – MAC NAMARA'S CAR – FIFTEEN MINUTES LATER PENN, TELLER and OFFICER MAC NAMARA are riding along the waterfront. It is almost sunset. PENN Well, I guess it's the slammer for me, eh? Maximum security. Solitary. Guards around the clock. There's no telling how far this wacko will go to kill me. Probably need a food tester. OFFICER MAC NAMARA You're not going to prison, Penn. PENN What do you mean? I don't mind. It's for my own good. OFFICER MAC NAMARA The p.d. cannot afford to put every asshole that wants to get killed in maximum security. Why did you go on TV and say you wanted people to kill you? Aren't you supposed to do card tricks, or something? PENN I know my rights. And I have the right to go to prison. Want me to give you a reason to lock me up? OFFICER MAC NAMARA You do one thing that's illegal, I'll make your wish come true, and blow your face all over the upholstery. It would save you some time and save the taxpayer some money. PENN Okay. If you aren't taking me to prison, where are you taking me? OFFICER MAC NAMARA pulls the car to a stop in front of a pier. OFFICER MAC NAMARA My place. She nods towards a wharf where old, crusty fishing boats are tied up, and surprises PENN with a sexy smile. OFFICER MAC NAMARA You'll be safe here. PENN (smiling) You're the cop. You know best. They get out of the car. OFFICER MAC NAMARA leads PENN among the boats. OFFICER MAC NAMARA Hurry up, Penn. Teller, you bring the luggage. She tosses the car keys to TELLER, who is none too happy with this treatment. He goes to open the trunk, grudgingly. EXTERIOR – MAC NAMARA'S BOAT – FIVE MINUTES LATER OFFICER MAC NAMARA and PENN hop easily onto the boat. TELLER struggles with the luggage. OFFICER MAC NAMARA unlocks and opens folding doors on the cabin. Inside is a 12– year-old's dream hideout. The style is a combination of comfortable, feminine, and spartan/military, i.e. cafe curtains and framed pictures of Chuck Norris and Bruce Lee. There is a TV, a refrigerator full of sodas, lots of snacks. PENN immediately makes himself at home. OFFICER MAC NAMARA Well, here it is. Home sweet home. PENN How long will we be here? OFFICER MAC NAMARA Till we catch that creep. Might be a while. Get comfortable. Would you like a cola? PENN Yeah. Thanks. PENN is looking over OFFICER MAC NAMARA'S record collection. OFFICER MAC NAMARA brings PENN a cola and a glass with ice and lime. PENN looks over at TELLER, piling the luggage. PENN You got a Yoohoo for Teller? OFFICER MAC NAMARA Yeah, in the fridge. Help yourself. Grudgingly, TELLER does so. He is resentful and suspicious of MAC NAMARA. Meanwhile OFFICER MAC NAMARA goes downstairs into the sleeping cabin. PENN pulls out a Velvet Underground album from her record collection. PENN (calling to OFFICER MAC NAMARA inside) You like the Velvet Underground? OFFICER MAC NAMARA sticks her head above deck. Her hair is down, and she is starting to look like a woman. PENN notices. TELLER notices PENN noticing and disapproves. OFFICER MAC NAMARA Yeah! Love 'em. She goes below deck again. PENN has pulled out the Velvet Underground album and started playing "Femme Fatale". It is a great sound system. PENN Yeah. They were the best. I had such a crush on Nico. I've always been a sucker for classy Eurotrash in sunglasses. OFFICER MAC NAMARA emerges. She is classy Eurotrash in sunglasses. OFFICER MAC NAMARA I don't wear them to look like the Highway Patrol. TELLER is starting to pull a record out to look at it. OFFICER MAC NAMARA pushes the record back in as she walks by. TELLER is starting to really dislike her. PENN It's amazing. You look so much less like a cop. OFFICER MAC NAMARA Oh, don't worry. You're still in good hands. OFFICER MAC NAMARA lifts her shirt, exposing quite a body, and shows PENN the pistol stuck in the top of her jeans. PENN is impressed. TELLER thinks it's cornball. OFFICER MAC NAMARA We got some time to kill. PENN With the Velvets playing I like to watch the Three Stooges. OFFICER MAC NAMARA Oh, I love the Stooges. MAC NAMARA selects a videocassette from her library. She puts it into her vcr. PENN You know, most women don't. Most women I've met just think they're stupid. OFFICER MAC NAMARA Oh, I don't think they're stupid. I think they're sexy. She hits the PLAY button, and shoots PENN an inviting glance. OFFICER MAC NAMARA Velvet Underground. Three Stooges. Cola beverage. I'm set. Meanwhile OFFICER MAC NAMARA has lowered a folding bunk bed from the wall right in front of the television. She sits down. PENN sits beside her. There is no room for TELLER, who stands looking at them. PENN (to Teller) You know, Teller, no one's trying to kill you. Why don't you go back to the hotel and pick up some of our stuff or something. Maybe catch a movie. OFFICER MAC NAMARA instantly tosses keys to Teller. OFFICER MAC NAMARA Take the car. We don't need it. Sullenly TELLER gets ready to leave. OFFICER MAC NAMARA Give a call from the pay phone before you come back. PENN You know, just so we don't think you're the bad guy. I wouldn't want my partner getting shot accidentally. TELLER memorizes the phone number, and leaves. The sun is setting, and it's pretty romantic. PENN points at the tv. PENN Is this the one where they're plumbers? EXTERIOR – NIGHT – MOVIE REVIVAL THEATRE – FOUR HOURS LATER A show is over, and among the people leaving we pick up TELLER. TELLER walks away down the street, but the camera remains to pan up to the marquee: "THREE STOOGES – ALL SHEMP MARATHON". TELLER walks up the ramp to the boardwalk. From beneath the boardwalk, the ranchwagon emerges. The FAN gets out. He follows TELLER. As TELLER walks along the boardwalk, he senses the FAN behind him. TELLER glances back then retreats into the nearest store, a PAWN SHOP. EXTERIOR – PAWN SHOP – FIFTEEN MINUTES LATER A

MAGIC FOR MIKE RED DOG

by

TELLER

It was early September and I was driving on Interstate 10 across the Arizona desert toward my home in Los Angeles in a little white station wagon, made in Japan. Penn had gone to Europe for six weeks with The Residents, an avant-garde band; I had been in Denver doing magic shows at a Renaissance festival and watching old hippies pretend to be knights.

I kept checking the thermostat to make sure the air conditioning wouldn't drive the engine temperature up too high. I had the soundtrack of *Psycho* on the stereo and was steering with my left hand, practicing the DeManche Change with my right. (The DeManche Change is a secret sleight-of-hand move magicians use to switch an object visible at the fingertips for one hidden in the hand.)

I was sick of the dazzling majesty of the Arizona desert. The big rocks just made me think how I'd be dead and forgotten before another eighth of an inch was worn into their colossal faces.

Dead and forgotten! When Jimi Hendrix or Liberace or even Camille, the piano player at Julio's Buffet in Hollywood, died, people were broken up about it. They missed not so much the music as the musician, the *personality.*

But nobody misses magicians. People rarely even remember their names. Their props, sometimes ("Remember that guy who pulled a brick out of your soup?"), but never their names. Anybody with any heart or talent gets out of magic early and becomes a comedian, a film director or a talk-show host.

So I was driving along, getting depressed, when I saw, half a mile ahead on the flat bright road, a short hitchhiker, a teenager, I guessed. I decided I would do a good deed and pick him up, making my pointless, obscure life of use to somebody.

I slowed down. As I got closer, I began to have second thoughts. This hitchhiker was short, but he was no teenager. He had a leathery look about him, dark and hard and dirty. I thought better of it and drove past.

But it was too late. He had already noticed me slowing down, and was jogging after me along the shoulder of the highway. I had to stop now. I leaned across the front seat and pulled up the lock. The hitchhiker opened the door.

He was in his thirties with small, hooded eyes, and a half-hearted goatee. He was wearing a black T-shirt which had turned brown with age, faded green work pants with a clothesline belt, and sandals. He smelled like very old chicken soup.

He closed the door, and as I pulled out onto the highway, he said in an accent that was half southern drawl and half something more exotic, Mexican perhaps, "Thanks. I was there five hours."

"Wow. You must be thirsty. There's Hawaiian Punch in the cooler back there. Help yourself."

As he leaned back over the seat, I got a look at his right arm. An eye a little bigger than a human's was tattooed on each side of his biceps, and a hooked nose with flaming nostrils was placed so as to coincide with his bent elbow. It looked like a full-size demon's head projecting from his T-shirt sleeve.

The violins on the *Psycho* soundtrack whined creepily. I was wondering if he had a knife, and trying to decide what to do if he pulled it on me. It occurred to me that I had my seat belt on, and he didn't. I could speed up and veer into one of the colorful sandstone monoliths. He'd go right through the window, and I'd end up with just some broken ribs.

"Where're you headed to?" I asked.

"Quartzsite. They said there's a pretty good mission in Quartzsite. I've been hitching around, staying at these missions. They have them all over . . ."

All of a sudden the *vreep-vreep-vreep* of the violins screamed out on the stereo. He paused. "This is strange music," he said.

"Yes it is. Let's hear something different." I popped the tape out of the deck. "What would you like to hear?"

"I like the Bee Gees."

"I think I have some Bee Gees. Reach me that tape case from the back, would you?" I asked. As he leaned into the back seat his elbow was staring at me again. "That's it. Just flip it open. *Saturday Night Fever* is in there somewhere."

Sipping his Hawaiian Punch, he opened the case, patiently took out the tapes one by one and looked at the pictures on the cover, until he recognized John Travolta. "This one?"

"Yup."

He pushed it in the tape deck, and "Staying Alive" started up. "Thank you," he said. "This is good. May I have more Hawaiian Punch? It was very hot out there."

"Certainly. Help yourself. Finish the can, if you like."

"Thank you."

After twenty minutes in the air conditioning, sipping cool beverages, he looked much more comfortable. "My name is Mike," he said, looking over at me with a smile. Every third tooth was missing or broken. "What's yours?"

"Teller. Where are you from, Mike?"

"Gila Bend. My wife and daughter are there. I'm out to find work." He looked through the windshield at the setting sun. "Those missions are good to stay at, except there is a lot of stealing, so you have to watch your belongings. Last night somebody took my belt." He turned and looked at me. "What are you doing out here, Teller?"

"Coming back from a show. I'm an entertainer. Magician. I was working out at a fair in Denver."

"Really?" he seemed excited. "What kind of music? Any Bee Gees?"

"No. *Mag*ician. I do magic tricks. You know, sleight of hand? Card tricks?"

His excitement faded. "You make a living?"

"I do okay."

"That's better than me."

We drove on, listening to music, thinking. Now and then I would look over at him. Sometimes he'd be sitting very erect with great dignity, and his profile would make me think of the sand-blasted cliffs outside. Other times he'd be bouncing his head and mouthing the lyrics like a passionate rock 'n' roller.

Abruptly he turned to me as if a thought had struck him.

"Can you float a lady?"

"Sure."

"No, I mean really."

"Well, not really, of course. It's a trick."

"If it's just a trick, then why bother?"

I paused, thinking. "Mike . . ."

"Yes, Teller?"

"Would you mind wearing your seat belt?"

We drove on through the long afternoon. I learned that he was not Mexican, but Walapai Indian. His full name was Mike Red Dog. He had grown up on the reservation and gone to the white school in the town nearby. He hated the classes (they taught false values, he thought) but developed a fondness for pop music and town girls. He and his girl had run away when he was seventeen and had been on the move ever since. We passed a sign: QUARTZSITE, NEXT THREE EXITS. Mike looked right at it with no reaction.

It hit me that he might not be able to read. " 'Quartzsite, next three exits,' " I read aloud. "Do you know which one is near the mission?"

"Oh. No. But just drop me anywhere."

"Listen, it's getting dark now. I'll pull off at the next exit, find out where the mission is, and bring you there. It'll take me ten minutes and maybe save you a couple hours."

"Really? Thanks!"

I turned off at the next ramp, CENTRAL AVENUE.

There was an open gas station, Flying A, complete with the red Pegasus and a little convenience store inside. "We'll get directions here." I went inside.

When I came out, I knew where the mission was, but, more important, I had a newspaper under my arm and a rolled-up twenty-dollar bill (the perfect size for the DeManche Change) in the top of my left sock.

I wedged the newspaper between the seats. As we drove out onto the main street, all the street lights popped on at once.

"Is that one of your tricks, Teller?" he laughed.

After about a mile, we came to an abandoned diner and turned left. The street had no houses on it, but about half a block down on the left was something that looked like an old firehouse. There were lights inside and a cross over the garage door. I stopped fifty yards from the building.

"Thanks a lot, Teller." It was funny how he kept using my name, like somebody who had been through a human-relations course. "I guess this is so-long."

"I guess so. Uh, Mike . . ."

"Yes?"

"I was wondering. Would you like to see a magic trick before you go?"

"Oh. Okay, I guess. It won't take long, right?" He looked over at the lights inside the mission. "They'll probably be eating soon."

"It will only take a minute. Here." I switched on the interior light, picked up the newspaper, and tore a corner off the back page. It showed a picture of a woman, holding a hook-rug. I handed the paper to Mike. "Look at the picture, and try to remember it."

"What do you mean, remember it?"

"Just look at it. So if you saw it again, you would recognize it."

He shrugged and studied the picture. Meanwhile, I leaned forward and surreptitiously took the rolled-up twenty-dollar bill from my sock. I palmed it in my cupped hand, ready for the DeManche Change.

"Okay. I got it memorized. A lady with a rug," he said.

"Right. Roll the picture up into a little ball."

He did it. "Now what?"

I took the paper ball from his hand. "Spit on your hand."

"Spit?" He held up a palm. "Here?"

I nodded.

In the moment that followed, while Mike was spitting on his hand, I quietly performed the DeManche Change, palming the newspaper ball, and flipping the rolled twenty-dollar bill into its place. Immediately I put the bill (which he still assumed was the newspaper) on his spit-covered palm. "Now take this newspaper, close your hand around it real tight, and rub the spit in good." He made a sour face, but closed his thick fingers around the paper ball and rubbed.

"Great." I turned off the interior light. "Keep doing that and walk outside. When you see me turn the headlights off and on once, open your hand, unroll the newspaper and look at the picture."

"This is disgusting, you know."

"Trust me. This is how I earn my living."

"No offense, but if I were you, I'd learn to play guitar. So long, magic man."

"Goodbye, Mike."

He got out of the car, his hand so tightly closed that the knuckles were all white through his deep tan. He stood there staring at his fist, rubbing. Then he looked up at me.

I blinked my headlights once, and drove off into the night.

window full of beautiful, sensuous firearms. The front door of the shop opens, and TELLER comes out. He is folding a credit card receipt around a package of shells. He slips the package into his side coat pocket, and the front of the jacket flaps out, disclosing, stuck in his trousers, a beautiful little revolver. He looks around. The FAN is nowhere to be seen. He spots a telephone, goes to it, picks up the receiver, drops in a quarter, dials. We hear the phone ringing. EXTERIOR – MAC NAMARA'S BOAT – CONTINUOUS ACTION From outside the boat, we can barely hear the phone ringing as a singer (Jad Fair of Half Japanese) sings on the stereo. HALF JAPANESE (SINGING, ON STEREO) Let's have sex! Sex at your parents' house. We're so naughty. We hear the volume is turned down, and MAC NAMARA answering. OFFICER MAC NAMARA (O.S.) Yeah? (pause) You were followed? Where are you? (pause) You lost him? All right! (pause) You coming up right now? (pause) Okay. We'll see you then. Be careful. B'bye. (to PENN) Says he'll be here in about a half hour. He was followed and everything. He's into it! The volume of the stereo is turned up again, good and loud. EXTERIOR – THE BOARDWALK – CONTINUOUS ACTION TELLER hangs up the phone. He looks at the gun and the bullets. He wants to load the gun, but looks around and notices that there are a few PASSERSBY and a POLICEMAN nearby. He sees the stairs leading to the beach. He goes down them. EXTERIOR – UNDER THE BOARDWALK – CONTINUOUS TELLER reaches the bottom of the stairs and looks around. He is alone. He figures out how to load the gun. He gets the feel of the gun and sticks it into his belt, under his coat. Thoughtfully he strolls under the boardwalk, then, perhaps out onto the breakers. He has a lot to think about. A quiet moment. He turns back and goes under the boardwalk again, toward the stairs. Suddenly two YOUNG MUGGERS step out of the shadows. The YOUNG MUGGERS are bigger than TELLER. They are not nicely dressed. They are not attractive or sympathetic in any way. They each have a big knife. YOUNG MUGGER #1 holds his big knife against TELLER's little throat. YOUNG MUGGER #1 Don't say a word. TELLER doesn't. YOUNG MUGGER #2 Give us your money, asshole. TELLER steps back, pulling his neck off the knife point. He reaches into his jacket. His hand curls around the gun. He has a clear shot, if he wants it. He pauses, with his hand on the gun. YOUNG MUGGER #1 It's not a fucking MENSA test, asshole. Just grab your money and give it to us. TELLER stares in their faces with his hand on the gun. YOUNG MUGGER #2 Maybe he can't find his money. Maybe he needs a little help. YOUNG MUGGER #2 starts to grab TELLER's jacket. TELLER gives him a powerful enough warning look that even a hood-junkie with a knife backs away. YOUNG MUGGER #1 C'mon, man, do it! We haven't got all fuckin' night! Just give us your fuckin' money. TELLER is still holding the gun and staring. YOUNG MUGGER #1 reaches up with his knife, and makes a very tiny cut in TELLER's neck, then withdraws the knife again. YOUNG MUGGER #1 C'mon! Do it. TELLER draws his hand rapidly out of his coat. We see that it is not the gun he has drawn, but his wallet. YOUNG MUGGER #2 reaches for the wallet. TELLER stops him with a look. He opens the wallet, withdraws all the bills, and with a faint smile coolly, deliberately hands the neat stack of bills to YOUNG MUGGER #2, then flips his wallet closed and puts it back in his inner breast pocket, and leaves his hand inside. The two YOUNG MUGGERS take the money, look at TELLER, look at each other, and start to jog away. TELLER pulls out his hand, with two fingers extended in the shape of a gun, aims it at their backs. With tiny, quiet movements he "fires" twice, blows the "smoke" off the barrel of the "gun", and sticks it back in his imaginary shoulder holster. TELLER turns, and walks on. EXTERIOR – MAC NAMARA'S BOAT – THE NEXT DAY OFFICER MAC NAMARA is banging a frying pan against the hull of her boat, and watching the surface of the water. A huge, bubbing gush of blood infuses the water like a "Jaws" shark attack. PENN bobs to the surface, carrying a two-handled logging saw. PENN I'm glad you showed up. Put on a tank. You gotta see this new bit. I'm sawing Teller in half underwater. Doesn't the blood look cool? It's Teller's same formula. I also cut and restore his air hose. There is another gush of blood in the water, and TELLER bobs up, blood running down his face mask. OFFICER MAC NAMARA Show's over. We got our man. PENN You sure? OFFICER MAC NAMARA Of course I'm sure. I saw him myself. PENN and TELLER climb on to the boat. TELLER is carrying a spear gun with cards impaled on the spear. PENN I want proof. OFFICER MAC NAMARA We don't do that head on the platter thing much anymore. PENN It's the guy in the alley, right? OFFICER MAC NAMARA Yup. PENN and TELLER take off their wetsuits. Underneath, a la James Bond, are their regular grey suits and ties. PENN The ranchwagon? OFFICER MAC NAMARA Yup. PENN And your sure he's the only one? OFFICER MAC NAMARA I hate to break this to you, but the vast majority of people don't care at all if you're dead or alive. Most of us aren't lucky enough to have even one psycho try to kill us. He sure loved you guys. You should see his apartment. It's Penn & Teller land. PENN We want to see it. OFFICER MAC NAMARA It's private property. We caught him. That's all that matters. We're done with him now. By now PENN and TELLER have dried their hair and put on their shoes. PENN Listen, it was our souls he was leaching off and we want to see Penn & Teller land. EXTERIOR – THE FAN'S APARTMENT BUILDING – HALF AN HOUR LATER A violent rainstorm with thunder and lightening gives the scene classic scariness. INTERIOR – INSIDE THE FAN'S APARTMENT – MEANWHILE The door is unlocked and swings open. PENN (once again in his gray suit), TELLER, and OFFICER MAC NAMARA enter and look around. Through the window we can see a storm outside, whose rumblings and flashings color what we see in the FAN's apartment. It is Penn & Teller Land. There are two life-size photographic cut-outs of PENN and TELLER. The walls are covered with autographed PENN and TELLER posters and photos, with warm personalized messages. OFFICER MAC NAMARA We checked. These aren't your signatures. On another wall they discover a bookcase of 3/4" videotapes neatly catalogued. Each tape is a single PENN and TELLER TV appearance, and is carefully dated and labeled. The last in the row is labeled, "Penn's Wish". OFFICER MAC NAMARA You want proof this was your nutter? Watch this. She plays the cassette. We watch full frame. The short section of videotape in which PENN said, "I wish somebody were trying to kill me," has been edited into a psychotic rock video by running it backwards and forwards at varying speeds against a "scratch" drum track. The effect is a video version of a "found audio" rap track. Interspersed are scenes of violence, of PENN and TELLER happy in various TV appearances, PENN saying, "My name is Penn Jillette and this is my partner, Teller," and PENN asking "Are we Live?" from the opening segment. Single words are excerpted from different interviews, and edited together to say, "I" "wish" "somebody" "were" "trying" "to" "kill" "me" in rapid montage. Also cut in are other wacky clips. OFFICER MAC NAMARA (sarcastically) Well I guess your "art" is inspiring somebody, eh? PENN Jeez. It's really pretty good. Could we, like, not press charges and hire this guy? OFFICER MAC NAMARA Attempted murder with a police officer present, whether you press charges or not, he's gonna do some time. Although when the judge sees your little "Weekend Live" spot, I think he could get off with aggravated assault. Bet you can't wait to get on TV and tell this story. Letterman will be rolling around laughing about how a couple of comedians got a man sent to prison. The weather outside is starting to clear. PENN C'mon! This guy was a little wacko to begin with, doncha think? I mean something was going to set him off. OFFICER MAC NAMARA I'm just concerned about you. Let's get out of here. This place gives me the creeps. By now sunlight is streaming through the window. As they leave, TELLER lingers behind, looks around with satisfaction, and throws his gun into the waste basket. EXTERIOR – THE FAN'S APARTMENT BUILDING – AFTER THE STORM PENN, TELLER, and OFFICER MAC NAMARA are parting. TELLER is nearby, leaning on a park bench covered with pigeons. PENN Well, thanks. You kept me alive, and taught me a very important lesson: One should never go on national TV and beg psychopaths to kill one. In the background TELLER jumps towards the pigeons, startling them into flight, then darts his hand into the flying flock, and snatches one of the pigeons in mid flight. He holds it for a moment, then releases it and sits down on the bench. PENN Isn't he great? OFFICER MAC NAMARA How does he do that? PENN It's a lot of practice. Will you be at the boat tonight when we come to pick up our stuff? OFFICER MAC NAMARA No. I start another case right away. Teller has keys. PENN Well, um, you know my number at the hotel. If you ever have the uncontrollable desire to see a card trick, give me a call. MAC NAMARA Thanks. I think I may have that urge. As MAC NAMARA gets into her car and drives away, TELLER catches another pigeon. PENN goes over to TELLER. PENN You're getting better at that. You don't even hurt them anymore. TELLER lets the pigeon go and they start to walk down the street. PENN It's not like we needed a cop. You had that guy on the run. You were getting pretty good with the ninja stuff. We could have done it alone. TELLER looks affectionately at PENN. PENN But, you know, it's good to keep the cops off the street. We got a lot of work to do. We got to get our careers back. But we got a hook. We can exploit this new Penn-and-Teller-Rage-To-Live-Peace-To-AllMankind thing in the entertainment market place. They set off down the street. There is a PEDESTRIAN coming towards them, head lowered. As they pass, the pedestrian lunges at PENN. PENN groans, collapses, and we see that he has been knifed in the stomach. TELLER gets a glimpse of THE PEDESTRIAN's face. It is the FAN. TELLER starts to chase him. PENN Hey, Teller, could you give me a hand over here? Is that that creep? TELLER runs back to help PENN. The FAN escapes. PENN Was that that nut? Was that that same goddam nut? That was that same nut! PENN I think we should go to a hospital. I have a knife in my stomach. Wait a minute! I thought Mac Namara locked that nut up. I hate that nut. Why did Mac Namara let him out? He's a nut! He should be locked up. TELLER is starting to help PENN up. MAC NAMARA drives by in her car. PENN Isn't that Mac Namara? (screaming) Why did you let the nut out? TELLER is in a frenzy. He sees Mac Namara, goes to start to chase her, and drops PENN in the process. By the time he has recovered PENN, MAC NAMARA is out of sight. He hails a taxi. INTERIOR – TAXI – A FEW MINUTES LATER TELLER rips part of his shirt off and wraps it around his fist as if in preparation for application of direct pressure in first aid. He reaches for the knife to pull it out. PENN What are you going to do? Twist the knife? Don't touch it! It hurts. Get away from me! It hurts and I don't want you to touch it. TELLER sits back in the seat. PENN Now don't pout. Very shortly I'm going to pass out. Then I'll go into a coma. Then I'll die. During any one of those times, you'll have plenty of opportunity to play around with the knife. Until then, keep your little paws to yourself. TELLER looks out the window resentfully. PENN Jesus christ, cut me some slack. I have a goddamn knife in my stomach. Jeez. PENN reaches down and touches the knife handle. PENN Ouch. Jeez! EXTERIOR – HOSPITAL – A FEW MINUTES LATER Taxi with PENN and TELLER pulls up. TELLER tosses a twenty dollar bill at the driver, exit the taxi, and walk towards the hospital door. PENN (tenderly) Hey, listen, Teller. I'm sorry I yelled at you. It looks a lot worse than it is. Blood spurting from the abdomen always looks bad. I probably have a couple internal organs that are still functional. Your partner's going to be okay. Forget the solo act. As PENN is speaking, the ranchwagon driven by the FAN pulls up where the cab let them out. PENN (pointing over TELLER's shoulder) Uh-oh! TELLER looks. The ranchwagon drives away. PENN I can get to the door myself. Catch that guy and kick his ass permanently. TELLER runs after the ranchwagon. We see it turn a corner as TELLER frantically chases it. Meanwhile PENN stands up straight, begins whistling, and strolls towards the emergency room door. EXTERIOR – STREET CORNER – MEANWHILE TELLER reaches the corner and looks around. The Ranchwagon is nowhere to be seen. Suddenly at an intersection a little further down the street he has been running on he sees the Ranchwagon drive across. It glides by at a leisurely pace. The FAN is in the driver's seat, smiling and waving cheerfully like a politician on a float. TELLER heads down the street at a dead run. INTERIOR – HOSPITAL EMERGENCY ROOM – MEANWHILE PENN is sitting in the waiting room with a knife in his stomach. A mother and a 12–year-old son hurry in. MOTHER (to Nurse) My son has a splinter in his finger. I can't get it out. I've tried everything. NURSE I'm sorry. This man here was ahead of you. KID Mommy, it hurts. It really hurts. PENN Aw, I'm okay. Help the kid. EXTERIOR – ANOTHER STREET CORNER – MEANWHILE TELLER turns the corner. He sees the Ranchwagon pull to a stop a long block away. The FAN gets out, opens the back door, pulls out a motor scooter, starts it, and leaves it standing on its kickstand. He gets back into the car and drives away. TELLER runs up, hops on the motor scooter and follows. The scooter is not very powerful, and he can't quite catch up with the Ranchwagon. He guns the accelerator in vain. INTERIOR – HOSPITAL WAITING ROOM – MEANWHILE NURSE The doctor will see you now, sir. PENN (looking at his watch) Sorry. Gotta run. EXTERIOR – STREET – A FEW MINUTES LATER The FAN's ranchwagon is parked at the curb. TELLER pulls up behind on the motor scooter and parks. He looks up. It's the FAN'S apartment building. TELLER runs in the door to the elevators, gets into an elevator, and the doors close. INTERIOR – THE FAN'S APARTMENT BUILDING – SECONDS LATER The elevator doors open and TELLER jogs out and approaches the door of Apartment 12H. TELLER hears from inside the apartment the FAN'S voice. FAN (O.S.) Are we live? Yeah! Are we live? Yeah! TELLER is perplexed. INTERIOR – THE FAN'S APARTMENT – CONTINUOUS ACTION TELLER cautiously enters the apartment. At the far end, facing away from the door, is the FAN, wearing the vest, shirt, and trousers of his business suit and hanging upside down by gravity boots from a horizontal bar. Also upside down, hanging from the bar is a life-size cardboard cutout of a second man's figure. FAN Now watch closely. See if you can see any strings or wires, as I perform The Bouncing Muffin. The FAN is re-creating the television appearance we saw in the opening segment for his small home video camera. The FAN is watching himself on a monitor. The cardboard cutout by his side is TELLER. The FAN bounces the muffin against the table top, catching it as it falls. The FAN spots TELLER on the TV MONITOR. With an amazing gymnastic twist, the FAN unhooks and rehooks his feet, so that he is still hanging, but now facing TELLER. He smiles proudly. FAN Ladies and gentlemen, my partner, Teller. The FAN provides crowd-cheering noises. TELLER breaks character to try and calm the FAN. TELLER Listen... The FAN is shocked and angry that TELLER is breaking character. FAN Come on, Teller. The audience knows Teller doesn't talk. With a swift flip, the FAN jumps down. He snatches down the lifesize cardboard cutout of TELLER and tears it in half. TELLER is intimidated into silence. FAN Okay, Teller, let's continue. He clamps some inversion boots on TELLER. FAN Up we go. He easily picks up TELLER by the ankles and hangs him over the bar. As TELLER is lifted, we see from his POV the waste basket with the loaded gun he left behind still in it. The FAN jumps into position with an easy somersault, hooking his ankles over the bar. The FAN hands TELLER a bagel. FAN Okay! And now Teller's Amazing Bouncing Bagel!... TELLER tears his eyes away from the waste basket. He

THE TIME I FELT FAMOUS

by

PENN JILLETTE

Teller and I have worked together since August of 1975. We played fairs, festivals, and small theaters for ten years and did fine. We didn't go on TV, we didn't play Broadway, we didn't make a movie, but in our first decade we made living wages, and we're proud of that.

We hit New York City in 1985. Our show was Off Broadway and we were on TV, *Late Night with David Letterman* and *Saturday Night Live.* We started getting recognized on the street. At six feet six and 230 pounds, with a stupid haircut, I'm not very hard to pick out in a crowd. After a few Lettermans, people on the street would say, "Hi, Teller." I would say, "Close—I'm Penn." They'd say, "Hi, Penn," I would say, "Hi," and that would be the end of it. It made me happy and it never got in my way.

The opening show of the second season of *Miami Vice* was a two-hour "movie" filmed in New York City, and I was the guest star. They took me, a big, goofy New England guy, a teetotaler who'd never had a sip of liquor or a puff of marijuana, and had me play a short Hispanic drug dealer. The part was "Jimmy Borges,"

58

and the description in the script was Puerto Rican and short. What on earth were they thinking? It took four weeks. *You* spend four weeks on the set of *Miami Vice* and see how much *you* want to live. It was the only thing I've done that I liked less than high school. The money was better but the popular kids were just as unpleasant.

A couple months later, "Prodigal Son"—that was the name of the *Miami Vice* "movie"—came out. I was no longer "Penn" or even "Teller" or even "one of those crazy magician guys." I was "that guy from *Miami Vice* who got shot in the head." Women would come up to me and give me messages for Don Johnson. I would explain that Don and I didn't play miniature golf together as often as we used to and he must have misplaced my phone number, but they would still tell me where Don could get in touch with them.

So, I was the guy from *Miami Vice,* but I didn't feel famous. Then one day, at Show World, I did feel famous. I felt like a superstar. I felt like Elvis.

Our theater was at Forty-third and Ninth and Show World is at Forty-second and Eighth. Show World is a sex shop. It has peep shows and talk-to-live-nude-girl things. It has magazines and plastic sex things that are painted badly. It smells like cigarettes and protein. To tell this story I have to admit that I was in there and it wasn't to use the phone. I really like the seedy atmosphere of these places, and although I'm too chicken to really talk to a live nude girl, I do like to go in and think about it. To talk to a live nude girl, one on one, is too real, but I have watched peep shows

59

and I have watched the live sex show, which is just like talking to a live nude girl except it isn't just you and her and you don't have to talk. Going to Show World is the fastest way for me to remind myself that I really live in New York City.

Now, I don't know if you know how these live sex show things work. Maybe you saw Madonna's video "Open Your Heart." It's the one where she's in leather and men are watching her through windows. Every once in a while, in that video, you see a metal sheet come down and block the man's view. What Madonna is depicting is a stylized version of a live sex show at Show World. The differences, I suppose, are obvious, but I'll just point out that the real live sex shows are less well maintained than Madonna's and the women in the real ones wear fewer clothes. You go into a little phone-booth thing and you put a quarter in a little parking-meter thing and the metal-window thing slides up and you can look in at the act. The women are bored and full of hate. They can look through the window at you but they don't bother. You watch them until your quarter runs out (about fifteen seconds), then the metal comes down and you have to put more money in to see how the show continues. We thought about charging for *our* show that way—but the performance has to be compelling every fifteen seconds, and I couldn't work under that pressure.

So, I walked into the live sex show and put in my quarter and the solid window went up and the clear window was there. I was watching the woman on the bed and I was lost in thought. The woman, a natural blonde, looked over in my direction, smiled warmly, and said, "Aren't you the guy from *Miami Vi—*" The metal window guillotined closed. I could have put in another quarter and said, "Yup," but I felt that it really should be her quarter. After all, *she* wanted to see *me.* When she smiled at me, I really felt famous and it was great. It wasn't worth putting up with Don Johnson, but . . . it was great.

THE DOMESTICATION OF ANIMALS

translated by

PENN JILLETTE

*Students of anthropology may be interested in the fragment
reproduced on the facing page. It is a literal translation
of a series of pictograms that archeologists recently found
on a wall in a cave in the Euphrates Valley. It is believed
to have been inscribed by late Pleistocene Man
around the close of the last Ice Age.*

NOTICE

(1) We're going to take over this planet, what with our opposable thumb and our ability to perceive our own mortality, and when we do, we will no longer forage for food.

(2) Those of you that we find useful, such as the Silkworm, the Ox, the Horse, and the Honey Bee, you can live with us on these farms and you'll receive food, shelter and protection from your natural enemies.

(3) It's no secret to any of you that we are carnivorous, and those of you that we find edible, such as Pigs, Cows, Sheep and Chickens, you can live on these farms under these same conditions; except, of course, when you reach adulthood you will be slaughtered and eaten.

(4) We do still have some openings for Pets: I'm talking Canines, Felines, certain small Birds, Reptiles, and Fish. As a Pet, you will live right in the family dwelling; you will eat the family food; you will share affection with the family members; but you will, of course, have no vote, nor any say in any family matters.

(5) The vast majority of you will choose to remain in the Wild. There are a few things I'd like to warn y'all about:

(a) First of all, many of you will be hunted for sport and for food.

(b) You will all be studied eventually in scientific experiments, and

(c) If you'd like to look many thousands of years in the future, as our species multiplies, we will need more and more homeland for ourselves, leaving less and less wild homeland for you. This means some of the more fragile, less adaptable species will become extinct.

All things considered,
if I were in your position,
I would opt for Domestication.

FORM No. 1

bounces the bagel against the counter, but drops it. FAN I'm sorry, my partner seems to be having an off night. TELLER swings towards the waste basket to get the gun. The FAN thinks he's reaching for the bagel. FAN Leave it! The show must go on. TELLER notices, in the MONITOR, that OFFICER MAC NAMARA has entered the apartment. FAN Are we live? (as AUDIENCE) Yeah! OFFICER MAC NAMARA (pulling out her gun) Get down from there! TELLER, relieved, starts to unhook himself. OFFICER MAC NAMARA Not you! The FAN gets down. He brings over the waste basket, in easy reach of TELLER and throws the props he has used into it. He leaves the waste basket in place. TELLER can see the gun clearly in the bottom of the waste basket. OFFICER MAC NAMARA spots a roll of silver duct tape among the rubble in the FAN's apartment. She tosses it to the FAN. OFFICER MAC NAMARA Tie him up. The FAN runs strips of tape around the inversion boots so as to fix them to the bar. Meanwhile OFFICER MAC NAMARA walks around to face TELLER and address him. OFFICER MAC NAMARA You know, Teller, when I first saw you and Penn on TV, and Penn was talking about someone trying to kill him, I really hated Penn. And I decided to scare him. And I hired this guy... She points to the FAN. OFFICER MAC NAMARA ...and he was great. We scared him. And then, the more I got to know you guys and the way you work, the more I realized that even if I could stop you from displaying your putrid disregard for life and death, there would be others, unless I could show them what happens to people who think that death is a joke. OFFICER MAC NAMARA tosses her gun to the FAN. OFFICER MAC NAMARA Penn's still at the hospital. Kill him. The FAN takes the gun and leaves. OFFICER MAC NAMARA smiles. OFFICER MAC NAMARA You're not uncomfortable up there, are you? You're used to it, right? TELLER is uncomfortable. And he is thinking about the gun in the waste basket. I hated Penn. But I watched the videotapes again. And again. And again. And I got to really hate you. Always standing there beside him, smiling, tacitly accepting. But you don't just accept it, do you? You think it up with him. And you're too sick to even express yourself in words. That's why I decided to kill him first. So you could just hang around here—forgive me—and smile passively while Penn learned how serious death can be. And I'll see how well you learn and then I'll decide what to do with you... In the meantime, I'll just sit here, and watch your blood vessels pop. TELLER grabs the waste basket, pulls out the gun, and, still upside down, points it at OFFICER MAC NAMARA. OFFICER MAC NAMARA Where'd you get that gun? I haven't seen that gun before. Where'd you get it? TELLER holds the gun as steady as he can as he swings back and forth from the bar. VOICE FROM BEHIND TELLER Hey, Teller, just chill out. A hand touches TELLER's shoulder. TELLER twists around and without thinking fires four bullets into the upside-down figure of... PENN. PENN is wearing a party hat. PENN (dying) No hard feel... PENN falls dead. Long pause. OFFICER MAC NAMARA starts to laugh. OFFICER MAC NAMARA (smiling, affectionate) You guys! She kneels down over PENN. TELLER That's Penn! What's going on? OFFICER MAC NAMARA (laughing) I don't know. You're the one that shot him. She takes off her wig and sunglasses. It's CARLOTTA. TELLER Carlotta? This was all a joke on me. It's a very mean joke. When did you switch the gun? CARLOTTA I didn't switch the gun. This is a joke on me. That's a fake gun. TELLER No. CARLOTTA (screaming) You fucking shot him with a real fucking gun?! TELLER I think so. She begins babbling and sobbing uncontrollably. TELLER watches CARLOTTA hugging PENN's dead body. TELLER Should I call an ambulance? CARLOTTA (screaming) He's dead! TELLER God damn it. TELLER takes the gun, puts it against his chest, pulls the trigger, and BAM! He's dead, hanging from the bar like a side of beef. CARLOTTA looks at TELLER and PENN dead. She gets a determined look on her face and jumps out the window. EXTERIOR – SIDEWALK OUTSIDE BUILDING – MEANWHILE The FAN and his FRIEND are walking toward the building. The FAN is carrying a cake box, and his FRIEND is loaded down with shopping bags of sodas and party goods. Faintly, in the background, we hear the SPLAT of a body hitting a pavement after a fall of 12 stories. FAN Well, it wasn't so much an acting job. I mean, it was an acting job. The most incredible acting job I ever had. We did this whole thing just for one person. Just for Teller. They enter the building, and wait for the elevator. FAN And I was the psycho PENN and TELLER fan, and Penn and his crazy girlfriend are, like, really obsessive. I mean they got my picture in the mug shot books, and I was, like, sneaking around with these real guns with, like, blanks in them. And Penn taught me to use this breakaway knife. It was great: even Teller didn't see me do the move. They get on the elevator. FAN And Penn was so pleased with my performance, he said they might use me in a movie or something. So it was good experience, and good for my career, even though they wouldn't let me tell anybody what I was working on. The elevator stops and they get out. FRIEND Are you sure they're not going to mind me going to Teller's private party? FAN Nah. They said I could bring somebody. It'll be fun. There'll be soft drinks, and snacks. You'll like Penn & Teller. They're wild. They'll do anything for a laugh. They arrive at the apartment door. They ring the doorbell. They push open the door. They see the dead people. FRIEND So this is their idea of a joke...? FAN Oh, jesus! Everything in this apartment has my name on it. It's all designed to make it look like I'm a psycho who wants to kill Penn and Teller. They'll never believe me. I can't go to prison. I can't take prison. I'll crack. I'll fall to pieces. The FAN pries the gun from TELLER's fingers. FAN Tell them it was Penn's idea. He pulls the trigger. BAM! The FAN kills himself. The FRIEND looks around. FRIEND My life in politics is over. I couldn't get elected to dog catcher after this hits the press. I never even met these people. God, I hate Penn and Teller. Not content to just destroy themselves... He pries the gun from the FAN's hand. We come in close on his face, and switch to slow motion. We all expect him to blow his brains out with full gore. We hear a CLICK. The gun is empty. FRIEND Fuck! Well, I'm sure one of these people has bullets on him. He begins searching through the pockets of the corpses on his hands and knees. He finds bullets in TELLER's pocket. FRIEND Here we go! The camera turns away, towards the window. We hear the SOUND OF THE GUN BEING LOADED. Then, A GUNSHOT. Then some GURGLING AND MOANING. Then another GUNSHOT. Through the window we can see a police car pulling up to the sidewalk outside. EXTERIOR – FAN'S APARTMENT BUILDING – CONTINUOUS ACTION An OLD COP and a YOUNG COP get out of the police car and walk towards the building. OLD COP In that building, it must just be some kids with firecrackers. But it still gives me the creeps. They say you get used to it, but you don't get used to it. Yeah, you change but you don't get used to it. I can never forget that night. That horrible haunting night. That deadly night when my first partner... He trails off, lost in dreadful recollection. YOUNG COP It must have been awful. I sure couldn't have taken it. I mean, I like the law enforcement business. But what I really like is the paperwork. I like watching the laws being interpreted day to day. But I can't stand violence, never could. I'm not cut out for the streets. Wish I could get back in my office. I really love office work. You know, my background is all clerical. INTERIOR – INSIDE AN ELEVATOR IN THE FAN'S APARTMENT BUILDING – A MINUTE LATER OLD COP You know, kid. When I listen to you, I hear myself forty years ago, when I first got out of the office. I liked the office too, and I didn't want to leave. You're right. You're gonna see things, kid. Awful things. I can't tell you when. But you'll see things. Look at what it did to me. Here I am, about to retire, about to enter my "golden years". And what have I got? Nothing. My wife left me. My kids hate me. On my retirement pay I guess I'll have just about enough money to spend my final days in a drunken stupor. I'm an alcoholic, you know. INTERIOR – APARTMENT BUILDING, ANOTHER FLOOR – A FEW MOMENTS LATER The elevator doors open, and the cops come out. YOUNG COP It's not the suffering per se that bothers me. It's the fact that so much of it is senseless. What apartment was it? OLD COP Right here, 12H. They knock on the apartment door. There's no answer. YOUNG COP looks nervous. OLD COP smiles reassuringly. They take a deep breath. They take out their guns. OLD COP Police! Open up. Guns out, they wait a moment, then open the door. As they stand frozen with horror, the CAMERA PULLS SLOWLY AWAY from their faces and out the window, and starts to LIFT AWAY FROM THE BUILDING. YOUNG COP (O.S.) Oh, god! Oh, jesus! Oh, god! Oh, god! I can't take it. I just can't take it. OLD COP (O.S.) Don't do it, kid! You'll get used to it. YOUNG COP (O.S.) I don't want to get used to it. Goodbye, my friend. We hear a GUNSHOT. A pause. OLD COP (O.S.) I guess there was no way I could have stopped him from taking the easy way out but... I can't lose another partner, not the same way. I'm just not strong enough. Okay, so I am a coward. So, my kids don't get the life insurance money. Bastards never write me. A pause. Then a GUNSHOT. MUSIC: "I STARTED A JOKE" (PERFORMED BY THE BEE GEES) CONTINUES UNDER THE ACTION FROM HERE TO THE END. Long pause as the CAMERA CONTINUES TO PULL AWAY. We see the whole neighborhood now. NEIGHBOR'S VOICE What is all the racket down there? Long pause. NEIGHBOR'S VOICEW(shaken voice) Ohhhh.... (yelling) Honey! I guess you should come down here. Or call the police. NEIGHBOR'S WIFE'S VOICE (yelling) I can't hear you. What? Long pause. NEIGHBOR'S WIFE'S VOICEW What? Very long pause. We hear a GUNSHOT. Very long pause. We see a passerby going into the building to investigate. NEIGHBOR'S WIFE'S VOICE Oh, no! The CAMERA CONTINUES TO PULL BACK. We are now looking down on the whole city. Another GUNSHOT. As the CAMERA CONTINUES TO PULL BACK to a DISTANT AERIAL SHOT of the city, we hear. PENN (V.O.) That's it! We're dead. Go home. It wasn't a gag. It wasn't a joke. We're just dead. Go home! As the CLOSING CREDITS START TO ROLL, the CAMERA CONTINUES TO PULL BACK through the clouds. Every once in a while for the rest of the movie we hear, in the background, growing fainter and fainter, GUNSHOTS. PENN (V.O.) And this camera pull-back, with the clouds and everything, the whole peaceful vibe here, this is not us goingto heaven. We're just dead. That's it. Go home. And even, if you buy the whole religious thing, we still wouldn't be going to heaven. Those were suicides, frowned upon by every major Western religion. And Atlantic City is in the Western world. We're dead. THE CAMERA CONTINUES TO PULL AWAY. It is now beyond the clouds. We can see the shape of North America. PENN (V.O.) So please clean up any litter you may have left around your seats, and deposit it in the trash receptacle on the way out. And if you do want to stay, make sure you're just staying to see that the gaffer on this shoot was Marc Garland, or who published the songs. Or maybe you really like reading the little disclaimer about any similarity between the characters and any persons living or dead (and "dead" is the operative word here) being purely coincidental. But unless you're staying to read that stuff, you might as well go home. There's no surprise ending. We're just dead. Go home. THE WHOLE GLOBE is now visible, and the camera is continuing to pull away. PENN (V.O.) You can imagine that the sequel thing is kind of a bitch. But it's too late to worry about that. We're all dead. Thanks for coming. Go home. The PULL-BACK continues PENN and TELLER ride up into frame on the credits. They are seated behind a desk, PENN What do you want out of us? We're dead. Go home. No cute surprise ending. Dead dead dead dead dead dead dead dead. They take out guns, put them to their heads. PENN Dead. They shoot themselves and slump over the desk, dead. They ride up out of frame on the continuing credits. The credits continue to run. On the disclaimer about similarity of characters to living or dead people, the word "dead" flashes brightly and prominently. The PULL-BACK ENDS. We see the earth hanging in space, and hear at irregular intervals, fainter and fainter GUNSHOTS. FADE TO BLACK.

THE END

Penn & Teller MTV Video Music Awards Penn & Teller enter with guitars. PENN One, two, three, four. Penn & Teller play a distorted E chord and let it continue to sound. PENN Good evening, were Penn & Teller. And these are electric guitars, the foundation on which rock and roll is built. Without electric guitars there would be no rock and roll and without rock and roll there would be no music videos and without music videos there would be no MTV and without MTV there would be no place to advertise hair care products 24 hours a day. My name is Penn Jillette and Im playing a brand spanking new Gibson ES-175-D guitar. Its the exact same guitar thats played by Issy of Guns and Roses. This is my partner Teller and hes playing an Epiphone Sheriden VSB. Its the same guitar played by Andy McCoy of the Iggy Pop band and the same classic style guitar played by guitar legends, B.B. King and Chuck Berry. One, two, three, four! They hit the chord again and smash the guitars. PENN Peter Townsend, throughout most of his career with the Who, would smash guitars. This was not vandalism; it was not mindless destruction. The reason Mr. Townsend trashed his guitar. (and, I might add, the reason Keith Moon destroyed his drums and Roger Daltry ran around trying to act out of control) was that the passion was so great that the tools of the trade could not contain it. He had more passion than the music and the guitar could contain. Even rock & roll could not express the wildness in his soul. It was a wonderful thing. We are magicians and this is the tool of our trade... Teller opens a cage R and removes a rabbit. PENN ...This rabbit is our guitar. And sometimes this rabbit cannot contain all of our passion. Penn brings out the swords. PENN This is our amplier. Teller brings the cage with rabbit C. and puts it on the magic table. Penn attaches a piece of paper to the front of the cage. Teller begins to draw on the paper with a magic marker. PENN My partner, Teller, is creating a depiction of a bunny in neo-primitive style. This will show you the position of the rabbit at all times Lets do some rock and roll magic. One, two, three, four. During each of the following sentences, either Penn or Teller takes a sword and thrusts it through the box, until the box fairly bristles with six swords. PENN People try to put us down. Just because we get around. Things they do look awful cold. Hope I die before I get old. Im talking about my generation. Why dont you all fade away? Swords are sticking out from the front and back of the box. Teller turns the table to show a prole view. PENN (criticizing himself, to Teller) That wasnt really rock and roll magic, that was more techno-pop or disco dance magic. Teller whips out a sword, ips open the top of the box, and rams the sword in from above. A stream of blood from inside the box hits him in the face. PENN (quoting Elvis) No, no, Teller, that dont swing. Lets get real gone. They put the box on the oor and smash it. They look at the phoney looking table on stage and smash that with the remains of the guitars. Penn stops smashing, Teller continues like a wildman. PENN My name is Penn Jillette, this is my partner, Teller, we are Penn and Teller. Teller cut it out. Show them that the bunny is okay. Teller pulls the bunny out of his coat, pets it, then drop-kicks it into the audience in a high, graceful arc. (Its clearly a fake rabbit).

THE END

THE SCLERAL SHELLS

by

TELLER

We were booked to appear on *Today,* the classic early-morning news-and-chat television show. We were complaining to one another about how little we looked forward to getting up at dawn when an idea occurred to us: We would go on the show in pajamas (matching gray, of course) and try to sleep through our appearance. In his phlegm-laden just-awakened voice, Penn would grunt how foolish he thought it was to expect stage performers to be witty at seven o'clock in the morning. Meanwhile I would snuggle up against Jane Pauley, one of the show's perky hosts, and take a nap. Then Penn would grudgingly agree to do a card trick. He would have Jane pick a card, then shuffle it into the pack. He would make an unenthusiastic attempt to find it. He would fail. Then he would awaken me to ask for assistance. I would awaken, and the viewers would see the number and suit of the card painted right on my eyeballs.

We liked the idea, cleared it with the producer of the show, and went to work figuring out how to make it happen.

Getting the right card was cake. Penn would use his "slip-

force," a surefire way of making people pick the card he wants them to pick. He would force the three of clubs.

But writing the name of the card on my eyes was trickier. We had seen *The Man Who Fell to Earth* and remembered that David Bowie wore some kind of special contact lens that altered the shape of the pupil of his eye. So Penn called his contact lens doctor, Dr. Julie Stein (known in underground circles as Julie the Eye), who knows magic and likes being involved in novel scams. Julie tried sandwiching card pips drawn on tissue paper between contact lenses, but it didn't show up well enough to be seen by the camera. He said what we really needed was scleral shells, thin curved plastic pieces that covered the whole visible surface of the eye. These could be painted however we wanted and would do no harm at all.

So he made some phone calls on our behalf and located a specialist in ocular prosthesis, Annette Kirszrot, who designs and makes cosmetic pieces for people who have had disfigurements of the eye. We made an appointment, and Penn and I went in together.

Her office was austere, full of trays of false eyes and sinister-looking apparatus for measuring and casting eyeballs. It looked great.

Annette Kirszrot greeted us and we explained our idea to her. In a strong foreign accent and a precise professional tone she answered our questions. Yes, it was possible. Yes, it was safe. Yes, it was an unusual project that held interest for her. But yes, it was also expensive. Quite expensive.

I'm ashamed to say it, but I hesitated. It seemed like an awful lot to spend for a two-minute bit on morning TV. I glanced over at Penn. "Jeez," he said, when he heard the price, and furrowed his brow in thought.

Then he brightened. "When people come to our show and give us their money," he said, "this is what they want us to do with it. Not buy Cadillacs for our friends. I vote yes."

There are times when I really like Penn.

"That's settled, then," I said. "So what's the next step?"

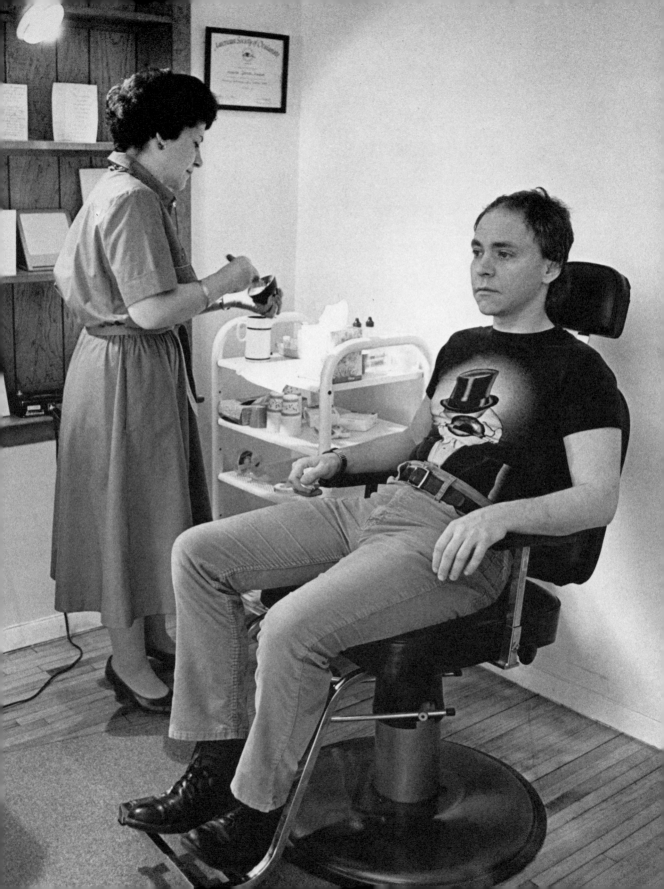

"Come with me." We followed her into a small examination room with a dentist-type chair in the middle and a small table full of strange medical instruments. "Sit down, please. We will take now the impression of the shape of the eye. From that we are able to cast the shell. It must fit perfectly the curve of the sclera, the white of the eye. Otherwise it will be most uncomfortable." She pronounced the last word syllable by syllable, so that I had plenty of time to appreciate what she might mean.

I wasn't scared, mind you. But I did suddenly remember a previous appointment. "We shouldn't do it now, should we?" I asked Penn. "I have to meet my parents at the train station in half an hour."

"Relax. I can go pick up your parents. If we get this done now, we'll be all set."

"Oh. Thanks. Okay. Let's do it."

Annette picked up a small bottle from her instrument stand. "First we must anesthetize the eye." She held open each eye and put in drops. While they took effect, she turned to her work table and picked up a small bowl, poured in a powder, added water, and stirred it with a small metal paddle.

"Anesthetics are good things," I said. "I'm sure glad I live in the modern world."

"That's very true. I am *certain* you would not want to feel *this.*" She had blended her mixture to the consistency of pancake batter and was using the little paddle to scoop it from the bowl and pack it into a syringe.

I looked at my watch. "Don't worry," said Penn. "I'll pick your folks up on time. I just want to see what she's going to do to you."

Annette leaned over me and pulled back my eyelids. She slipped something in, and the next thing I knew, cool moist goo was squishing out from under my lids.

"That looks terrific!" Penn exclaimed. "Wow! My partner is so cool!"

continued on p. 74

CRUEL TRICKS FOR DEAR FRIENDS by Penn Jillette and Teller OPEN ON A closeup of PENN and TELLER. As yet we cannot see the background. PENN: Hello. We are PENN and TELLER. The title of this videotape is "CRUEL TRICKS FOR DEAR FRIENDS". Please do not take that title lightly. The tape is a tool for you to humiliate your friends and take their money. Although you may experience a great deal of pleasure in using this tape, it is not good clean fun. We are encouraging you to laugh at your friends and not with them. If you want good clean fun, ask your aunt to take you bowling.TITLES roll over the picture as the camera pulls back.Over the titles we hear a LIGHT JAZZ RIFF (SPOOKY STUFF by Penn Jillette).As the camera PULLS BACK we see that we are on a simple set representing the VIEWER'S HOME. It is as dazzlingly bright as a Stanley Kubrick film, and contains principally a HIGH SNACK COUNTER with TWO HIGH STOOLS next to a REFRIGERATOR, and a second area featuring a TV, a VIDEORECORDER, and a couple of COMFORTABLE CHAIRS. This area also has a DOOR IN A FRAME, representing the entrance to YOUR HOME.We also see that, in the economical, bare-bones, frankness which will pervade the style of the tape, our MUSIC has been played by PENN and TELLER (we could not see their hands before) on ELECTRIC BASS GUITAR and A LITTLE CASIO KEYBOARD INSTRUMENT. They set down their instruments. PENN takes a seat on a stool by the refrigerator. PENN There are over forty billion people in this world. 11% of them own televisions. Only 39% of all the television-owners have VCRs. And, of those owning VCRs only 93% will buy this videotape. As PENN speaks, TELLER opens the refrigerator door next to him. Using the refrigerator door as a blackboard and a fat felt marker to write with, TELLER does the figuring for PENN's calculations in scientific notation shorthand. PENN That's 735,676 of us and 3,369,405,579 of them. That's at least 66,784,934 for each one of us. Sucker-wise, it's an embarrassment of riches. We are tight on PENN. PENN If you follow our instructions carefully, and have the capital to fund your betting, you're gonna make a profit off of us. Even if you paid as much as the full list price of three dollars and ninety five cents for this videotape, you're going to increase your money by an order of magnitude in the time it takes to say knowing falsification of advertising claims resulting in irretrievable financial loss by the aggrieved party. PENN and TELLER lead the viewer on a tour of the set. We watch from a HIGH ANGLE. PENN: This set is your classroom. It represents the parts of your home in which you will bilk the dunderheads. We have not spent a lot of money on this set, because we wanted to save as much of the budget, at least the below the line budget, as possible, for the payoffs. Ah, the payoffs! Right now on this set we will teach you how to set up seven swindles. Each of these swindles is followed by a payoff that happens when you play a segment of videotape. Let's get to work. CUT TO: TITLE: SCAM #1 CARD TRICK WITH VIDEO STING INSTRUCTIONS MUSIC : SPOOKY STUFF. PENN Some of the tricks are easier to do than others and this first one... The camera backs off and we see that the title was printed on a large card hand held by TELLER. PENN ...requires you to learn how to do a simple card force. If you can't handle this, go down to the video store and swap this for an aerobics tape. Let's look at what the trick would look like in your home. Now, I'll be you...PENN hangs a large sign around his neck, reading YOU. PENN ... if Teller doesn't mind playing your dear friend. TELLER doesn't look entirely pleased, but he shrugs consent. He puts a sign around his neck which reads "DEAR FRIEND". He goes around to the door of the set. He rings the door bell and walks around the door frame to re enter. (NOTE: Every time there is a camera edit, the note around TELLER's neck changes. It goes from DEAR FRIEND to IQ 63, to DOESN'T HAVE A THOUGHT IN HIS HEAD,to MAN WITH WIND WHISTLING THROUGH HIS EARS, to HEAD THICKER THAN A MC DONALD'S MILKSHAKE, etc.) PENN Well, there's my "friend" Think I'll invite him in. TELLER comes into the living room. PENN (hustler, aggressive) Well, come in, dear friend. I've got a great card trick to show you. TELLER attempts to break away to leave. PENN pulls him back, pulls out the deck of cards, and leads TELLER to the snack-counter. PENN C'mon, this will just take a minute. I want you to take this deck and cut them about in half. TELLER cuts the cards. PENN Okay, put them down here. TELLER puts the half of a deck he has cut down onto the table. PENN puts the other half of the deck crosswise on top. PENN Let's just put the other cards down cross-wise-to mark the cut. Would you like some refreshments? TELLER shakes his head no. PENN Well, I'm going to have a soft drink. PENN opens the refrigerator, which is full of JOLT Cola. He grabs one, and snaps the pull tab noisily. It sprays a bit into TELLER's face. TELLER wipes his face as PENN pulls the top card of the bottom half of the deck out about an inch and squares the rest of the deck. The card now protrudes from the middle of the deck. PENN Okay, now, look at the card you cut to and remember it. TELLER pulls the protruding card out of the deck and looks at it. He shows it to the camera. it is the three of clubs. PENN Now lose it in the deck. Make sure you remember it. TELLER sticks the card into the middle of the deck, gives them a little shuffle. PENN Would you be amazed if I could show you your card without so much as touching the deck? TELLER nods his head with a "Yeah,sure" attitude. PENN Would you care to bet on it? TELLER shakes his head no with a "Do I look like a putz?S attitude. PENN C'mon, I'll give you odds. Twenty gets you]thirty.TELLER is slightly tempted. PENN I'm just trying to make it more fun.. Tell you what. Twenty gets you fifty. TELLER, unable to pass up such odds, pulls a twenty from his pocket. PENN pulls his money out. PENN Well, alakazam, alakazoo! PENN reaches smugly into his pocket and pulls out the king of hearts. Is this your card?- the king of hearts. TELLER smirks and laughs up his sleeve at PENN PENN That's not it. Oooo. I thought I knew how to do it. TELLER is enjoying feeling superior. TELLER takes the money from PENN and puts it in his shirt pocket. PENN Boy, do I feel like a dink. I could'a really used that twenty, too. Oh well, might as well do something else. Let's watch TV. PENN and TELLER move to the "living room" area with the tv and VCR. PENN turns on the TV. He looks out at the viewers. As the camera comes in on TELLER looking smug, we hear what PENN is thinking... PENN (vo) Look at my friend. He feels great. He's savoring this moment like he personally solved the Kennedy assassination. NEW ANGLE: We watch them watching the news. After a beat, PENN turns smugly to the camera. We hear what he is thinking. PENN (vo) So, the two of you are watching the news.He's just about forgotten the trick. All that's left is the warm feeling in his stomach. Yeah, you're watching the news.... PENN turns back to watching the screen. NEWSCASTER (on TV) ...It looks more like a damned phone booth than a piece of fruit. On TV, a hand reaches into frame and hands NEWSCASTER a piece of paper. NEWSCASTER (on TV) This just in. On TV, NEWSCASTER turns paper to camera to reveal that it is an oversized three of clubs. NEWSCASTER (on TV) Is this your card? TELLER responds with true amazement. It was obviously his card. PENN plucks the money from TELLER's pocket, reclaiming his losses and adding TELLER's twenty. PENN Thanks, pal. All right, then. The tape of the newscaster is the punchline. We supply the punchline. But first, we're going to show you how to force your slow-witted playmate to pick the three of clubs. Piece of cake.TELLER breaks from his amazed look abruptly. He and PENN walk around so they are both facing the camera. TELLER has the deck of cards. PENN We're going to teach you a card force.There's hundreds of ways to make a person take the card you want him to take, when HE thinks he has a free choice. This one's pretty easy. But anyway you can force your dupe to grab the three of clubs is fine. First, we'll let you in on our secret preparation... TELLER looks through the deck of cards. PENN Before Professor Stupido comes over make sure that the three of clubs is on top of the deck. Now, we're going to mark the back of it with a big black X. That's just you can follow it easily in this demonstration. Don't you do this. If you even thought about marking your three of clubs, somebody should be using this tape on you. TELLER shows the three of clubs, marks the back of it with a big, black X and puts it on top of the deck. PENN Tell your brain dead buddy to cut off about half the cards. Teller, if you don't mind. TELLER cuts the cards. PENN Tell your victim to put the cards he cut off the top down onto the table. Okay, Teller. Put the cards you cut down on the table. TELLER puts the top half down on the table PENN Now, take the other half and lay them cross-wise on the first half to "mark the cut". PENN takes the remaining half and lays it crosswise on the half TELLER put down. We can clearly see by the marked back that the three of clubs is the top card of the bottom half. PENN The three of clubs is the top card of the bottom half or the first card beneath the "mark of the deck". PENN points to where the three of clubs is. PENN All you have to do is distract your friend's attention for a moment so he loses track of which half is which. The distraction could be a simple question. (to TELLER) Would you like some refreshments? TELLER nods his head "yes". PENN noisily pulls open the tab on a can of JOLT cola, spritzing it a bit in TELLER's eye. PENN Or the distraction could be an unexpected surprise. RUN DMC burst into the living room for a twenty second rap. PENN Or anything in between. You're not distracting the lunkhead from any tough sleight of hand move. You just want to give him a moment to forget which half is which. This way, when you put the halves together with the top card of first half purposely poking out a bit and tell him to look at the card he cut to, he'll have no idea that it was originally the top card- the three of clubs and not the card he cut. PENN lifts the half of the deck now on top, aligns it with the other half, sliding the clearly marked top card (the three of clubs) out about an inch. This is done openly, casually, as if this is a fully legit step of the procedure. PENN Have him look at the card and the dirty work is done. Look at the card you cut to, my friend. TELLER pulls the card out of the deck looks at it. PENN Now, remember what I did next. No, after Iran the wager up. Right. I screwed up. Let's roll the tape. On the tv in the living room set, we see an "instant replay" of the scene just played (MOS). We see PENN failing in the trick, and TELLER gloating. PENN Look, I'm showing him the wrong card. I've made a mistake. And look how he's reacting.He's gloating. He's showing his true colors,all right! As TELLER gloats easily, his expression stops in a freeze-frame. PENN Yup! He's scum. And that's why we made this tape. It's wrong to gloat. And evil-doers must be punished. "Instant replay" continues as PENN narrates. PENN Appear humbled and contrite and clumsily try to change the subject. Suggest some TV. On the "instant replay" we see the newscaster delivering the punchline, and TELLER's reaction of amazement. PENN So play the tape, let him see the card, feel like a jerk, and hand over the cash. Isn't justice great? PENN takes a twenty out of his pocket and hands it to TELLER PENN Here's your twenty back, pal. PENN pulls a telephone from under the counter. PENN Okay, now you got work to do. Get on the phone. Call the prospective pigeon. Make a date for chips with the dip.- Before they arrive, put your three of clubs on top of the deck. TELLER demonstrates. PENN Be ready to mark the cut and distract your friend. TELLER demonstrates. He marks the cut and readies a JOLT. PENN Pretend to screw up the trick, and suggest to your friend that you watch tv. Don't just turn on the tv, but rather sneakily turn on the videotape. Not the videotape of us teaching you how to do the trick, but the videotape that follows the 5-second countdown. That's right. No guesswork involved. A real, professional 5-second countdown. Here it comes: TITLE: SCAM #1 P CARD TRICK WITH VIDEO STING PUNCHLINE ELECTRONIC SLATE COUNTDOWN - from 5 to 1.CUT TO: LOGO: NEWSBREAK. CUT TO: newscaster sits at newsdesk. There is a key screen behind her with a photo of the capitol building. REPORTER Hello I'm Jean Prysock and this is NEWSBREAK. They say that power is the ultimate aphrodisiac and within the last quarter century Washington has proven that sex and politics are not really strange bed-fellows. Another scandal is rocking the capitol. It all is happening in the same building in front of which Rita Jenrette, former wife of Congressman John Jenrette, posed nude for Playboy. The same building where Congressman Wilbur Mills cavorted with his mistress, stripper Fanny Fox. But no scandal, not even Gary hart throwing away his political future over a dalliance with a swimsuit model, compares to the story now coming out of Washington. We've received reports that a member of the Supreme Court has been using government research funds to maintain a Virginia lovenest for one of the pages on his staff. Our sources assure us that positive identification will be made within 48 hours but we are hopeful that we will be able to learn...Someone hands a piece of paper into the frame to the REPORTER. Wait. This just handed me....The REPORTER holds the "paper" to camera and leans forward. ...Is this your card? is. And after giving it a moment to register, the REPORTER pulls back to regular position.REPORTER Also in the news in Washington, a fundraising dinner held by the wives of Democratic Senate leaders was held this week. The talent show portion of the dinner was deemed a rousing success by one observer, specifically for the absence of both ventriloquism and mime. Stay tuned to this channel for further developments. This has been NEWSBREAK. FADE TO BLACK INTERIOR: Studio. PENN is leaning on TELLER's shoulder. PENN Hello. When you're really doing this scam for your friend, try to remember to turn the videotape off before now, okay? FADE TO BLACK AGAIN TITLE: SCAM #2 P TV SCREEN CLEANER P INSTRUCTIONS. MUSIC: SPOOKY STUFF.Over this we hear the sound of a spray-bottle, and see a mist sprayed onto the title. As we widen out to reveal TELLER industriously cleaning the title off of the FREEZER DOOR, PENN addresses us...PENN One thing that's very important when doing this type of interactive video con is that your equipment is in top working condition. To get the most out of this video it is important that your TV screen is as clean as possible so you don't miss any subtle video signals we may be giving you. TELLER notices a couple of tiny black specks (dead luminous dots on the viewer's television screen?) floating on the picture between him and the viewer. He takes paper towel and reaches to wipe them away. PENN This tape can bring hours of entertainment but only if you adhere to the proper preparation. Equipment maintenance is perhaps the most obvious. TELLER is having no effect with his paper towel. He grabs his bottle of spray cleaner, sprays some onto his towel and continues wiping. But now, everywhere he wipes affects the picture we see. Where he rubs, video tears appear. When he squeezes the towel, the colors of the picture run like watercolor. Where he tries to repair the damage,the picture wrinkles.PENN is oblivious. PENN For a complete video maintenance kit, send$18 to PENN and TELLER at the address now on the screen. The address is unreadable. The entire picture is well mutilated.NEW ANGLE: The picture is back to normal as PENN and TELLER stroll towards the "living room" tv viewing area of the set. PENN This is our next trick and, like playing Bach fugues or performing micro-surgery, it's a lot more fun to do than it is to watch. TELLER turns on the VCR. As PENN does the following explanation, TELLER cues up the tape to the title card SCAM #2 P TV SCREEN CLEANER P PUNCHLINE. He watches through the electronic countdown and pauses the tape at the first frame of some footage of an old

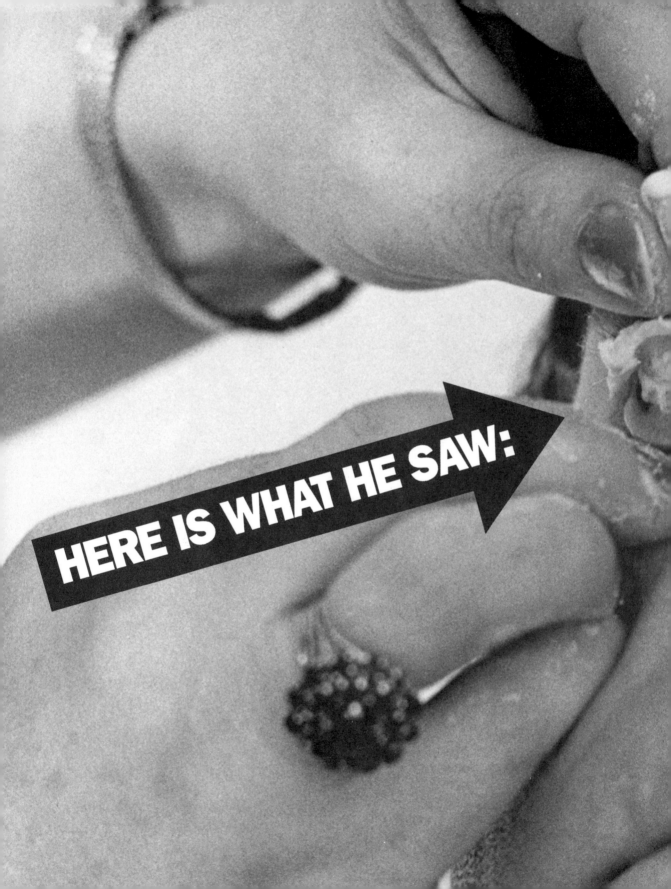

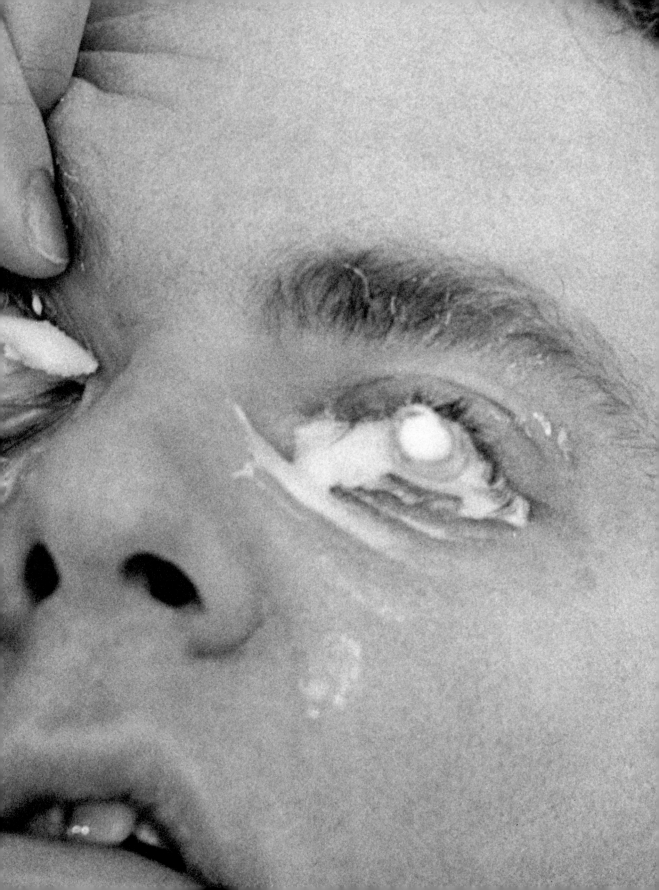

"Okay, Teller, I'm going now. Don't you worry about your parents, little buddy. Just get this done. If you could see the tubes and stuff sticking out of your eyes, you'd know it's already worth every penny. It looks great. Just like *Clockwork Orange.* Bye, Annette. Nice meeting you. Take care of my friend."

"I will take care of your friend. Goodbye."

I remembered the scene in *A Clockwork Orange* Penn was thinking of. Malcolm McDowell is strapped to a chair, and a foreign doctor puts awful metal clamps in his eyes to prepare him for a brutal session of aversion therapy.

I heard Penn saying goodbye to the receptionist. Then silence. Sightless, with tubes sticking out of my eyes, and alone with a stranger in an office full of plastic eyeballs, the thought darted through my mind: I wonder if I'll ever see Penn again?

"He is a very large man," Annette commented.

"Yes, very large. How long does this stuff have to stay in?"

"Why? Are you un-com-fort-a-ble?" I was sure she was genuinely concerned, but her voice, with its strong hard-to-place accent, began to seem sinister in the darkness. It reminded me of somebody. Who?

"No. Not uncomfortable. It's . . . almost pleasant," I lied.

"Pleasant? I have never heard someone call it that before. Don't worry. It is all perfectly safe."

Safe. That's who the voice reminded me of: Lawrence Olivier in *Marathon Man,* the scene where Olivier, playing the diabolical Nazi dentist, straps Dustin Hoffman to a chair and asks him, "Is it safe? Is it safe?" while drilling his teeth without anesthetic to ensure his cooperation.

"So," said Annette, "you are a magician, eh?"

"Umm, sort of."

"Then you know how all the tricks are done, yes?"

"Well, I . . ."

"Of course you do. You are famous. You are on television. So tell me: How is it that they saw the woman in half?"

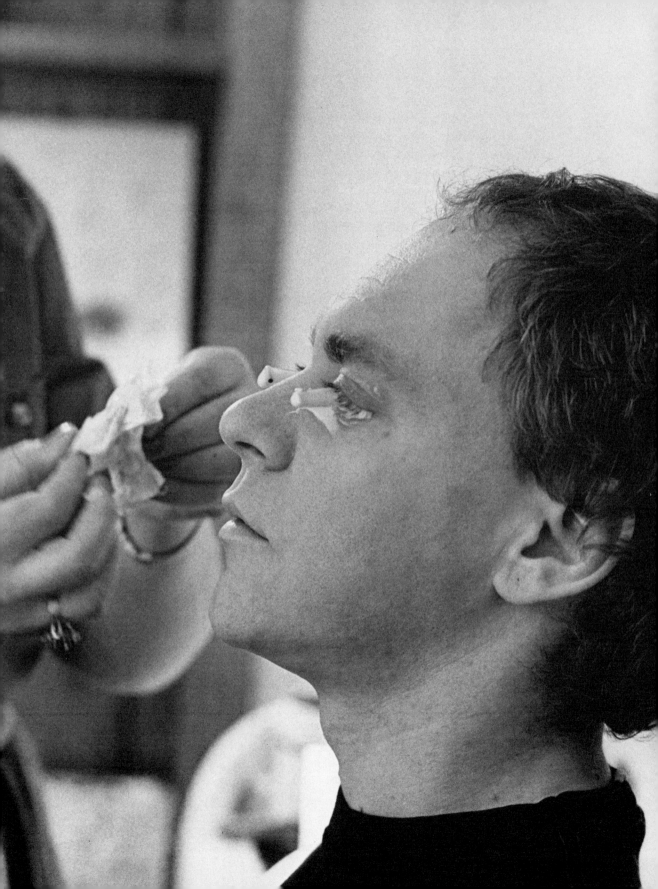

A magician's sacred obligation is to keep the secrets of his brotherhood. Nothing brings about the ruination of the art form more quickly than low scum who betray their brethren and expose the methods of classic tricks.

"Two women," I said. "One curls up in the head half of the box. The other is hidden in the tabletop and sticks her feet out when they are turning the box around. You don't notice the thickness in the tabletop because it's beveled. Anything else you want to know?"

movie, "Nothing Sacred". Carole Lombard is lying in bed recovering from a hangover while Fredric March discusses her funeral arrangements. The sound on the tv is turned down very low. PENN This one's extremely simple. You and you brain dead companion are watching a movie.In this case "Nothing Sacred", starring Carol Lombard and Fredric March.- You pretend to see some dirt on the screen.You bring out a bottle of glass and window cleanser with the RNEW IMPROVEDS sticker included with this cassette. Anyhow, you wax poetic about how great this stuff cleans TV screens. Show them how you spray some on a paper towel. When Fred says, "Oh, about half a million, I suppose," start wiping the screen. TELLER starts wiping the screen on cue. Wherever he wipes, the picture is damaged. PENN The picture will seem to rip and tear and become distorted like a water color being rubbed by a wet sponge. TELLER smears with his towel, and the picture smears and blurs. PENN The more you practice this one, the better it looks. Just run it a few times and try to get your timing right. TELLER is demonstrating as PENN describes. He gives it the works, looking more and more fretful and frustrated. By the time he finishes, the picture is utterly ruined and obliterated. TELLER acts appalled. Meanwhile, PENN narrates... PENN The closer you mirror the distortion on the screen, the better the illusion. You can fret a bit and try to put the sections you've affected back correctly. The important thing is that our sapling believes that there is an over the counter product that can pull pulsing dots of light off of a TV screen and onto a household paper product. This one just makes your friend look bad.No money to be made here. But money isn't everything. Stick your sticker on your cleaner, grab a cloth and get to work. You'll have your usual five seconds to cue it up. TITLE: SCAM #2 TV SCREEN CLEANER PUNCHLINE ELECTRONIC SLATE COUNTDOWN from 5 to 1. There is a BEEP on each number change.TWO MINUTES OF FOOTAGE from "Nothing Sacred" In the scene where Carole is recovering from a hangover and Fred is planning her funeral, right after Fred says, "Oh,about half a million, I suppose," the picture is wiped, distorted, crushed, torn, crumpled,smeared, and obliterated as if being damaged with some supernatural paper towel. It is reminiscent of a wet sponge running over a water-color done on bleeding crepe paper. TITLE: SCAM #3 DEMON FROM HELL. INSTRUCTIONS. MUSIC: SPOOKY STUFF.The TITLE CARD folds closed inside the cover of a Bible which TELLER carries away. PENN sits comfortably by the television. He turns on the videotape recorder and plays a segment of tape. We watch an electronic COUNTDOWN, and then a preacher, a typical tv evangelist, starts to preach. (Astute viewers may recognize that this is PENN in disguise.) PENN turns down the sound on the television. PENN Teller and I both have our favorites on this tape. His is coming up a little later, but this one's mine. I got a couple of reasons for liking this one. First off, you don't have mess around with any props. You got your TV, you got your tape, you got your dunce you're golden. Secondly, in this one you get a chance to make money using the Devil's name. I like that. Now, Teller and I love fundamentalist preachers. You probably never thought these wackos were laying the groundwork for you,the Penn & Teller fan, to cheat someone out of some cold, hard-earned cash. But that's just what they're doing. These preachers are always talking about "Backwards Masking" secret, satanic messages that are hidden backwards in records, films and television. Obviously, this is hysterical grandstanding. Use your head!If backwards masking worked, wouldn't Ozzy Osbourne be prime minister of England? Anyway, you tell your friend you've been watching these preachers and you're starting to receive and understand their backwards messages and he's gonna think you're crazy. Great! He thinks you're crazy and you know he's stupid. This is how kingdoms are won.- Tell him that you've taped one of these preachers and you'll bet him that there's backwards masking on it. PENN He'll jump at the bet because the burden of proof is on you.- Play the tape.-PENN turns up the volume on the television. We can hear the preacher speaking faintly. PENN About a minute and a half into it, the preacher will start to pray. That's your cue to pause the tape and make believe you're putting it into reverse. PENN pauses the tape. PENN When it starts to "go backwards", prompt your friend. The first thing you'll hear backwards is... PENN releases the pause control. PREACHER (ON TV) ...eeeshnot veldo eeblay oxto sateen...PENN pauses the tape again. PENN Swear to him that Reeshnot veldo eeblay oxtosateenS is "Satan is our Lord", clear as a bell.And say you won the bet. PENN releases the pause control and plays more of the tape. PENN He'll still think you're nuts but as the voice gets clearer, he'll start to doubt his own sanity. PREACHER (ON TV) Leeeoord Satan is my master. I will heap tribute on him. I will take of his sacraments. I drink the blood of slaughtered masses. I dance in the shadow of sin. PENN turns down the volume on the tv. PENN Just don't let him doubt that he owes you the money from that bet. I do so like to see the Devil get his due. TITLE: SCAM #3- DEMON FROM HELL- PUNCHLINE, ELECTRONIC SLATE-COUNTDOWN from 5 to 1. There is a BEEP on each number change. INTERIOR: SET FOR TV EVANGELIST SHOW. Potted palms and a cross projected in light against the backdrop. ORGAN MUSIC fades out as the camera closes in on...PENN, gray hair swept back, aged and disguised as a tv evangelist (a la Jimmy Swaggert),with a faint southern accent, is just beginning an altruistic sermon... PENN This week marks one of our Hebrew brothers high holy days, the holiday called Simchat Torah. The word Simchat means happy in Hebrew and the Torah is the name the Jewish people give to the first five books of the Old Testament. So, this holiday literally means "happy Bible". What does that mean? PENN drinks a few gulps from a glass of water. PENN In today's hectic world, full of temptation and sin, it is important to take time and find joy in the eternal truths found in the Bible.And so seldom in the whirligig of activity do people pause long enough to let the wisdom of the Lord's word to sink in. The troubles of the world, the troubles with our young, the troubles with ourselves can all be traced to inadequate Bible study. But,today's Jewish holiday, Simchat Torah,focuses a much needed light on this important book and it is with a heart full of gladness that I wish our Jewish friends a happy holiday in their native tongue- Chag Soma-och, may the books of the Bible fill you.PENN finishes off the glass of water. PENN And what better way to be filled with the spirit of the books of the Bible then to all bow our heads now in silent prayer? PENN bows his head. IMAGE FREEZES for a moment and begins going backwards. With his head bowed in silent prayer it is momentarily impossible to tell if the tape is going forwards or backwards. (This gives the user of the tape some margin of error in the moment he chooses to PAUSE the tape.) As the tape plays "backwards" only the Hebrew sounds remain the same. PENN...eeeshnot veldo eeblay oxto sateen Chag Soma-och eshtap iktar oshneat wurshepsatun simchat torah. Gradually, the voice becomes clearer. PENN Leeeeord Satan is my master. I will heap tribute on him. I will take of his sacraments. I drink the blood of slaughtered masses. I dance in the shadow of sin. The screams of torture are the music of my dance. I breathe deep the stench of burnt-flesh and illicit lust. PENN spits half a glass of water into his tumbler. PENN Take crack in Beezlebub's name. Offer yourself into shallow sexual promiscuity to circulate venereal diseases from hell. Spit upon the flag and all that is holy.Worship at the altar of the dark arts. Wear leather and stalk strangers. By now the voice is totally clear and almost conversational. PENN Steal from the rich. Steal from the poor. Take your own life. Take someone else's. Don't take your own first, of course.PENN spits the rest of the water into the glass. It is full. PENN The opinions expressed here are those of one dark angel serving Lord Satan, prince of Darkness and do not necessarily represent those of PENN & Teller, the producers, any of their subsidiaries or employees, nor the teachings and beliefs of Beelzebub, the Beastmaster himself, one true ruler of the univ... Horns suddenly appear on PENN's head. (This is done by having horns pulled off PENN's head quickly right before he starts preaching. Backwards, it will look as if they suddenly appeared.) TITLE: SCAM #4 - VIDI-KOPY INSTRUCTIONS - MUSIC: SPOOKY STUFF.A brilliant bar of white light sweeps from left to right, obliterating the title and revealing... INTERIOR: THE LIVING ROOMS PORTION OF THE SET. PENN Next we're going to show you how to turn your TV set into a modern video equivalent of a high speed office copier. TELLER turns on the tv and inserts a cassette labeled VIDI-KOPY. As PENN speaks, on the screen are displayed computer codes and symbols in rapid, flashing succession. It appears that a computer program is being loaded. PENN Using up to the minute modular technology coupled with existing computer chips and relays used in the standard home VCR this video-cassette can be used to put any image pressed against the screen- onto the screen. First, let's copy a random piece of paper. On the television screen we see a COPY SCREEN: PENN picks up a piece of paper and hands it to TELLER. TELLER holds the piece of paper against the screen. Teller touches a button/indicator light labeled COPY on the TV screen. A blinding white bar of light, like that seen in standard copy-machines goes from left to right on the TV in the living room. PENN Be careful, Teller. Don't touch that copy filament. TELLER moves the paper away and a second later, a life-scale copy of the paper pops onto the screen. PENN Why don't you save that into the memory so we can call it up later? TELLER hits the - SAVE- button/indicator. The copy scrolls off the screen as a numerical printout labeled - BUFFER MEMORY - appears in the column to the left. When the copy is gone, the message, - SAVED TO UTILITY FILE - appears. PENN Show them the magnification mode. Use a common, handy piece of paper, a dollar bill. Don't forget to compensate for scan line ratio for magnification. PENN takes a dollar out of his pocket, hands it to TELLER who places it against the screen and hits the- "size change" - button/indicator. The bright white copying bar goes across the screen. PENN Be careful of that filament, little buddy. TELLER gives PENN a "what a wimp!" look. Teller moves aside and we see that the dollar bill has been copied onto the screen. The reproduction is much larger than the bill, and just fits on the screen. The detail work is not very good and the green of the seals on the bill is the lurid electronic color of a color computer terminal. PENN That's .6070 scan line change. Teller, why don't you demonstrate the second step of the magnification mode. TELLER hits the - "size change" button/indicator light. The bill magnifies again. TELLER keeps holding his finger on the button. The bill magnifies again (like a freeze-frame magnified in an assassination documentary). The screen is now filled with the cameo portrait of George Washington. PENN Isn't that amazing? TELLER plays with the screen a bit, touches a couple of buttons. PENN Teller! Don't mess around with that. TELLER shoots an even more withering look towards PENN. Full of contempt for him, TELLER places his hand on the screen and pushes the - COPY - button with his other hand.The white copying bar travels across the screen. When it hits, TELLER's hand, all hell breaks loose. There is a horrible electronic noise, some bright shards of light emanating from the TV, video break-up, etc. TELLER (screaming) AAAAAARRRRRGGHHHHH!!!!! TELLER jerks his hand back from the screen and tucks it protectively in his armpit. The image on the screen has settled and we can begin to make out a video photo copy of a horribly burned and mangled hand. PENN stares at the screen for two beats before he turns back to address the camera. PENN Now, of course, you weren't fooled... TELLER takes his hand out from under his arm and shows it to be unharmed. PENN After all, you were smart enough to buy this tape. And that means you're smart enough to see the implications there's money to be made here. PENN Demonstrate this to the vegetable that walks like a man and then sell it to him. The price? Let me put it this way...if Lieutenant Doofusis the buyer and a Penn & Teller fan is the seller, it's pretty safe to call it a seller's market. I would start at least $250, though. So let me tell you what you need to know. Start by giving your friend with the room temperature IQ the rap about utilizing existing computer chips and relays. It's the same rap I gave you before. You can rewind and learn it later. There's an instructional voice on the tape and little chimes and sound effects. They are recorded very quietly, so you should turn the volume way up. That way the burning hand effects can be ear piercing. Now, you've got the volume way up loud,and the tape all cued up. First comes the random piece of paper. Yeah. Random piece of paper! Just make sure you have the "right" random piece of paper ready near the TV. Get a piece of paper and hold it up to the screen and trace the piece of paper I'm about to show. FULL SCREEN we show the RANDOM PIECE OF PAPER for the viewer to trace. It is a series of doodles, phone numbers, and shopping notes. PENN (V.O.) If you don't have a piece of paper handy, don't run around like a crazy person looking for one. That's why the Japanese invented the pause control. After a few seconds we see PENN and TELLER again. PENN See this READY light? TELLER points to a flashing green block on the screen labeled READY. PENN That will blink five times. Then the action starts. You got to have your piece of paper against the screen by the fifth blink. If you want to be really hip, you can do what Teller likes to do and act as if these lights are heat sensitive buttons, and learn the timing so that you can press them just before they light. So: First you copy your manufactured "random" sheet of paper, then you magnify your dollar bill. And use your head: put the picture side of the bill against the screen. Once you've done the whole bit with the 'in for a ridiculously high price. That's why there are extra labels. Just stick them on old copies of Masterpiece Theatre. TELLER holds up a handful of cassette label stickers, imprinted with a very high tech logo for: VIDI KOPY PENN After you got the cash, start the tape again,and the real fun begins. There's an instructional voice that will warn you to keep your hands and face away from the copier filament just like I did. Make fun of this. Talk with your friend about all the times anyone you know copied any part of their anatomy. If he's as dumb as he seems, he'll think this is a great trick. Watch for the READY button blinking five times, then put your hand on the middle of the screen. When the light bar reaches your hand, all hell will break loose. Scream, tuck your hand out of sight under your arm and roll around in agony. PENN puts his arm around TELLER. PENN A gory laugh and high yield profits. This may be the purest example of our goals. TITLE: SCAM #4 VIDICOPY PUNCHLINE ELECTRONIC SLATE countdown from 5 to 1. On each counted number there is a BEEP. A FULL FRAME SIMULATION of a computer program being loaded. (Momentary flashes of ASCII codes, color bar, strings of figures and data with jargon, etc.) At the end of this process, the basic screen comes up:This is a two tone screen with a pale blue over most of the screen, and a dark grey frame on the left side and at the bottom. Superimposed on the larger blue area, in a slightly different shade, are the words: COPY AREA DO NOT TOUCH. At the bottom is a row of small rectangular buttons or indicator lights. They are labeled: READY, COPY, SAVE, and size change (see drawing). A voice giving instructions is smooth and modulated. MODULATED SOOTHING VOICE VIDI-KOPY is activated. System test in progress. Do NOT touch the copy area during VIDI-COPY operation. Two second pause. COPY button lights. CHIME. In the vertical area to the left, red warning letters flash DO NOT TOUCH COPY AREA. The words COPY AREA DO NOT TOUCH disappear, and a white bar like that

About "Invisible Thread"

Magicians spend a lot of time trying to pretend that what they do is classy. They think classy is good. They're embarrassed by the magic stores that rip off little kids. Ripping off little kids is not a classy thing to do. Teaching little kids to lie for fun is not a classy thing to do. But the seedy side of magic stores is the only good part. I love the fact that the tricks themselves are a rip-off, a lie within a lie within a lie. My friend Elliot thinks that if he had been ripped off in a magic store as a child, he might not have been ripped off by getting his master's degree. A sleazeball with sponge bunnies might have saved him a few years and several thousand dollars.

I wrote this story and gave it to Teller to read, because he's my friend, and he liked it, because he's my friend. When we wanted to do a little movie for Showtime, we dug up this story and rewrote it as a Penn & Teller script. Major changes had to be made to fit us in and make it filmable. It was important that the aliens not be stupid Spielberg puppets, so in the movie, the aliens were just a refrigerator. A refrigerator was also cheaper. The movie featured Andy Warhol, G. Gordon Liddy, Dick Cavett, Whodini, Lydia Lunch, Joe Franklin, Peter Wolff, Bob Balaban, Amazing Randi, and Teller and me, none of whom appear in this original story.

INVISIBLE THREAD

The original short story by

PENN JILLETTE

This is the story of how Abner-Cadabra Milstein saved at least the human race and possibly the entire planet Earth. In all the excitement, I never got that straight. My name is Wally Lonsberry and I'm a clown, who also happens to be a four-star general. I'm a skill clown—I don't just put on makeup and a yama-yama suit and fall down. I juggle, do balloon sculpture, hand shadows, and a little ventriloquism. Up to eight years ago I still rode my giraffe unicycle, a ten-footer. But my first love has always been magic.

I don't love the magic that lies to people, the "magic" of astrology and mind reading, and I don't love the magic of Broadway or Las Vegas TV with their big glitter boxes and scared tigers. I love the magic of a seventeen-year-old tuxedo with special pockets. The magic of red "BEE back" playing cards and gimmicked "half-a-dollars." The magic that wears a Snydley Whiplash mustache even when the magician works in a hardware store eleven and a half months a year and only performs a show every couple of months plus two shows in the magicians' convention competition. I love magic books and magic stores and I love the people who write them and run them.

There was a magic shop in my town, the Sultan's Magic Emporium, and it was run by one of the sleaziest con artists that ever stalked the Earth looking to scam a quarter, Abner-Cadabra Milstein. You remember Abner—he's the one who saved the world.

I started going to the magic store (no one called it the Sultan's Magic Emporium) with my mom when I was four years old. And I can still recall my first visit: It smelled like an old man making money off kids; cigar smoke and spilled colas. What a magical smell! And Abner was greasy, really greasy, and he had spots on his head and long single strands of hair. What a guy! I loved him. As I got older, I spent all my time at the magic store, and I even worked there through high school. Abner taught me all the stuff you're supposed to learn on your first job: weird politics and the facts of life the way he saw them. But everyone learns those things. Abner also taught me how to hide things in my hand and lie to someone's face. He taught me things about magic props and things about people that most folks never even dream of knowing. And he saved the human race, but I'll get to that.

My eighth birthday was the best I ever had. I always got magic stuff for my birthday, but Mom and Dad always picked it out, with Abner's help, and bought it for me. On my eighth birthday Mom said I could go to Abner's alone and buy anything I wanted, up to ten dollars, while she went to get the cake and beverages for my party. Now I knew that Abner behaved differently when parents weren't around. He'd sell you more professional illusions if you were a real magician and not just laymen like a magician's parents.

"Hi, kid, what can I do ya for?"

"I need ten bucks' worth of performance-quality props, Abner. My mom is out shopping. I've got an hour to decide."

"Okay, kid, look around. If ya got thirty cents, I'll get ya a cola from the fridge."

"Here you go, Abner. Now I've got nine dollars and seventy cents to put toward my show."

"So look in the case and see what would look good in *Wally's Wondershow.*"

I looked through the case and couldn't take my eyes off a lined file card with the words *Invisible Thread—ONLY $3.50.*

"Abner, I'd like to see the invisible thread, please."

"If you could see it, it wouldn't be worth a damn, Wally. . . . Ya want the full demo?"

"Yes, Abner."

He reached into the case with his fat finger and thumb and fished around on the card until he got hold of it. He very carefully and slowly pulled out the strand of invisible thread. He stretched it up in front of his face and said: "You got better eyes than me, kid. Can you see it at all?" I got my nose right up between his hands and stared and stared and I still couldn't see a thing. This must have been the best batch of invisible thread ever.

"Hey kid, you're breathing on my fingers, get away."

"Sorry, Abner. It sure is a good batch this time, isn't it?"

"Yeah, kid, it's a great batch. Now, watch the routine. It's real

continued on p. 90

in an office xerox machine moves from left to right across the screen, and goes out. Red warning letters go out. COPY AREA DO NOT TOUCH reappears superimposed on the large blue area. COPY button/indicator light goes out. MODULATED SOOTHING VOICE Test completed. VIDI-COPY system is ready for use. The READY indicator flashes green five times. CHIME.COPY button/indicator lights. MODULATED SOOTHING VOICE DO NOT touch the copy area during VIDI-COPY operation. In the vertical area to the left, red warning letters flash DO NOT TOUCH COPY AREA. The words COPY AREA DO NOT TOUCH disappear, and a white bar like that in an office xerox machine moves from left to right across the screen, and goes out. Two second pause. A copy of the random piece of paper appears on the screen. Red warning letters go out. COPY button/indicator light goes out. Ten second pause. CHIME. SAVE button/indicator lights. MODULATED SOOTHING VOICE File mode. Two second pause. The "copy" rolls off the screen to the left as a printout labeled BUFFER MEMORY appears in the column to the left and quickly rolls totals from 0% to 100%. As we hear a CHIME, the message SAVED TO UTILITY FILE appears in the column to the left, holds for a second, and disappears. The screen is restored as it was before the copy operation took place. Five second pause. The READY indicator flashes green five times. CHIME. The size change button/indicator lights. MODULATED SOOTHING VOICE Magnification mode. Scan Line Ratio Compensation on. Do not touch copy area during VIDI-COPY operation. In the vertical grey area to the left, the title SLR COMPENSATION .6070 U appears. Simultaneously, below it, the familiar red warning letters ash DO NOT TOUCH COPY AREA. The words COPY AREA DO NOT TOUCH disappear, and a white bar like that in an office xerox machine moves from left to right across the screen,and goes out. Spanning the copy area a reproduction of a dollar bill appears. The detail and color are what could be expected from a high-end home computer graphics generator, i.e. the green is a bit on the lurid side. SIZE-CHANGE button lights. This holds for one second, then moves to a still bigger enlargement. The SLR COMPENSATION changes to .3125. This holds for a second then moves to an enlargement in which the eye on top of the pyramid fills the screen. The SLR COMPENSATION reads .0190. Red warning letters go out. COPY button/indicator light goes out. Six second pause. CHIME. SAVE button/indicator lights. MODULATED SOOTHING VOICE File mode. Two second pause. The "copy" rolls off the screen to the left as a printout labeled BUFFER MEMORY which appears in the column to the left quickly rolls totals from 0% to 100%. As we hear a CHIME, the message SAVED TO UTILITY FILE appears in the column to the left, holds for a second, and disappears. The screen is restored as it was before the copy operation took place. Five second pause.The READY indicator ashes green five times. CHIME. COPY button/indicator lights. MODULATED SOOTHING VOICE Do NOT touch the copy area during VIDI-KOPY operation. In the vertical area to the left, red warning letters flash DO NOT TOUCH COPY AREA. The words COPY AREA DO NOT TOUCH disappear, and the bar of white light starts to move from left to right across the screen. Suddenly all hell breaks loose. There is a loud burst of electronic noise and feedback. The bar of light breaks into shards which go in all directions in garish colors. After a moment, the image clears to reveal a video copy of a seared human hand. Five second pause. CHIME. SAVE button/indicator lights. MODULATED SOOTHING VOICE File mode. The "copy" rolls off the screen to the left as a printout labeled BUFFER MEMORY appears in the column to the left and quickly rolls totals from 0% to 100%. As we hear a CHIME, the message SAVED TO UTILITY FILE appears in the column to the left, holds for a second, and disappears. The screen is restored as it was before the "copy" operation took place. PENN's VOICE Yeah, babe. You might want to add some more toner. That's right. You've been suckered, pal. Here, put your head right up to the screen. I want to make one last copy. COPY indicator/button lights. CHIME. MODULATED SOOTHING VOICE X-ray mode. The bar of white light travels across the screen, leaving in its wake a cartoony x-ray of a skull with a peanut in place of a brain. This holds for five seconds. MODULATED SOOTHING VOICE VIDI-KOPY operation terminated. Thank you for using VIDI-KOPY. TITLE: SCAM #5 THE DIAMOND AND THE DOPE INSTRUCTIONS. MUSIC: SPOOKY STUFF. PULL OUT to reveal that the TITLE is printed on a playing card on the face of the pack. TELLER's HAND comes in, passes over the title card, and it changes to a Joker. PENN and TELLER are back at the HIGH SNACK COUNTER. PENN Enough of the fun stuff. Let's do another card trick. Get your deck and find the five of diamonds. TELLER produces the five of diamonds PENN Now take the five and very carefully cut out the center diamond with a razor blade. This is one of the few examples in life where neatness actually counts. TELLER begins cutting the center diamond from the five. PENN We call this the DIAMOND AND THE DOPE trick and it's so simple that it has no right to be so good. Let's run through it. TELLER gives PENN the doctored FIVE OF DIAMONDS. PENN Put the doctored five of diamonds back in the deck, leave the cards near the TV and wait for the doorbell to ring. When micro-brain comes over and you tell him that PENN and TELLER are going to be on TV with ALAN HUNTER. You switch on the tape cued up to pay-off for this scam. TELLER cues up the tape on the VCR and we see Alan Hunter on the TV. PENN In that segment we appear on with Alan and say that we're going to perform a magic trick with the people at home. You encourage your low-wattage goombah to participate with you. Let them take the role of the magician. Here Teller, you be the magician. TELLER takes the cards with a self-important flourish, and prepares to act the role of the sucker. PENN Now listen to my directions on the TV. TELLER turns up the volume on the TV. PENN(on TV) Okay magician, have your victim choose a card. TELLER has PENN, playing innocent, pick a card from the deck. PENN(on TV) Don't let the magician see it, victim.Remember your card and put it back in the deck. PENN puts the card back in the deck. PENN (on TV) Now put the deck on top of the TV. Teller will now find your card. Concentrate on your card. TELLER, on TV in the talk-show, reaches up out of frame and pulls down a playing card as if from the top of the set. He and Penn look at it. PENN (on TV) Okay, victim, what was your card? PENN Here's all you got to remember...when I ask this, you respond "the four of diamonds." It doesn't matter what card you picked. Say the four of diamonds. All you gotta do is lie. PENN The four of diamonds. On the talk show, PENN and TELLER look sad. PENN (on TV) And we were so close, too. PENN At this point, Mister Mental Velocity will think that this was a pretty lame trick. But let him keep watching. PENN (on TV) Turn it over, Teller. It's such a shame. We were just one off. Teller, on the screen, turns the card over to reveal the five of diamonds. PENN (on TV) You did say the four of diamonds, didn't you? PENN Yup. PENN (on TV) Gee, Teller, we should be able to do something about that. After all, it just off by one. TELLER rubs the middle diamond of the five. When he moves his hand away, it is now miraculously the four of diamonds. PENN (on TV) Much better. Teller, why don't you return the card to our dear friends and we'll talk about our new home video... TELLER (on TV) reaches out of frame and seems to return the card to the deck atop the set. PENN switches off the TV. PENN The simplest thing here is transforming the five of diamonds into the four of diamonds. You notice that Teller was wearing a red and white striped tie. TELLER produces the red and white tie he was wearing on the talk show. He demonstrates the vanishing diamond. PENN Now that's not a bad trick at all and all you had to do was lie to make it work. Give your friend all the credit in the world. After all he did the trick. PENN winks. PENN But there's another sting coming. The same card that we used on TV, the card with the diamond cut out, to do this move... TELLER continues moving the card from the red section of his tie to the white,so that the diamond disappears. PENN ...is already in the deck. But you have to let the idiot find it himself. So, ask old Mr. Cranial Density... FULL SCREEN (MOS) we see PENN asking TELLER how he thinks the trick was done. PENN (VO) ...if he has any idea how PENN and TELLER turned the five into the four. If he says yes, ask him to pull the card out of the deck and show you. TELLER nods, pulls the card out of the deck, holds it up to the light so we can see the hole cut out of it. TELLER is amazed. Again, we see PENN, full frame, addressing us. PENN If he hasn't figured it out, ask him to hand the five of diamonds to you and you'll show him. Either way, he has had a gimmicked card appear mysteriously from on TV to his hot little hands. It's a great trick, and needless to say, there are three separate betting points in this trick and even someone who couldn't attend a UN summit and understand everything without translator headphones doesn't need me to point them out. Ya' got your gimmicked five of diamonds in the middle of the deck, the deck some place near the TV where you can get at it easily,the videotape cued up, and you're ready to go. TITLE: SCAM #5 THE DIAMOND AND THE DOPE PUNCHLINE ELECTRONIC SLATE COUNTDOWN from 5 to 1. INTERIOR MTV SET WITH ALAN HUNTER. PENN, TELLER, and ALAN HUNTER chat on the MTV set. NOTE: These lines are a guide post. Feel loose and free with them. ALAN HUNTER ...two weeks from now on the anniversary of the death of lead singer Keith Relf, the surviving members of the Yardbirds will reunite for a benefit concert. Guitar freaks don't need to be reminded that three guitarists for the Yardbirds were Eric Clapton, Jeff Beck and Jimmy Page. So far, plans call for an all instrumental concert. And that's the week in rock. Joining me now are modern day Houdini's, kind of the New Wave equivalent of magicians, Penn & Teller. PENN Hi ya Al. TELLER nods hello. ALAN HUNTER Guys, you know I saw your show four times. I'm like the biggest PENN and TELLER freak around. So. I hate to be the one who has to say this. PENN Spit it out, Al. ALAN HUNTER It's just that live you guys are so great, but everytime I see you on TV, I'm disappointed. PENN Yuh? ALAN HUNTER Don't get mad or anything, but what was so great about your live show was the way you got everyone in the audience involved. On TV, it's just like..a spectator sport. PENN You know Alan, you're right. I'm glad we told you to say that. You see, we have a trick for the audience at home. ALAN HUNTER Oh...what? You're going to teach the folks at home how to do a trick? PENN No, Alan, we're going to do a trick with them. Its interactive. ALAN HUNTER Oh, we set up a nine hundred number phoneline or something? PENN No, Alan, this is pure interaction. All the people at home need to do is decide which one of you will be the magician and which will be the victim. Why don't you folks at home figure that out now. And, oh yeah, you're gonna need a deck of cards...As a matter of fact, you're the only one who won't really be able to see it here. You're going to be the spectator in this case. So, why don't you just go over there while we do this and we'll call you over when we' re done. Okay? ALAN HUNTER Uhh...sure. Fine. ALAN HUNTER walks out of frame. PENN Ok, I'm sure everybody who plans on doing this trick has had time to get their cards now. Let's see. Okay magician, have your victim choose a card. Don't let the magician see it, victim. Remember your card and put it back in the deck. Now put the deck on top of the TV. Teller will now find your card. Concentrate on your card. TELLER reaches up out of frame and pulls down a playing card as if from the pack on top of the home-viewer's TV set. He and Penn look at it. PENN Okay, victim, what was your card? PAUSE. (as if replying to the homeviewer) What? PENN and TELLER look sad. PENN And we were so close, too. TELLER snaps his fingers in disappointment. PENN Turn it over, Teller. It's such a shame. We were just one off. Teller turns the card over to reveal the five of diamonds. PENN You did say the "four of diamonds," didn't you? Gee, Teller, we should be able to do something about that. After all, it just off by one. TELLER rubs the middle diamond of the five. When he moves his hand away, it is now miraculously the four of diamonds. PENN Much better. Teller, why don't you return the card to our dear friends and we'll talk with Alan about our new home video. Yo, Alan, come on back. TELLER hands the card out of the top of the frame, as if he is replacing the card in the home-viewer's pack. Alan comes back. ALAN HUNTER Penn and Teller, was that it? PENN Yeah? ALAN HUNTER Well, I guess it looked a lot better at home. I couldn't really see what you were doing. I'm sure it was great. PENN Thanks Alan. ALAN HUNTER Anyway, we got a real blast from the past here. Let's take a look at the first video PENN and TELLER ever made. It's RUN DMC and ITS TRICKY. CUT TO: The first few moments of the ITS TRICKY video. TITLE: SCAM #6- BEGINNER'S LUCK- INSTRUCTIONS. MUSIC: SPOOKY STUFF. This TITLE is printed on the flyleaf of a book. TELLER closes the cover over it. The cover reads, "Magic For Fun and Popularity". TELLER throws the book in the trash. PENN is sitting comfortably at the snack counter, enjoying hors d'oeuvres. PENN There's two groups of people, addle-brained though they may be, that present a problem to this tape being used effectively. People who know that you have the Penn &Teller video may ask to see it while at your house. Lord knows they're too cheap to buy it for themselves. That's probably why they're visiting, too cheap to buy their own refreshments. Anyway, anyone requesting to see this tape is not going to be fooled by a phony copying machine or same fake backwards masking. The other type of person who may be a problem is the mook you already suckered with one of the other tricks on here. Even a dumb animal is once bitten, twice shy. Of course, we wouldn't have told you that these people could be problems if this next trick wasn't a solution. In the video pay-off of this trick, Teller and I appear to be giving some rudimentary, if you'll pardon the "M" word, magic classes against a shoddy background with mediocre production values. For the person requesting the tape, it merely looks like we have sold out our integrity. And just tell the bone-head you've already stung that there's also instructional stuff on the tape and now they can learn to catch their friends. They'll jump at the opportunity. Remember how they gloated. The first thing on the tape is the request that only the person who bought this tape learn the tricks from it as our livelihood depends on our peddling of our simple skills. That's not strictly true in this day of multi-picture development deals. But when you see ol' hollow-head flagrantly disregarding our plea, you'll be reminded of just why these tricks exist. Now, here's the trick they're going to see us teach. Teller takes three cards. TELLER takes three cards. PENN I'll tell you to take three cards. What'll happen is you'll take three and Mr. or Ms. Third Wheel will take three. For now, I'll take that role. PENN takes three cards. PENN Begin with the three cards face down. Turn two face up. Put the face down card in the middle between the two face up cards. Then turn them all face down and do the move: insert your little finger under the top card, allowing the pad of the finger to grip the back of the middle card, and flip it, so that it is face down like the others. PENN and TELLER demonstrate this. TELLER's three are perfect. PENN's has one card face up. PENN I give the directions slower and more clearly in the punch-line segment, but it doesn't matter. No matter how many times he tries,the village idiot's hand will come out like this—wrong. PENN and TELLER show their respective hands. TELLER points out the difference between them. PENN On the other hand, it will come out perfectly for you. Don't make fun of them in any gross, crude way. We repeat the trick several times, so pretty." He reached under the counter and pulled out a deck of playing cards. "Now, being invisible it won't hold much weight, but it'll handle a card nicely. You *can* get a freely selected card to the top of the deck, can't ya, Wally?"

"Yeah, Abner, I can't do the *Pass* good yet but I use an *In-Jog.*"

"Okay, so the spectator's card is on the top. Now watch this. If you try to tie a knot in this thread you'll end up blind as a bat and crazier than a shithouse mouse. So ya take a little tiny glob of magician's wax and you roll it up. See, it looks like a little ball of snot." It did. "And you fix that little ball right to the end of your thread." It seemed to take Abner a long time to get the wax onto the thread, but he did it. "Now, that's all done before the trick, of course, it's part of your *Advanced Preparation.* Now, after you got the card to the top of the deck, while you're *Pattering* a blue streak, you get a good strong bend lengthwise in the selected card and put your little snotball with the thread right on the face and push the card down so the wax holds it flat." Abner now had a perfectly normal deck of cards except the top card was bent and stuck in place all ready to pop up, as soon as you pulled the thread.

"Now let me get hold of the other end here..." He felt around the deck of cards with his thumb and index finger and ran them along the thread to the edge of the counter. "Damn! I lost it." He ran his fingers along again, lost it again, swore again, and repeated this entire procedure twice more.

"Now I got it. Watch." There was a long pause and his forefinger and thumb holding the end of the thread tugged just a little and the top card of the deck popped up. "Is *that* your card?" I reached for it. "Go ahead, pick it up. Look at it. Ya won't see anything but a little glob of snot on the face. You see, I just let go of the thread and you'll never find it. It's a pretty thing, Wally, a real pretty thing."

"Okay, Abner, I want the invisible thread. Now what else ya got that I can use?"

"Wait just a second, kid. Ya want the method on the Invisible Thread routine?"

"Well, yeah. I mean no. I mean yeah, I want the thread."

"You know the rules of the shop, Wally. What you're buying here are secrets, and once you know the secret you can't return it. So give me your three and a half bucks and I'll tell you all about the invisible thread."

"Okay, Abner, but my mother's going to be here soon and I've still got six dollars and twenty cents to spend."

"You got time, kid. The Invisible Thread routine may be the most important trick you ever learn. Now give me the money."

I counted out three dollars and fifty cents and handed it to Abner. Abner took a deep breath and put on his quiet-secret-method-voice. "The whole trick on this one is the demonstration. You can't really do a trick with invisible thread, because there is no such thing. It's just a piece of magician's wax and a bent card. But if you learn to perform the Invisible Thread routine, kid, you can perform any trick in the world. It's pure showmanship. It's acting. Now watch."

I could barely hold back the tears, I was so disappointed. But Abner went on. "The first thing you have to know is if ya bend a card and put a little magician's wax on the face, then press it down flat on top of the deck, it'll pop up on its own, as soon as the wax loses its stickum. But right before it pops up, you'll see it wiggle, just a little. When you see that little wiggle you *mime* pulling the thread and the card pops up, on its own, but it looks just like your thread triggered it. That's the easy part, kid. The hard part is setting it up.

"Now ya got a little card that says 'Invisible Thread' on it, and it says it in real official-looking print. I'll give you that card. So you talk to 'em like you're letting them in on some sort of big secret. Like you're not supposed to tell. Real secret and quiet you tell 'em you got some invisible thread. Then you spend all this time squinting and feeling around for the end of the thread. And take your time, kid—half the entertainment value is making the poor asshole that's watching you (pardon my French) climb the walls watching you squint and fumble around. When you finally got the 'thread,' spend some time stretching it out in front of them. Now, this is the great part: Ask them to look for the thread while you're holding it out for them. You'll have great fun watching them squint, lookin' for nothin'.

"When you're sick of laughing to yourself, show 'em the little glob of wax, pretend to hitch up the thread, look for the wiggle, and fake the pulling."

"You gypped me, Abner."

"Let me finish, Wally. Once you learn how to do this trick you will have learned the basis of all magic. All the acting and showmanship you need is right in the old Invisible Thread trick. And I saved the best part for last. I sold this to ya for three-fifty. That's cheap. And I'm going to give you some extra wax and some extra cards. You can do it for your friends and sell it for up to *five* bucks apiece. And even if you only get fifty cents each from the kids, you'll still make a profit after just eight performances."

Abner paused and looked at me. "It's really a great trick, kid."

Abner took the rest of my ten bucks and gave me lots of other little magic tricks so my mother wouldn't be upset, but I was in a daze. Riding home with my mom, I swore to myself that I'd get back my money and I'd do it by learning to perform Invisible Thread.

I learned to perform it and got good at performing it, but I still never made my money back. Friends made me feel guilty, and I was always afraid strangers would just beat me senseless. But Abner was right—the three-fifty was well spent and taught me all the basics of magic.

When I graduated from high school, all I cared about was magic. I still didn't feel I had the talent to be a professional magician, I couldn't make a living as a birthday clown, and I didn't have the money to open a magic store. So I joined the army.

I did very well in the army. I'm a very rare breed. I'm a smart-ass that people seem to like. In Basic I did little magic shows for everyone. I even did the Invisible Thread Routine for the sergeant in front of the guys and got away with it. I started to like the army. They gave me time to do my clown magic shows at birthday parties and they promised me a good enough pension that I could retire young and open a magic store. So I became a lifer, an army career man.

Everybody on the base liked me and ignored the fact that I had no military skills. They would move me from one unimportant desk job to another and they kept bumping up my rank until I was a four-star general who could open a hell of a magic store on pension and savings in a couple of years. Things had gotten easier and easier, and when the cush job of the century opened up, I got it.

Because of pressure from cranks who had seen too many movies, they had to open a department to prepare and deal with the problem of UFOs. A buddy of mine became head of a department that had to take phone calls from crackpots who were unable to identify things they saw in the sky. It was hours on the phone with loony tunes and endless paperwork. There was a sister department to "prepare for diplomatic relations with intelligent alien life." I became the head of it. It was great—the phone never rang. I had a secretary and an office where I sat, reread old magic books, and practiced sleight of hand all day long. Couldn't be better.

After about six months my secretary could do a passable

French Drop with a quarter and was learning to *Back-Palm* a card. On the rare occasions that it rang, we answered the phone, "Operation Little Green Man," and generally prepared for my retirement.

Then it happened. Aliens landed on planet Earth and said the modern equivalent of "Take me to your leader." The press found out. The government denied it, waited four hours, then leaked it to all the major UFO groups and tabloids, who had cried UFO so many times that no one would believe them anyway. The secretaries to the powers-that-be looked though their computerized-buck-passing Rolodexes and sent the spacemen to my office. If the aliens had wanted a clown for their kid's birthday party I was ready, but other than that I was totally unprepared. Whenever I'm really nervous I practice coin tricks, so the first official sight the aliens saw was an old, incompetent general running a half-dollar across the knuckles of each hand.

Goddam! They were ugly. Not like the movies at all. I mean, *no* recognizable parts. They didn't have insect eyes. They didn't even have holes, you know, like mouth, nose, and ears. Their skin looked like Tupperware and they moved with part crawl and part crippled hop. They had patches of very bright lumps hanging off them, and they smelled like raspberry mothballs and a little oily. I smiled and said, "Welcome to planet Earth." I'm sorry, it was all I could think of at the time. They didn't move, they just started making these farting and squawking sounds. Then they pulled out what I guess was an intergalactic "See and Say" toy and pointed it at me. Their army escorts pointed M16s at the space slugs, and I told the men to get out of my office and leave me alone with Zip and Zap.

"What's up?"

The machine farted and squawked and they farted and squawked and the machine said in a woman's English-accented voice: "We are from the intergalactic conference."

"Yeah, and I'm Captain Kirk. What's the skinny, compadres?" I wanted to see how good that machine really was. Well, like an irritating high school teacher, this machine understood slang but would not speak it. We talked for about three hours. I asked to touch them, and they let me. They must have been 150 degrees, and everything quivered under their skin every couple seconds.

Unpleasant. Having gotten preliminaries out of the way, they got down to their squawking and farting business. It was a difficult concept for me to understand. It seems there is a whole bunch of intelligent life in the universe and most all of it knows about the others. And, I guess like all those grade-B movies, they all really do have one intergalactic government and I was talking to a couple of space cops.

Now, from what I figured, either the human race or all life on this planet (I told you I never got that straight) was on trial for b̷ ̶̶redundant. That's some sort of super space sin. Everything ̶̶̶̶̶—central nervous system, endoskeleton, one-heart circulation, carbon-based DNA, the whole shebang—was enjoyed by some other life form in the universe. So what they were saying was that although we were the only human beings in the universe, there was nothing special about us. We had no quality that wasn't covered by some other intelligent life form. Okay, that was fine, I bought that. Then they said we had a really nice planet. I said thanks. Then they said they couldn't afford to squander a grade-1A habitable planet on some 4F redundant critters like us. They said it nicer than that, and that made it even worse. And the bottom line was that they were going to waste us and put some nonredundant ugly-as-a-mud-fence alien space slime on our day-at-the-beach planet. It was monster-movie panic time.

As soon as little Zip and Zap had arrived, the army had given me a staff of over a hundred people, all top-drawer, all top-secret, and I put them to work. I explained as much as I could without panicking them and sent them out to find what made us *homines sapientes* unique. Meanwhile the slug brothers just stood there in my office. I guess their unique *raison d'être* was the ability to stay in an office for three days without sitting down, eating, or peeing. I left the office a couple times and I had a few cheeseburgers sent in, but I pretty much stayed there with them. I sent out for the top scientists, gave them the lowdown, and sent 'em out. But I stayed in charge. As the reports came in I'd scan them really quickly and hand them to the E. T. Starsky & Hutch to evaluate. They'd slide the reports into their machine and tell me ten seconds later that they checked that and we were wasting our time. One time I said, "Where?"—referring to some filter system of the

continued on p. 98

you can offer to help. Be gentle. Condescend. Patronize. TELLER is doing the trick by sleight of hand, so that he can flourish the faces of the cards to the camera, thus disarming any suspicion the victim may have that you are using gaffed cards. You will be using gaffed cards: a double faced card. If you, however, flourish both sides of the double-faced card, you will look foolish indeed. You will also come off as a jerk if you a) put the card in the wrong position or b) deal the gimmicked card to the victim by mistake. Take two playing cards and glue them together face to face. You now have a double backed card. TELLER glues a card together in the fashion PENN described. PENN So Teller's gonna teach it, you're going to get it right off the bat. And your friend who can't get a ripple on an EEG machine is left staring at his thumbs. You've beaten him in head to head competition. And if there was money riding on it — well, that's Entertainment. So, glue two cards face to face and put the double backed card five down in the deck and remember to give your dear friend his cards first. You want to get the gimmicked one so the trick will work. TELLER demonstrates this. PENN Go nuts! TITLE: SCAM #6 - BEGINNER'S LUCK - PUNCHLINE. ELECTRONIC SLATE COUNTDOWN from 5 to 1. PENN and TELLER are at a glitzy demonstration table in front of a showbizzy backdrop. PENN Hello, We're Penn & Teller. And Welcome to "Cruel Tricks For Dear Friends." We are going to teach you how to do magic tricks to amaze and delight your friends. Your purpose in learning magic should be the same as ours: To make your friends and acquaintances happier and make the world just a little better place to live. May we ask you one favor? We have tried to price this tape so that everyone that wants to learn these tricks can purchase his or her own copy. All we have to make our living is the secrets we are selling to you. Please do not watch someone else's copy of this tape, but buy your own, and help protect our livelihood. Everyone loves card tricks. So let's start by learning the basic sleights. We'll start with a simple move, the flip-over. This is a very simple move, and will only take you seconds to master. But please be patient with us. We'll get to the good stuff later. TELLER demonstrates all of the following along with PENN's description. PENN Take any three cards from a pack. Turn two of them face up, leave one face down. Take the face-down card and put it between the face-up cards, then turn the whole pack over. Now here comes the flip-over. Insert your little finger under the top card, allowing the pad of the finger to grip the back of the middle card, and flip it so that it is now face down like the other two. All set? You probably had no trouble with that, but just to make sure, let's try it again. Begin with the three cards face down. Turn two face up. Put the face down card in the middle between the two face up cards. Then turn them all face down and do the move. Once again, insert your little finger under the top card, allowing the pad of the finger to grip the back of the middle card, and flip it, so that it is face down like its brothers. Even though it's easy, it really is a lot of fun. When Teller and I are on tour, we take time to work with the children in special classes, and this is the move they have the most fun with. If your grip feels even slightly uncertain, maybe moistening the finger would help. This is like training wheels on a bicycle however, and should be dropped as soon as possible. One final time, then, right along with us: three cards face down; two face up; face down card in the middle; turn em all face down. Little finger under the top card. Execute the flip over, and, voila, your first successful feat of sleight of hand. MUSIC: SPOOKY STUFF. TITLE: Using a Flipover-Type Move in a Game of Blackjack. Again we see PENN and TELLER. PENN The following application of the Flipover was developed by professional gamblers for use in casino-type situations. A lot of money was stolen using this move. We present it here for entertainment purposes only. PENN starts to deal blackjack hands to himself and TELLER. I'm sure that you've realized by now, that if the Flipover move is done end-to-end rather than side-to-side, and 360 degrees rather than 180, if it's done left-handed with the middle finger it could be pretty damn useful to the unscrupulous gambler. Let's show you what we mean: Here's the hand you got. TELLER shows his cards, a lousy hand, and turns them face-down. PENN And here's.. TELLER does a slight flipping move. He turns the cards face up. They form a great hand... PENN The hand you want. FADE TO BLACK. TITLE: SCAM #7- BEHIND THE BACK- INSTRUCTIONS MUSIC: SPOOKY STUFF. This TITLE is written on the back of PENN's shirt. He turns around and addresses the viewer. TELLER is sitting placidly in the living room portion of the set beside PENN. PENN Here we are at our final sting and Teller has asked me to make two announcements. One, he wants you to know that this is his favorite trick and secondly, don't ever call what he does "mime." The great thing about this one is- not only will you make some money but there is a perfect chance to introduce the element of sexual embarrassment. And like all episodes of sexual embarrassment, you'll be working with a partner. Your friend may have only scored 300 on their verbals but somehow they have built a relationship with someone that you deserve more. Here's how you can drive a wedge into that relationship. You're home watching TV when this couple comes over. You talk to them about the simpatico that some couples have. Tell them that it verges so close to ESP that it's almost eerie. Offer to be the medium for a little experiment. Of course, this rap can be modified to accommodate any two people, even strangers. And a small crowd of people watching won't hurt. In this case, TELLER will be playing you, I'll be playing your friend and as your friend's date — please welcome Miss Lydia Lunch. LYDIA LUNCH enters. TELLER, PENN and LYDIA don signs reading respectively --YOU, YOUR FRIEND and YOUR FRIEND'S DATE. PENN Now TELLER's going to stay in character and not talk, so even though he's playing you, I'll describe what's going on in voiceover. Take it. PENN, TELLER, and LYDIA act out the scene as PENN narrates. PENN (VO) You've laid the simpatico/ESP thing on pretty thick and they're ready for your little experiment. Seat your friend and their date back to back. TELLER seats PENN and LYDIA back to back so that PENN's back is also to the TV set which is still playing in the background. PENN and LYDIA ad lib small talk while following TELLER'S directions. PENN (VO) Get a random book or newspaper. Begin leafing through it. Have your friend tell you when to stop. TELLER picks up a book and begins leafing through it. . PENN Okay, TELLER, stop. TELLER stops leafing through the book. PENN (VO) Have your friend pick a random number of lines down and words across. PENN TELLER, twelve lines down and seven words in. TELLER counts down then across. We do not see the page of the book. PENN (VO) Write the word down and give it to your friend. Make sure your friend's date doesn't see it. TELLER writes a word on a slip of paper, folds it half and gives it to PENN. PENN (VO) Now tell your friend his date will be able to read his mind. PENN looks at the word on the piece of paper. TELLER encourages PENN. PENN scoffs. PENN Your friend may scoff and not want to participate. There is only one thing you can do in this case. TELLER leans towards the camera and rubs his thumb against his forefinger. PENN That's right. It's time to bet. You've told this half-wit that his date will read his mind. Now, you're getting him to bet that his date can't do it. This drives the wedge of greed in between lovers. To be fair, your friend will humor you and at least pretend to concentrate on the word. PENN, with the YOUR FRIEND sign around his neck plainly visible, makes mentalist faces as he pretends to concentrate on the word. TELLER stays in plain sight of PENN. LYDIA seems to be suppressing a giggle. LYDIA Is the word "bundle?" PENN, as YOUR FRIEND, is shocked. PENN What? How did you know that? PENN shows the unfolded paper. It reads "BUNDLE". LYDIA I just knew. We had a bond. And you didn't think so! You bet against it! I don't want to see you anymore! Teller, would you join me for some herb tea? TELLER nods his head "YES.", holds his hand out for money from PENN. PENN gives him money and TELLER and LYDIA walk off arm in arm. PENN breaks out of the scene and addresses camera. PENN Look how you can leave your friend - embarrassed, economically injured and alone. Perfect. But what just happened? Lydia, Teller, c'mon back. TELLER and LYDIA come back in and thank PENN. PENN puts his arm around LYDIA. PENN You remember the film we used in the SUPERCLEANER sting a while back, "Nothing Sacred" starring Carole Lombard and Fredric March? Well, we like it so much (and we already bought the rights to it) that we're going to use it again. If you remember, Teller was careful to seat YOUR FRIEND. PENN points to the sign around his own neck. PENN ...with his back to the TV. He was equally careful to have YOUR FRIEND'S DATE... He points to LYDIA's sign. PENN ...face the TV. The tape with a chunk of "Nothing Sacred" was playing. No one even noticed it. What happened next Lydia? LYDIA I was just sitting there. I got a little bored because no one was talking to me. I started looking at the TV. We see the TV segment. In it we see a few seconds of the same section of the movie that we saw before. But this time through the magic of cheap blue-screen TELLER enters the picture. One by one he holds up signs that tell LYDIA what to do. LYDIA describes them. LYDIA Suddenly, TELLER appeared on the screen. He was jumping up and down to get my attention. He was holding a sign telling me not to say anything. So I didn't .Then he held up a sign saying that the word was "BUNDLE." I believed him and he was right. Once again we see PENN, TELLER, and LYDIA. PENN But how did Teller know? Was there some great psychic feat of prediction involved? Of course not, there's no such thing! All you have to do is lie. Your friend is convinced that they are the one picking a random word. Once you put down the book or paper there is no way for them to check it. CLOSE-UP of TELLER'S hand counting down ten and across seven words of a page. His finger lands on a random word and he writes down "BUNDLE" on a little piece of paper and folds it. PENN (OS) Just write down the word "BUNDLE". This is a bald-faced lie. No matter what the word on the page really was, write down BUNDLE. Write down the word BUNDLE, seat your rival with his back to the TV, and make sure your other guest can see the TV so that they can be your unsuspected accomplice. Thank you, Lydia. LYDIA ad libs goodbyes and exits . PENN Okay, here we go. Last stop everybody out. This is the last punchline on the tape. You've seen the piece of film before, so, for right now, fast-forward up to the good part. The clip itself is only entertaining when the joy of being alive is being sucked from your friend's soul into yours. Get them good. TITLE SCAM #7 - THE WEDGE OF GREED - PUNCHLINE. ELECTRONIC SLATE COUNTDOWN from 5 to 1. We now see the film footage. After a while TELLER walks into frame (he is blue-screened into the film). He waves and gestures wildly to get attention. He then proceeds to hold up a series of signs which read in the following order: 1) Shhh! Don't say anything. 2) This isn't an ESP experiment. 3) It's a trick 4) And now you're in on it 5) Your partner will be shocked when you guess the right word 6) Your partner is a chump and is not a very attractive person 7) Concentrate before you say the word 8) The word is "BUNDLE" but maybe you don't want to say it yet 9) Maybe you want to spell it out 10) BUNDLE 11) B 12) U 13) M, no it's an "N", I think 14) D 15) L 16) E 17) Go ahead. Say it. BUNDLE 18) Don't let on. 19) Carry this secret to your grave. 20) Have a nice day. 21) Don't let on 22) See you soon EXTERIOR HAWAII THE PRESENT. PENN and TELLER are in casual resort clothes and sunglasses, lounging on beach chairs in front of panoramic stock footage of an Hawaiian beach. They are surrounded by beautiful woman and the cast and crew of the video tape (these two groups are not mutually exclusive). They are sipping soft drinks and relaxing. PENN Learn all the tricks on here and maybe you'll be able to move on to bigger swindles and make millions of dollars from people just like you, friends. Make sure you buy Cruel Tricks 2. Aloha. PENN and TELLER pick up their bass and Casio and play a laid back version of Spooky Stuff, while the friends around join in on island instruments. MUSIC : SPOOKY STUFF. Roll Credits

THE END

EXTERIOR A WHARF BY A PARK NIGHT Close on PENN and TELLERs faces. PENN Hey, I sure hope Bill Shatner narrates our footage after were dead. Were Penn & Teller, and we are not part of this so-called tribute to Houdini. There are liars on this show and we refuse to be part of it. What bigger lie can you imagine than pseudo-duplications of Houdins unique feats? The Pendragons are trying to make you believe that by doing the same trick 4 seconds quicker than Houdini they are paying homage to his memory. This is not paying tribute! This in oneupsmanship. Lies, lies, lies, lies, lies, lies, lies! And we are not part of it. We now widen out to see PENN and TELLER strapped in matching strait jackets. TELLER tries, with increasing discomfort, to escape. PENN We allowed our names to be used on this special because someone had to give Houdinis point of view against this posse of bbers. We knew Houdini. He was our friend. We admired him. And he often referred to himself as Penn & Tellers biggest fan. When he died, he left all his equipment to us. But you know Bess, yapyap-yap-yap-yap-yap-yap until we gave the stuff to her. But the one thing she couldnt wrench out of our deserving hands was the friendship we had with Har, as we called him. And if theres one thing we learned, over our thirty years of friendship with Harry Houdini, it was that he never wanted anyone to duplicate his miracles. And he also suggested that Teller keep his mouth shut if we ever wanted to make any money. We are wearing two of the actual strait jackets that he used. Teller is wearing one from an early part of his career, and I am wearing one from right after he gained sixty pounds to play the part of a washed-up prize-ghter in a Scorsese lm. PENN and TELLER turn around showing the backs of the jackets. PENN As you can see these are buckled rmly in place with a crotch strap running between our legs, stopping us from slipping it off over our heads, and making our trousers t in an attractive way. Only the king of escape could liberate himself from these bonds. How ya doin, Teller? TELLER is still trying to wriggle out, but making no progress. PENN Yeah. I havent got a clue either. Marc, would you let us out of these things? Marc, do me first, would you? MARC GARLAND enters and unbuckles PENN and TELLER from the jackets. PENN Damn, Houdini was good. Several PASSERSBY from the park have come into the shot, hanging back like a crowd in a typical news shoot. Some have traces of Halloween costumes on. PENN But dont take our word for it. (to PASSERSBY) Hey, any one of you guys want to be on television? How about you? PENN invites PAT. RHONDA eggs him on. PAT Is this Saturday Night Live? PENN No. Have you heard of Houdini? PAT Yeah, I saw them at the Garden with LL Cool and Run D. PAT sings a little of their hit. PENN No, not that Whodini, the old dead one. Long pause as Pat thinks. RHONDA The magician. PAT thinks. PAT Oh yeah! The Tony Curtis guy. PENN Yeah. PAT He drowned, or something, didnt he? PENN No. Do you think his escapes were hard? PAT I guess so. But there was probably some trick to them. TELLER brings out a packing case, handcuffs, kidney or something that some egghead had come up with. "Where you got that?" They told me there was no Earth term for that planet or even that solar system because we hadn't even discovered it yet. I was getting so sick of that woman's teabag accent coming out of their little machine. I was hungry, I was tired, the future of the whole goddam human race and maybe all life on Earth was on my shoulders, and these two trash bags full of brightly colored hot mud were having some machine tell me, in an English accent, with no emotion, that we were redundant. I was irked.

In the army the rule is C.Y.A., Cover Your Ass, and I did. I did everything short of telling the public. We told all the other countries, even Russia and China, about the problem. They sent in all their suggestions, and finally we just hooked the aliens right up to the teletype and computers. About every ten seconds they'd say, "Sorry, no. You are wasting your time."

I was watching all the facts pour into their machines from all over the world, in every language, and I said, "Really, you got *all* that stuff somewhere else?" They said they did and tried to reassure me that nothing was being lost. That we had to look at the big picture. They were even nice enough to say that before we were snuffed, they would answer all the questions we had about the universe and even about theology and philosophy. All the hard questions. They would end our wondering and snuff us. The way they said it, it didn't sound that bad. I was really tired, but suddenly it struck me that I was the guy. I was the guy in 2001 that faced the truth, the most important guy in the history of all human evolution. I was the last guy, or at least one of the couple billion handfuls of last guys. And they'd probably take a few of us and stuff us or suspended-animate us for a museum, and that might be me, quintessential Earth Man, maybe in my dress uniform with clown shoes.

I got really philosophical and said, "You got the Velvet Underground?" And they said that they had cultures that produced sound as art.

"I didn't say 'sound as art,' I said 'the Velvet Underground,' Lou Reed's band in the sixties."

"You don't seem to understand. Your mind can't grasp the universal picture."

"So there are no fartin', squawkin' trashbags that can play 'White Light/White Heat,' huh? And we're *redundant? REDUNDANT?* You got Elvis?"

"We are not talking about individuals, we are talking about species."

"What about Houdini?" I said it very quietly, and I repeated it: "What about Houdini?"

"You are not looking at the universal picture."

"I got your goddam motherfucking, 'universal picture' hanging, you assholes. *Houdini* redundant, you scumbags?" I was upset. Then I got an idea. I paused and said, really cool, "You guys got Invisible Thread? You got that out in starworld?"

They farted and squawked and the machine said, "Please explain further."

"Invisible thread. You know, thread that you can't see."

"We've explained this before. We 'see' very differently from you. We don't have lenses or rods and cones. We see a much different and much broader spectrum than you."

"I'm talking *invisible,* can't be seen by any creature in this whole great beyond. *Nada* on every spectrum."

"No, we don't. And you don't either. It's impossible."

"Well, it may be impossible, but we've got it. It's not very strong, so it's only used here on Earth for magic tricks. I have some right here in my desk. You've got better eyes than me—can you see it?" I held it right up to what I thought was their eyes and later found out was more likely their secondary sex characteristics. But they couldn't see it.

I did Abner proud. All the bells and whistles, every nuance. When the top card popped off the deck I said, "And here on Earth we sell it for only three-fifty."

Well, they farted and squawked at each other for the longest time and then started packing up. I thought that I'd really pissed them off and we were dead meat. I started begging for them to hook back up to the teletype and look over the material that was coming in. But they just kept getting ready to leave. I hadn't fooled them.

Then they said it was okay. They said we weren't redundant. I guess they figured that no other living creature anywhere in the whole universe would ever lie about a thing like invisible thread.

So that's why I suggested to the President that he declare Halloween to be named Abner-Cadabra Milstein Day, but he didn't believe me. No one ever believes me after I show him that Invisible Thread routine.

A Postscript by TELLER

When Penn was in the throes of writing the "Invisible Thread" short story, he came to me one day and asked me if I knew of a trick that would simulate the presence of invisible thread in the pitch. No such trick existed. "Does it have to work?" I said.

"Of course not. It just has to be plausible." So after a little discussion we came up with the idea of the card with the bend, held flat against the deck by a ball of wax, which eventually releases when the wax gives out. We tried it. It didn't work. The card would lose the bend. Or the wax wouldn't stick. Or it would stick too well. But it suited the story just fine. And there was something neat about even the trick behind the trick being mythical.

Later, when we decided to adapt the short story as a film script, we wrote the trick into the stage directions, just as though it existed. Nobody questioned it. It was the producer's first project with us and he assumed we knew what we were doing. It was only after we were well into pre-production that we realized that a camera would have to **photograph** the Invisible Thread routine, i.e., we'd actually have to do it.

So we had to cheat.

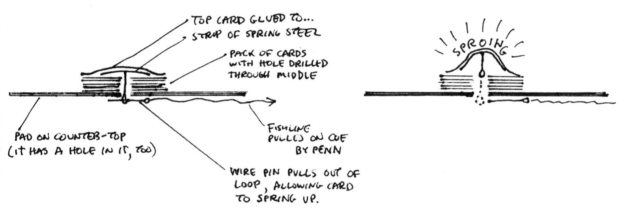

TOP CARD GLUED TO...
STRIP OF SPRING STEEL
PACK OF CARDS WITH HOLE DRILLED THROUGH MIDDLE
SPROING
PAD ON COUNTER-TOP (IT HAS A HOLE IN IT, TOO)
FISHLINE PULLED ON CUE BY PENN
WIRE PIN PULLS OUT OF LOOP, ALLOWING CARD TO SPRING UP.

If you ever see "Invisible Thread" on video, watch carefully. You'll notice that there is a camera cut between the action of showing the bent card being put on top of the deck and the moment that it pops up. Between shots we switched in a gimmicked pack of cards. The top card was loaded up with bent spring steel to give it a good jump. The rest of the pack was all glued together in a block and had a hole drilled through it. There was a short piece of fishline that ran from the middle of the top card through the hole in the pack, and hooked onto a wire under the red pad on the counter. That wire, in turn, was tied to a string, which Penn pulled on cue while he said his lines.

You don't see the fishline and steel on the face of the card when I hold it up to Wally because, as I pick it up, the card drops out of view below the lower edge of the television picture into

101

the hand of a waiting prop man, who instantly substitutes a plain bent card with a little wax in the middle.

Later we found out that some magic-store owners had contacted their suppliers, inquiring whether "Invisible Thread, as Seen On TV" was available. Wherever Abner-Cadabra Milstein is, I bet he's proud.

*   *   *

UNIMPORTANT THINGS
THAT YOU DON'T CARE ABOUT

Right now, before you do anything, while you're thinking of it, remove and destroy the page that told you to look here. You don't need it anymore. You can remember the title of this section, and it's listed in the table of contents. You don't want anyone else to read it. This is secret.

There is one big rule for using this book: **EVERYTHING PRINTED IN RED INK IS A LIE!!!!** The attention-grabbing red instructions throughout this book are bogus. They are lies to make fools of your friends. Lies for you to use. Lies that will be your new friends.

The following sections are the only real instructions in this book. If you try to work the tricks according to the instructions in red *without* reading this section, the tricks will screw up and you will look like a bonehead. You will look stupid. Very stupid. *Very* stupid. We have buried these real instructions so that the putzes, chumps and dunderheads—your "friends"—will not be apt to notice them. Your bird-brained cronies will ignore this dull black ink and go right for the exciting red print like a parakeet to a reflective piece of metal or a disco fan to a mirrored ball. This way you can leave the book in plain sight on your coffee table and still scam the suckers. We think this is a nice touch.

Some people will buy the book and ignore the instructions to read this section first. Red and black, fiction and fact, lie and truth will be taken as the same. For them this book is a rip-off and we're glad. We hate them. They are not our kind of people. You, on the other hand, are reading this section. We like you. We want to help you prove that you are superior. If you read and follow these instructions you will be able to make your fellow human beings feel shame. We are all going to have fun.

The book itself is gimmicked to the gills. Keep it handy and always ready to torture your guests. But it is more than just cheesy magic tricks in book form to make a quick couple/three bucks for a pair of two-bit swindlers. This book is also real literature. In your solitary moments, when there's no one to humiliate, don't forget the other stuff, the filler. Some of it was written by Penn & Teller, some by just Penn, and some by just Teller but we each put in the same amount of effort and we're both proud of everything in the book.

We have tried to answer questions that we've been asked a lot. We have photo-essays explaining how we dumped cock-roaches on *Late Night with David Letterman* and cut a snake in half on *Saturday Night Live.* We have disgusting pictures of Teller with gunk in his eyes getting ready to have trick plastic shells fitted over his eyeballs. We have the original short story, "Invisible Thread," by Penn, that turned into "Penn & Teller's Invisible Thread" on Showtime. Whether you read books all the way through from beginning to end, like Penn, or browse, like Teller, we sincerely hope you'll enjoy every page of this book and find it well worth the purchase price.

We enjoy funny, creepy short stories, and there are plenty in *WOULD/COULD/SHOULD*, the little book that came packaged right with the big book. These are also written by us, but, for reasons you will learn later, are credited to various nonexistent authors. If you want to know who wrote what, look in the biography at the beginning of each story. If it says the author is a member of the New England Science Fiction Society, it's really Penn. From any other science fiction society, it's Teller.

VERY IMPORTANT NOTE: When you read the stories in *WOULD/COULD/SHOULD*, make sure you skip the first line on each page. That is a scam we'll explain later.

continued on p. 106

out of frame. PENN Pat, would you examine this packing crate, please? PAT (examining crate) What am I looking for? PENN Any gimmicks? Trickery? Go ahead, bang on it. PAT bangs on the wall of the crate. Its heavy and solid. PAT Seems okay to me, but what the hell do I know? TELLER clicks the handcuffs on PAT. PAT Ow. PENN Could you get out of those? PAT No. But Im not a magician. I work in vintage clothing. PENN So you couldnt get out of them. PAT No! Its not my job. I dont know jack about this. Listen guys, is this going to take long? I got a Halloween party to go to. PENN What about these leg irons? PAT, still handcuffed, examines them. PAT What about em? PENN Could you get out of them? PAT Hell, no, I couldnt get out of them. I cant even get out of the damn handcuffs. TELLER locks the leg-irons on him. PENN Teller, make sure he doesnt have any picks hidden on him. PAT Why would I have picks on me?? Im going to a Halloween party. Meanwhile, TELLER has unbuttoned PATs shirt, gone through the pockets and pulled it down over his wrists. PENN No picks in any of his pockets. No picks in the small of his back, none in his nose, his armpits, his hair. How bout below the waist? TELLER goes through PATs trouser pockets, and starts to undo his belt. PAT resists. PAT Yo, creep! PENN (looking to camera) Okay. Fine. But Houdini would have been completely stripped. As PENN talks, PATS GIRLFRIEND tries to come into the shot. PATS GIRLFRIEND Pat! MARC GARLAND (pushing her out) Mind your own business, honey. He drags her off camera. MARC GARLAND (O.C.) Come on everybody! Nothing to see here! Move on,come on. Lets go! PAT Houdini was a magician! Im a clerk! By now TELLER is winding chains around PAT and padlocking them around his neck. PAT Okay! Thats it! You guys are dead! PENN Struggle though he may, hes no match for the great Houdini. MARC GARLAND and another GOON grab PAT and force him into the packing case. TELLER closes the lid and, sitting on it, padlocks the hasps. PAT (from inside box) Somebody help me! These guys are crazy. Someone call the police. PENN Now thats a padlock. Anybody can pick a padlock. PENN and TELLER walk out of frame. PAT struggles, rocking the box to and fro. The box comes to rest. PAT (from inside box) Rhonda! Rhonda! Call 911. TECHNICAL NOTE: At this moment we will stop tape, take PAT out of the box, and continue. PENN and TELLER re-enter frame, each carrying hammers and nails. PENN Were nailing the lid onto the box with tenpenny spikes. PAT (from inside) When I get out of this box Im gonna nail you. PENN Not as easy as you thought it was, eh, smartie pants, now youre inside. Youre no match for Houdini. PAT (from within) Help! Rhonda! Help! PENN (sarcastically) Help me, Rhonda! Help, help me, Rhonda. Big baby. Houdini didnt cry for his girlfriend. PAT (still incarcerated) Shut up and let me out of here! PENN (to PAT) You shut up or youre really in trouble. PAT (in box) Youre the one thats in trouble. PENN I dont think youre in any position to give orders. Just shut up. TELLER grabs a can of gasoline and begins dousing the box. PENN I dont know if Houdini actually ever did a aming box thing, but he could have. PAT (trapped) You gonna light this thing on re? PENN Its just a trick. The re will go out as soon as the box hits the water. PAT (through the reeking walls) Water!!? Dont throw me in the bay! Please! Please! Please! Please! Houdini was the greatest. He was the king. He was the Elvis of magic. He was bigger than Elvis! Please! Please! TELLER lights the box on re. PAT AHHHHHHHHH! ...and starts coughing. TELLER pushes the box into the water. He takes out a stop watch and starts it. He watches the bubbles until they stop. We can now see the illuminated Statue of Liberty in the background. PENN You know, I dont want to get saccharine. But when I look out at the Statue of Liberty and think about our good friend and hero, Houdini, it makes me think of really what a great country this is. Where a man, born in Budapest, can come to this land of ours and be embraced by the entire nation. TELLER shows the watch to PENN. PENN Yup. Houdini would have been out by now. Its sixty one years since Houdinis death, and the people that loved him, Penn & Teller, are giving a humble, teary-eyed, tribute to the immigrant they loved. PENN and TELLER look out at the water where the box fell in. PENN:

> Give me your tired, your poor,
> your huddled masses yearning to be free.
> The wretched refuse of your teeming shore.
> Send these, the homeless, tempest-tost to me.
> I lift my lamp beside the golden door!
>
> —EMMA LAZARUS

THE END

SHARPENING STONE OPEN ON: CLOSE-UP of a shot (the metal ball used in the shot put track and eld event). It is on a carpeted oor. A hand REACHES into frame to pick it up. PULL OUT to reveal it is PENN. He holds the shot as he addresses the camera. PENN This is a six pound cast iron shot of the type used in track and eld events. Melted cast iron is molded in a sand mold and then ground to the correct weight and to remove the seam. It is then sand-blasted to its correct surface texture. PULL BACK to reveal TELLER sitting next to Penn on a bed. There is a piece of carry-on luggage between them. PENN Teller and I have been together for more than thirteen. We are obsessed and, indeed, make our living from deception, lying, cheating and swindling. Though these skills do come naturally, it is important that we do keep them razor sharp. So, since about the second year, we have carried with us this thing we call the sharpening stone. We transport it in this piece of carry-on-luggage. Teller and I have made a blood vow that no airline employee nor any member of their family will ever see this shot. We have snuck this six pound iron ball through metal detectors in just about every airport in the country as we zig zag the nation on our tours. PULLING BACK a bit further reveals they are in a hotel room of a Holiday Inn. We see their luggage which has stickers from all of their travels. There are also a few souveniers scattered around. PENN Sure, its not illegal to carry sporting goods on a commercial airline. If we told them we had it, theyd say `Bring it on. BUT, to Penn and Teller, that would be cheating. Penn and Teller exchange a glance like a blood oath. Teller RISES and sets up a portable, folding movie screen. PENN So, to get our sharpening stone through these metal detectors, we are forced to keep our deception, lying and chicanery skills honed to a ne edge. Let me point out that this is called a shot. The shot put is the competition. In our case, we put the shot through hundreds of metal detectors. And like many competitors, we tape our maneuvers for later study. We thought wed share a few representative ones with you now. Teller walks over to a portable lm projector and switches it on. CUT TO: Jerky super 8 footage from a camera in an airport. A crude cardboard sign is held up. It reads: SHARPENING STONE NUMBER 64. LOGAN AIRPORT. BOSTON MASS. HAND-OFF 6C. The sign is removed and Teller gives a questioning thumbs up to camera. PENN(VO) This is an example of our simplest move. We use this one quite a lot. Satised that the camera is on, Teller walks through the metal detector with no problem. He stands on the far side of it, stalling, looking at his ticket and boarding pass. PENN(VO) Now here I come. Watch closely. Penn walks up and starts talking to the guard at the metal detector MOS. Penn leans against one side of the metal detector. He passes the shot around to Teller on the other side. PENN(VO) And there goes the shot. A very simple hand-off. Right there. Many strategies grow out of this simple hand-off. CUT TO: New angle in a different airport. This footage is a bit better technically, as if their equipment has been upgraded slightly. We see this from the exit side of the metal detector. Another crude sign is held up. It reads: SHARPENING STONE NUMBER 285. OHARE INTERNATIONAL. THE RED HERRING. Teller puts the carry-on bag on the conveyor belt next to the metal detector. He then walks through without any trouble. He waits for his bag to come down the belt. PENN(VO) In this case, the hand-off is augmented by a bit of misdirection, a red herring and a slightly more complicated move by Teller. Penn walks through the metal detector, palming the shot. The detector is set off. As he turns to go back through the detector, Teller turns, unzipping the carry-on bag. Penn drops the shot into it. Teller nishes his turn, zipping the bag and walks away. Penn hands the guard a big ring of keys he seemingly forgot about. He then walks back through without a problem. PENN(VO) Teller has a nice move there. But if I do my job as a red herring, you dont even see it. Watch Teller really closely. Boy, hes good. In this next move, misdirection is coupled with brute force in an adagio of subterfuge. CUT TO: Another hand held set-up in a different airport. Another crude title card is held up: SHARPENING STONE NUMBER 108. NATHANIEL GREEN AIRPORT. THE TOSS-UP. In this one, the metal detector cuts the screen in half. Teller APPROACHES on the left. The GUARD POINTS at the carry-on bag. Teller BACKS AWAY suspiciously. The Guard APPROACHES him. Teller CLUTCHES the bag to his chest frantically. Everyone around the area is staring at the suspicious-looking Teller. Everyone is oblivious to Penn who ENTERS from left. Just as he ENTERS metal detector, he lobs the shot into the air very casually. PENN(VO) Let me just remind you, that shot is a whopping six pounds of cast iron. That toss took strength, timing and accuracy. Penn STEPS through the detector and casually CATCHES the shot as he exits. Teller, seeing this, becomes suddenly co-operative and gives the guard the bag and strides through the metal detector. CUT TO: Another jerky hand held airport shot. This time we are back to the less sophisticated equipment and therefore a jerkier picture. There is another crude sign: SHARPENING STONE 24. LaGUARDIA. HUMAN NATURE. PENN(VO) Weve stopped doing this one because, frankly, its just too damn easy. Penn walks up to security guard and points to the carry on bag he is carrying and converses with him MOS. The guard looks down at his feet sheepishly and nods his head yes. Penn takes out a bunch of money and gives it to him. The guard switches off the metal detector, allowing Penn to walk through unhindered. CUT TO: Another hand held shot at yet another airport. This time good equipment has been used. The picture is sharp, clear and relatively steady. A crude cardboard sign is held up. It reads: SHARPENING STONE NUMBER 793. LAX LOS ANGELES. THE FALL GUY. This is set up on the entrance side of the metal detector. Teller WALKS through carrying a stiff paper shopping bag with handles. Once he PASSES through the metal detector, he PUTS the bag down and KNOCKS it over with his foot. The bag is now lying on its side with the open end facing the metal detector. PENN(VO) A move like this next one not only serves to keep us sharp but also satises one of the basic human desires-the need for vengance. There are many variations on this move, but it is always called the Fall Guy. Camera PANS from Teller back past metal detector and across a wide area of the airport. HOLD for a couple of beats on a MAN. He is wearing cowboy boots, designer jeans, a silver Porsche racing jacket and slightly tinted sunglasses. He is in his mid-forties with nicely styled siver-grey hair. Needless to say, he is a dickwad. PENN Look at this guy. Remember him. He copped an attitude with the ticket guy. Then he cut in front of us in the coffee shop. We dont like him. Camera CONTINUES on its pan until it discovers Penn way across the oor. Penn WINDS UP in a bowling stance and SENDS the shot across the oor. A FLOATING RED ARROW SUPERED on the screen helps the audience keep track of its progress. It ROLLS right through the metal detector just as the Dickwad steps into it. The detector is set off and a number of security guards converge on the Dickwad. In the background, we see the shot ROLL right into Tellers overturned bag. The force of it rights the bag and Teller blithely LIFTS it and WALKS away. CUT TO: Penn and Teller in the hotel room. Penn is HOLDING a big hunting slingshot. Teller is pulling the shot back in the sling. He relaxes the tension and JOTS down some gures in a notebook. PENN Well, those are just the tip of the swindling iceberg. Staying sharp is a 24 hour a day job and were constantly looking for new ways to utilize our sharpening stone. So long, well see you at the airport.

THE END

PENN & TELLER in INVISIBLE THREAD OPEN ON: INTERIOR. THE MOFO MAGIC COMPANY. It is 1:00 p.m. in PENN and TELLERs small magic shop on the second story (walk up) above a Pizza Parlor in a neighborhood business district in Washington D.C. In one of the two windows an air conditioner is humming, and just above it, if you looked hard through the grime on the window, you might be able to make out the top of the Capitol dome poking above the other buildings. PENN (O.S.) Yeah. Yeah. Well, let me put it this way, the magicians we represent are all top ight professionals. Right! Some of the brightest up-and-coming young stars in the magic business. Every one of them has a live rabbit, presents a neat and attractive appearance, and does an entertaining show with plenty of color and audience-participation. No one is in the showroom of the shop, with its display counter full of close-up magic props, and its wall case behind the counter full of metal tubes and boxes painted in Chinese motif. Magic tables are hung from the walls and ceiling, as are posters for magic acts from the past and present, and autographed 8x10s of famous magicians. Prominantly displayed is a large sign: PENN and TELLERs MOFO MAGIC COMPANY. EVERYTHING FOR THE MAGICIAN. BeginningAmateur-Professional, Close-Up Parlor Stage. Elsewhere is a sign: HIRE A MAGICIAN, Special Effects for Your Special Event, World-Famous Professionals Available, ReasonableReliable, Comedy Magic Mentalism Adults Children Trade Shows Industrials Malls Boutiques Balloon Animals Hand Shadows Parties Schools Participation Rabbit Magigrams, Also Clown Magician Available. Another reads: Creative Consultants for T.V. And others: Caveat Emptor, Mundus Vult Decipi Ergo Decipiatur. Just behind the beaded curtain that leads to the back room, PENN is in the midst of a phone conversation. PENN Tough audience? What do you mean? How tough? (listens) No, thats no problem. Theyll love it. Its perfect: rehabilitation. Troubled teenagers love magic. Its an escape for them, away from their problems with the law, and into a fantasy world. Illusion! Fantasy! Its perfect. (listens) Oh, no, no. No problem. Magic is the international language. Meanwhile TELLER is in the back room. He is standing at a work table, apparently cutting open a U.P.S. box with a utility knife. He is watching himself do the action in a mirror. As he cuts, the knife seems to slip and accidentally cut a long gash in his hand. He looks critically into the mirror, approves. He wipes the blood off his hand with a paper towel. He dips the utility knife (to which, as we can now see, is attached a squeeze-bulb like the kind used on squirting owers) into a jar of water and squeezes the excess blood out of the bulb until it is clean.

You will use this book mostly against people who visit you in your home. Except for the occasional Jehovah's Witness, these people will, most likely, be your friends, your *dear* friends. Over the years you have forged relationships with these people. In the jungle of day-to-day life, in the lying, cheating, dog-eat-dog world, you have formed a circle of friends who allow you to let down your guard, let down your hair, and say what's really on your mind.

But, more important, these people trust you. When they're around you, their guard is lowered. They feel secure that you won't pull a fast one. You are their friend. You've spent hours, days, weeks, months and years nurturing an intimacy that, with the help of this book, you can exploit. You will take that trust and twist it so you can steal dignity (and in some cases real cash money) from these poor saps.

You may wonder why we think you would want to pull cruel tricks on your dear friends. It's a stupid question and you shouldn't have even asked it. Someone should have bought this book and scammed *you*.

There is no better feeling in the world than hooking a chump and reeling him in. Take it from us, it's worth it. We dropped cockroaches on David Letterman and it felt good. It felt really good. It felt great. And after we did it, after we dropped vermin on this man, on his own show, on national TV, he had us back on. He still likes us. How did we do that? Read on.

Once you've stung a few suckers successfully, your work has

just begun. If you do it perfectly and show them that they have gravel for brains, they may no longer want to be your friends. They may think you are an evil person who has taken advantage of a sacred trust. They may yell at you. They may call you names. They may try to storm out of your house. But don't worry. The person who truly understands *Cruel Tricks for Dear Friends* takes this as just another challenge. The real con *artiste* takes this as an opportunity to really pull a fast one and win their trust back. You must get them to think you're a good person. It's not hard to weasel out. Remember, human nature is on your side.

First, try the "You're a good sport" ploy. Just act like being made a fool of and forgiving the person that did it to you is a good character trait. Remember *Candid Camera*? Their slogan was "People caught in the act of being themselves." This was just a lie. They were really caught in the act of being the butt of a malicious prank. But Alan and the boys got them to pretend they liked it. They made them think it was part of being a *mensch* to allow themselves to be ridiculed. If you can pull this one off, you can humiliate them again and again.

If this doesn't work, try saying this: "I'm sorry, it was Penn & Teller's scam. They said in the book it would be fun for everyone. They lied to me. I don't even know why I bought this book. I never liked them. I especially hate the little one." It's fine to sell us out. We'll be the scapegoats. You bought our book. It's our job.

And if all else fails, if you can't get them to be "good sports," if they won't shift the blame to us, it's time to escalate to the practical joker's nuclear weapon. This one always works: "Let's do it to someone else." Try it. It never fails. Teach them the trick and let them make someone else look like a jerk.

Cruelty heals all wounds.

There's a world full of latent chumps just waiting for you to pounce. Read the following instructions up through page 127, closely and . . . happy scamming.

THE MAGIC DECODER GLASSES
(An exercise in peer-group humiliation)

Did you notice these pages are a bitch to turn to? When you tried to find "Unimportant Things That You Don't Care About," it sure as hell didn't fall open to these pages, did it? It wasn't your fault. The book is made that way. All the pages are specially cut. If you play with this book a little, you'll notice that if you put your thumb on the edge and flip it front to back, all the pages look like itty bitty tiny irritating psycho-print with patterns printed over it, and if you flip it back-to-front it's all big, stupid print. It's fun to do by yourself, but this book is not called *Fun Things to Do at Home Alone*, this book is called *Cruel Tricks for Dear Friends*. Here's a way to use this nice neat crazy printing thing to make a friend of yours look like a jerk:

You can do this with just you and Lieutenant Zero, alone, but it's better if his or her peer group is there watching. That way they can laugh at the putz along with you. Peer-group humiliation is the best. And if you can get the peer group in on the gag before the wazoo shows up, so much the better.

Show the book to the sucker and say, "This book is Penn & Teller's *Cruel Tricks for Dear Friends*." This is the truth, and if you're anything like us it may be a little hard to say it with a straight face, but give it a try.

Once you've said that, you can start lying. "The secret behind every single magic trick in the world is in this book and the book only costs five dollars." Pause while it sinks through the three inches of skull. "There is one catch, though. The book looks like this . . ." Flip the book from front to back so they see nothing but itsy-bitsy unintelligible little print. "... so you have to buy these special Magic Decoder Glasses for one hundred and twenty-five dollars." Pull out the glasses that we gave you packaged with this book. (If you bought the book used, I guess you're screwed.)

"It's a lot of money, but it's worth it. Check it out." Have the numskull put on the glasses. The glasses are specially designed to make whoever wears them look goofy. There isn't a peer group around that won't enjoy this immensely. Give the peer group a wink so they will all know that your friend is a dimwit.

"Look how well the glasses work." Flip the book from back to front so the sucker sees the big stupid print. He or she will think that the glasses did it, and all of the peer group will know that he or she is less than swift.

See if you can get him or her to repeat the whole process. Flip one way when he or she has the glasses off and the other way when the glasses are on. By the second or third time, the peer group should be rolling on the floor laughing. Memorize all their faces and make a mental note to catch each one of them on a different scam later.

WOULD/COULD/SHOULD
(A Tool for Reading the "Minds" of the Simple-Minded)

The little book that came with this bigger book is called *WOULD/COULD/SHOULD: The Science Fiction Society Anthology, 1988.* But it was not put out by a Science Fiction Society. That's a lie. The stories aren't really science fiction. That's a lie, too. It's not an anthology. That's also a lie. We wrote all the stories, even though other people's names are on them. The little book is a trick. It's a prop you can use a few different ways. Below are two sets of directions for using *WOULD/COULD/SHOULD.* The first set of instructions tells you how to do a mind-blowing trick just using the little book and a little bunkum. The second set of instructions tells you how to use the book with the phony instructions on page 45 to really do permanent damage to someone's life. Both are really mean tricks that are easy and fun to do.

If you would like to read our short stories in *WOULD/ COULD/SHOULD* for real: Skip the first line of *every* page. Ignore every first line! Do *not* read the first line of each page or the stories will not make sense.

We like the stories in *WOULD/COULD/SHOULD*, but their tone wasn't right for the main book. So we put them in a little phony book and made them into a scam. We would like you to read them, but when you do, remember that the top line of every page is added and has nothing to do with the story. The top line of each page is just there so you can fake the power of ESP and make your friends look stupid.

Here's how to do the trick with no hoo-hah:

1. Put *WOULD/COULD/SHOULD* in some easily accessible place in your home. Throw it on your coffee table.
2. Wait until the pigeon that you want to pluck is a guest in your home.
3. Give the pigeon a little ESP mumbo jumbo: The "There are lots of things that science doesn't understand" line works well. And don't forget "Haven't you ever had the phone ring and known who it was?" Just talk with the sucker a little about psychic phenomena.
4. Tell him or her you know that you're psychic and this test is going to prove it.
5. Bet money (at least the price of this book) that you can read the pigeon's mind.
6. Hand the pigeon a "random" book or magazine. **MAKE SURE THAT "RANDOM" BOOK IS *WOULD/COULD/SHOULD* OR YOU WILL REALLY LOOK LIKE A DIP!**
7. Now say, "Open the book to any page at all. Read the top line to yourself and make a mental picture of it. Now, concentrate on the image." Here's the fun part: Really make your victims concentrate—it makes them look goofy with their empty brow all furrowed.
8. Make faces like Uri Geller, act like it's really hard, and draw this picture: It looks like a spider. It looks like a transistor. It looks like

the sun. It looks like the top of a volcano. It looks like an octopus. It looks like a squid. As a matter of fact, it looks like everything that's the first image on every page. Pretty cool, huh?

9. Show the pigeon the picture and say, "This is the psychic image I got. Is this the image you had?"

10. Collect your money.

11. Laugh behind the pigeon's back after he or she leaves.

12. Send a check for half the money collected in Step 10 to:

Penn & Teller
c/o Villard Books
201 E. 50th St.
New York, NY 10022

THE PSI TV SCAM, OR GILDING THE LILY
(Sucker instructions on page 45)

If you enjoy misleading others with half-truths ("Mother isn't quite herself today," says Norman Bates), you may want to try an elaboration of the *WOULD/COULD/SHOULD* scam. We call it PSI TV.

Use it to punish "enlightened" believers in the occult—you know, the ones who scoff at demonic possession but read up on trance channeling; laugh at astrology but schedule their lives around biorhythm charts; sneer at fairies but spend their vacations watching the skies for the UFOs that built the Pyramids.

When a New Age nincompoop drops in, pick up this book and excitedly point out the article entitled "PSI TV" on page 45,* and watch the expression on his face as he reads. The article is full of brazen insults to simps like him ("People believe anything in print. . . . Most of the people who claim telepathic powers are not too bright"). But just you watch. The jackass won't realize you're pulling his tail. He will furrow his brow and nod, embracing the specious arguments. He thinks he's open-minded but *you* know he's empty-headed.

* Be sure to read the fake instructions on page 45 before you attempt the trick. That way you'll know what's going through the victim's "mind."

continued on p. 114

He dries the knife, and drops it into a box labled: Bleeding Utility Knives $12.98. Meanwhile, PENN continues his conversation. PENN Thats the best part. Its only $150. Amazing, eh? (listens) Its a professional from New York, working the Hotel Washington on weekends. He gures that getting maximum exposure while hes here cant hurt, what with all the exclusive parties politicians throw. So he gave us permission to book him at $150. Thats a third his normal fee. SOUND OF a disagreeable Radio Shack buzzer. The alarm that indicates that the front door of the shop has just been opened. PENN pokes his head out from the beaded curtains. WALLY, an 11 year old boy has just entered. PENN waves to WALLY with a Ill be with you in a second gesture, and resumes his conversation. WALLY amuses himself looking in the cases and studying the photographs of PENN and TELLER shaking hands with famous magicians and performing for large audiences in shopping malls. PENN (O.S.) Great. Just send your check right here, Mofo Magic Co., 2164 N. St. N.E., Washington, D.C. Youll need to have in in to me by the 5th to allow 2 weeks for it to clear before the show on the 19th. Righty Right. Thank you very much. PENN sticks his head out from the behind the curtains while he dials the phone again. PENN Hi, Wally. What can I do ya for? WALLY (holding up a $20 bill) I got twenty bucks for my birthday, Penn. I need... PENN interrupts him with a hold on gesture. He speaks into the phone. PENN Hello, Mrs. Carter. Is Dennis in? This is Penn from Mofo Magic. PENN puts his hand over the mouthpiece of the receiver. He calls to TELLER. PENN Get Wally a coke from the fridge, Teller. TELLER goes to a wicker basket with swords stuck through it, sitting in one corner of the shop. He opens the door. Inside is a small refrigerator. He takes out a can of coke, opens it, sticks a straw in, and gives it to WALLY. He takes WALLYs $20 bill behind the counter, makes change from a small cash box, and lays the change on top of the counter. WALLY picks up the change and starts to put it away, notices he has left a nickel on the counter top, and tries to pick it up. He cant. It is stuck on the inside of the glass display case top. PENN (into phone) Dennis. Congratulations. Youve got a booking on the 19th. Get a pencil. 4660 15th St. S.E., 8 p.m. (listens) Its a professional gig. Do your homework in the afternoon. (listens) Twenty ve dollars, you can use our rabbit. There is a rabbit in a cage asleep in the back room. It is lying on its side with its ankles crossed. PENN Youth group, but great exposure. The adults there see you, and before you know it, youre working their parties too. (listens) Yeah. I know. I know. But somebody must have seen you at the Cub Scout show, because these people requested you, specically. (listens) Right. Yeah. Bye. PENN comes out into the shop. PENN Sorry about that. We do bookings, too. So when your act is ready for the public, let us know. WALLY Okay, Penn, I will. PENN Are you working on your rabbit production? Lay people love live animals. WALLY I know, Penn. Im working on it. I got twenty bucks for my birthday, Penn, and I need twenty dollars worth of performancequality props. My moms out shopping. Ive got an hour to decide.

PENN (correcting WALLY) Nineteen and a quarter after the coke, but take a look around in the cases and see what would look good in Wallys Wondershow. WALLY points into display case. WALLY Whats that quarter do? TELLER pulls out a cigarette and lights it. He picks up the quarter...

PENN You switch this quarter in for a borrowed quarter. You borrow a cigarette. TELLER puts the cigarette into Wallys mouth, then borrows it back from him. TELLER pushes the cigarette through the quarter. PENN Its one of the best after-dinner tricks. Its only $6.75, and the professionals we have in here have been buying them up. As a matter of fact that demos our last one. They come out of Denmark. I dont think theyre making them anymore, are they, Teller? TELLER shakes his head. WALLY Ill take it. TELLER makes change from a cash box. PENN totals up the sale on a little printing calculator. PENN You got $12.50. Need any stage illusions? WALLY Yeah, but show me how that one works rst. PENN Okay. DISSOLVE TO: MONTAGE of PENN and TELLER demonstrating magic effects to WALLY who likes some and refuses others. Each time WALLY buys, we see change being made across the counter. MONTAGE ends with WALLYs hand pointing in the display counter to small display with card that reads, INVISIBLE THREAD $4.95. WALLY Penn, Id like to see the invisible thread, please. PENN If you could see it, it wouldnt be worth a damn, Wally. You want the full demo? WALLY Yes, please. TELLER reaches into the case with his forenger and thumb, and shes around on the card until he seems to get hold of a thread. He slowly and carefully pulls out the strand of invisible thread. He stretches it out in front of his own and PENNs eyes. PENN You got better eyes than us, kid. Can you see it at all? TELLER leans over and holds the thread up to WALLYs eyes. WALLY stares between TELLERs ngers. PENN Back off, kid, youre breathing on my partners ngers.

WALLY Sorry, Teller. Sure is good batch, isnt it. TELLER nods. PENN Yeah, kid. Its a great batch. From AustraliaSidney. They do ne work down under. Now watch the routine. Its real pretty. TELLER reaches under the counter and pulls out a deck of cards. PENN Now, being invisible, it wont hold much weight, but it will handle a card nicely. You can get a freely selected PENN(Cont.) card to the top of the deck, cant you, Wally? WALLY Yeah, I cant do the Pass good yet, but I use an Injog. PENN Okay. So the spectators card is on top. Now watch. If you try to tie a knot in this thread, youll end up blind as a bat and two beans short a burrito. So you take a little tiny glob of magicians wax and you roll it up. See? It looks like a little ball of snot. TELLER shows it to WALLY. It does look like a little ball of snot. PENN(Cont.) And you x that little ball right on the end of your thread. TELLER has a lot of trouble getting the snot ball onto the end of the thread. PENN(Cont.) Now thats all done before the trick, of course. Its part of your Advanced Preparation. Now after youve got the card to the top of the deck, while youre pattering a blue streak, you get a good strong bend lengthwise in the selected card, and put your little shot-ball with the thread right on the face, and push the card down so the wax holds it at. TELLER does each action as PENN describes it. So he now has a perfectly normal deck of cards, except that the top card is bent and all ready to pop up, except for a little piece of sticky magicianswax thats hooked to a piece of invisible thread. PENN Okay, Teller, get a hold of the other end. TELLER feels around the deck of cards with his thumb and index nger and runs them along the thread to the end of the counter. He loses the end accidently, swears under his breath, nds the end, loses it, swears, and nds it again. PENN Now hes got it. Watch. Pause. Wally watches intently. TELLER tugs the thread. The top card of the pack pops up. PENN Is that your card? Go ahead. Pick it up. Look at it. You wont see anything but a little glob of snot on the face. Ya see, he just lets go of the thread, and youll never nd it. Its a pretty thing, Wally, a real pretty thing. WALLY Okay, Penn. I want the Invisible Thread. Now I got a nickel left, right? Telephone starts to ring and continues during the following two lines. PENN Wait just a second, Kid. You want the method on the Invisible Thread routine? WALLY Well, yeah. I mean no. I mean yeah: I want the thread PENN Hold on, Wally. Let me get this. (i.e. the telephone) PENN answers the telephone. PENN Mofo

Magic: all your amazing needs. (listens) Yeah, Teller works here. But maybe I can help you. (listens) Yeah, Teller. (spelling) T-E-L-L-E-R. But youre more likely to know him as half the team, Penn & Teller. (listens) Yeah, thats him. But people just call him Teller. (listens) (to TELLER) Are you the Dr. Teller that taught classics at Oxford, and speaks seven dead languages? TELLER enjoys the question. PENN (into telephone) Sure. (listens) Yeah, hell be here all afternoon. Listen, if you want a magic show in Latin... (the other party hangs up and PENN realizes he is cut off and hangs up too. Then, to TELLER...) I dont know, but he knew your rst name. You know the rules of the shop, Wally. What we sell here are secrets. And once you know the secret, you cant return it. So gimme the $4.95 and Ill tell you all about Invisible Thread. WALLY Okay, Penn. But my mothers gonna be here soon. And you guys still have to show me how to do my Hippity-Hop rabbits. PENN You got time kid. Invisible thread may be the most important trick you ever learn. Now give Teller the money. WALLY gives his last $5 bill to TELLER, who gives him a nickel back. PENN addresses WALLY in a condential tone.

 PENN The whole trick on this one is the demonstration. You cant really do a trick with invisible thread, because there is no such thing. Its just a piece of magicians wax and a bent card. But if you can learn to perform Invisible Thread, kid, you can perform any trick in the world. Its pure showmanship. Its acting. Now watch. WALLY is shocked, disappointed, and about ready to cry. TELLER follows PENNs explanation with the appropriate actions. PENN The rst thing you have to know is: if you bend a card and put a little magicians wax on the bottom, it will pop up on its own, as soon as the wax loses its stickum. But right before it pops up, youll see it wiggle, just a little. When you see that little wiggle, you mime pulling the thread, and the card pops upon its own! Looks just like your thread triggered it. Thats the easy part, kid. The hard part is setting it up. Now you got a little card that says invisible thread on it. And it says it in real ofcial-looking print. Tellerll give you that card. Now you talk to them like youre letting them in on some kind of big secret. Like youre not supposed to tell. Real secret and quiet, you tell them you got some invisible thread. Then you spend all this time squintin and feelin around for the end of the thread. And take your time, kid. Half the entertainment value is makin the damn poor idiot thats watching you, pardon my French, climb the walls while you squint and fumble around. When you nally got the thread, spend PENN(Cont.) some time stretching it out in front of them. Now this is the great part. Ask them to look for the thread while youre holding it out for them. Youll have great fun watching them squint, looking for nothin. When youre sick of laughing to yourself, show em the little glob of wax. Pretend to hitch up the thread, look for the wiggle, and fake the pulling. WALLY Yeah? You guys just ripped me off! PENN Lemme nish, Wally. Once you really learn how to do this trick, youll have learned the basis for all magic. All the acting and showmanship you need is right in the old invisible thread trick. TELLER winks at PENN and points to some extra Magicians wax and invisible thread cards. PENN takes the cue. PENN And I saved the best part for last. We sold this to you for $4.95. Thats cheap. And Tellers gonna give you some extra wax, and some extra le cards that say invisible thread really ofcially across them. You can do it for your friends, and sell it for up to 12 bucks apiece. And even if you only get 50 cents each from the kids, youve still made a nice prot after only 10 performances. TELLER smiles and nods at the kid. PENN Its really a great trick, kid. Teller and I have made quite a little career out of it. When Harry Blackstone Jr. or Doug Henning or David Coppereld or Bernie, that guy who does the great dove productions, or any one of those guys comes in, this is the trick they want to see us do. And they take notes. Coppereld actually asked to borrow a pencil from Teller. He wrote down some performance notes, and not the trick, but PENN(Cont.) some of the style you saw here this afternoon, ended up in one of his national television specials. And he wrote us that thank-you note over there on the wall. One thing about Coppereld, he never forgets where he learned something. WALLY Which special? PENN The big one. The one he did in a foreign country. WALLY Im never gonna make any money off this. If I do it for my friends, theyll think Im a crook like you guys. And if I do it for strangers, theyll just beat me up, take my money, leave me to die, and Ill end up with my picture on a milk carton. I hate you, Penn. And your dummy crook friend. PENN He can talk. He just doesnt like to. WALLY Probably because he doesnt want to lie, like you. PENN Thats not a very professional way to act. And if youre not a professional, Im gonna have to charge you tax. And youll have to go get another $1.46 from your mom. WALLY Thats a good idea. Ill go tell my mom, and see what she thinks about a couple of grown men stealing birthday money from her only 11-year-old son. And, if she tells my dad, you guys are dead. PENN Wally Wally Wally Wally Wally! You better stick with a straight dove act. Make me a promise right now that youll stay away from comedy magic. You have no sense of humor! We were pulling your leg, kid. We wouldnt charge you $4.95 for some magicians wax and a few Invisible Thread cards. The retails on em is only a buck-seventy ve. And with your magicians discount, its a buck and a quarter, and with the wax and the cards, you also get a little dog that smokes cigarettes. Wally! If theres one thing Ive learned about really great professional magicians is, theyre always jokin, pullin each others legs. (pause) And Invisible Thread is a great trick. Now you got $3.75 left. What do you want. WALLY Give me a vanishing cane. TELLER gives him a vanishing cane in a little plastic package. PENN There ya go, Wally. Thanks a lot. And remember the Magicians Code. And keep this stuff secret from your mom. TELLER whispers to PENN. PENN And your dad. WALLY (a little sarcastically) Yeah. Thanks. WALLY looks out the window. WALLY(Cont.) Here comes my mom. WALLY exits. Two GOVERNMENT AGENTS entering the shop pass WALLY as he leaves. They are wearing matching dark suits and mirrored sunglasses and are nearly indistinguishable from one another. AGENT 1 Were looking for Mr. Teller... AGENT 1 checks a notebook he is carrying. AGENT 1(Cont.) Mr. R... PENN cuts him off before he can pronounce the rst name. PENN Yeah. What do you guys want? We have the best stage illusions in town. I got a disembodied princess and a sword suspension. Both real good stage illusions that I can let you have cheap. TELLER has pulled back a curtain from a little alcove in which there is a mini-stage. On the stage is a tacky painted sarcophagus with a round window for the face of the occupant to be seen. He gets inside, closes the door, and sticks his face out through the hole. PENN(Contd) You guys new in town or just on the road, passing through? AGENT1 Were not magicians. TELLER gets out of the sarcophagus. PENN You should consider it. You guys got a look. Teams are popular. You got the shades. You got the kind of Blues Brothers thing working. Vegas is just waiting for an act like you. AGENT 2 We already have jobs, Mr. Teller... PENN Well, you want to consider some close-up magic. Its great for business. If you guys like drab suits like that, why not add a little boutonniere? TELLER puts a little boutonniere on his lapel. PENN When you need an ice-breaker, BOOM! TELLERs boutonniere jumps to his other lapel. PENN No skill required. Seven bucks. No sales tax, cause youre professionals. AGENT 1 Were not here to buy tricks. PENN corrects him. PENN Illusions. AGENT 1 We dont want to buy any illusions. AGENT 2 We work for the government. The AGENTS show their badges. PENN We sell those. AGENT 2 continues, ignoring PENN AGENT 2(Cont.) And we need to bring you to the ofces.

When he gets to the directions, he'll ask you to be his partner. When he reads the sentence "Remember, intelligence is not a plus in PSI experiments," he'll make a cute joke about you being a good choice. Smile serenely.

He'll ask you to pick up a book and think of an image. Pick up *WOULD/COULD/SHOULD.* Follow his directions and leaf through it. When he tells you to pick an image and concentrate on it, act as though you are looking at the top line of the page and trying to picture what the words describe. Close the book.

The chucklehead will then draw a childish picture of a television set, as we've told him to in our fake instructions. He will wave it in front of his face and think he's going into a trance. Then he will draw something on the screen of his little TV. Watch him carefully. As he draws, think of something his drawing looks a little like. When he's finished, he'll show it to you and ask you what you were thinking of.

Lie. Tell him what you made up while he was drawing. Act skeptical at first. Force him to point out the similarities between his drawing and what you've told him. Then act impressed. Say you want to try it yourself.

Hand him *WOULD/COULD/SHOULD.* Have him flip to any page, note the first image, and close the book. Go through the whole rigmarole with the drawing of the TV. Yes, we know it's embarrassing. For a moment you will look like a dunce. This is your investment.

Show him your picture, which, of course, will look like this:

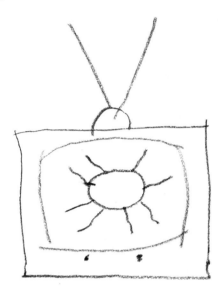

He will be thrilled that he has projected his thoughts so well. He'll want to try again as the "receiver." Humor him. Pretend to select a new image and concentrate. Let him wave his paper and draw his drawing. Then lie to him again, and tell him how amazingly accurate he is. But now, before he asks you to take another turn as "receiver," make some excuse for ending the experiment. Send the cretin away.

You have worked hard to set a wonderful mechanism in motion. Now relax. Sit back and imagine. Imagine how much confusion and shame the dunderhead will feel when he goes into a party or out on a first date and tries to impress somebody with his marvelous newfound talent.

THE BACK-COVER PUZZLE
(People Who Like Brainteasers Must DIE!)

We hate brainteasers. Those stupid goddam little questions that people try to pass off as social fun. "If a snail is climbing up a wall of a well and he climbs up three inches every day and falls back two inches every night, how many days would it take to climb out of a twelve-foot..." We just want to rip the little bastard slug's shell off and douse him with salt. "You are sitting around a table with three other people. Each of you either has an X or an O on your forehead. There are no mirrors in the room. Three have Xs and one has an O. How do you know if..." Just wipe off your forehead and get three different friends.

There are millions of these stupid brainteasers, and up until now, there was only one way to prove your superiority to the irritating puzzle-loving dorks,* and that was to not play their stupid little games. When one of these brainteasers came up in casual conversation, the noble person walked, took a powder, hit the trail, and never called the boor with the puzzle on the telephone again.

But now there is another way. The best defense is a good offense, and the best offense is always cheating. The back cover of this book is set up with a fake brainteaser that the pig can't win and you can't lose. A phony brainteaser that will drive the dorks crazy and move money and self-satisfaction from them to you. It's in a standard style for these hateful things. It's a dumb-ass test of observational abilities where you count how many times a certain letter appears in an arbitrary sentence. You know, you're supposed to read the sentence and count the *s*'s. You get the wrong number and they laugh at you because you missed an extra "so"

---

* No one with a brain in his head cares about these puzzles, *and* we're sure you know someone who cares. A person who loves puzzles. A person who must be punished. A person who probably chews shrimp salad with his mouth open. Goddam, we hate people who like puzzles. They're as bad as magicians. They must be crushed like bugs, and if they had a cockroach, a rabbit, a head of lettuce, and a fox to get across a river, two at a time in a boat... but we digress.

116

or something. Goddam, we hate those. Who cares how many *s*'s? No matter how may *s*'s there are, it's bad prose.

Here's how it works. Packaged with the book, with all the other sneaky little props, was a piece of white plastic that says on it, "How often does the letter *s* appear in this sentence?" Punch out the rectangle in the center and peel it off the stiff backing. Then press it lightly on the book cover right over the block that says "How many times does the letter *s* show up in this sentence?" Get it? Huh? Yup, just stick the little piece of plastic on the cover and hold it up in front of the puzzle-loving loser to look at. The directions on the book say to only look at it for seven seconds, so the dirtball will probably time it. When the puzzle-loving dog has said his answer, open the book to page 175 so he can see if he's right. When you open the book, peel the little piece of plastic off, and dispose of it inconspicuously into your hand or onto the floor. Let the sucker look up his answer in the book and see that he's wrong. (Note: The plastic answer is two off, so even if the toad miscounts he'll still get it wrong.) He will look at the back cover again, and it will be easy to count the right number. It will have changed, but he won't know it. Trust us. It will make him crazy. It will break him.

If you want to gain something besides satisfaction, make a bet while the sucker is looking right at the plastic. He'll insist that the right answer is four. Bet him he's wrong. While the plastic is on, the right answer *is* four, so he will take the bet. But the next time he checks, the plastic is off and the right answer is six. You win the bet and the sucker can *never* figure it out.

This is cheating, and that may seem wrong to you. We ask you to think of it this way. If your victim were a noble human being, when you said, "Do you want to try a brainteaser?" he would have said, "No!" and he would have left with his money and dignity. The fact that he played the game means he deserved to lose. Remember: The only so-called people you will injure are puzzle-loving scum. Scum that probably shouldn't really have a mean trick pulled on them. Scum that should have a .44 Magnum put against their head and the trigger pulled slowly. "If one tribe *always* tells the truth and the other tribe *always* lies, how would you find out which were which in three—" BANG!!!! Suck death, puzzle-loving pig!

THE NO-WORK HIGH-YIELD,
ALL-ELECTRONIC COMPUTERIZED CARD TRICK
(Sucker directions in red on page 3)

There is nothing even slightly computerized about this trick. It is just a hoax.

Get a pack of cards handy. Take out the three of clubs and put it in a convenient pocket. We use the outer breast pocket of a suit jacket, but fit the trick to your own style of dress. (This scam has no dress code. Dress any way you like. It is one of the few rights you have left.) Leave the book open to page 3 when your simian companion comes to visit.*

He or she will learn immediately that there is a chance to get something (a secret phone number) for nothing (*you* paid for the book). Out of the corner of your eye, watch the greedy lout surreptitiously copying the phone number onto a matchbook. Then you say, "Oh, that's a neat trick. Wanna try it?"

"What, this? Well, okay, if you think it's interesting." The chump is *dying* to try it. So you say:

"Good. Why don't you follow the directions on page 4 where it says, 'Here's how to use it.' "

Your "friend" will, after reading the red instructions, start to deal cards facedown on the table and instruct you to say "Stop!" whenever you want. Then he'll tell you to take the card you stopped at, and look at it in private.

Do it. Take the card and turn your back. While your "friend" is using the telephone, calling the number that we've thoughtfully provided, switch the card you stopped at for the three of clubs hidden in your pocket. Meanwhile the voice on the phone (Penn's) will put your friend through an elaborate, pseudo-computerized rigmarole, designed to convey the impression that the computer is calculating which card you hold.

There's no computer at all, of course. It's just an answering machine with a tape that always ends up saying the same thing: that the selected card is the three of clubs. But it sounds very "computerized," like the "random-access compact disk" that your friend thinks it is.

* Take a moment right now to turn to page 3 and look over the sucker's instructions.

Here, be prepared to do a little acting. The voice on the tape cues your "friend" to ask, "Is it a black card?"

Reply, "Yes," in a tone of "Big deal!"

Now the voice cues your "friend" to ask, "Is it a club?"

This time say, "Yes," a little more impressed.

Finally the voice cues your "friend" to ask, "Is it the three of clubs?"

Go to town. Act thunderstruck. Pretend you've just seen Jesus, Mary, Joseph, and Jimi step off the elevator. Say, "Yes!" as though your "friend" is a genius. Of course you know the truth: He or she is a dunderhead who will now go off into the world and try to get something for nothing. This time there will be more at stake than pride.

B372 PERSONALITY TEST

There is a Personality Test scam on page 154 that has so many lies in it, even we're a little ashamed of it. This scam is so ridiculously easy, and so stupidly mean, there isn't a reason on earth not to do it.

There is one arts-and-crafts thing to do first, but you can handle it: Take out the 6″-by-7″ pink-and-white plastic sandwich that came with the book. Remove the piece of paper that's nestled inside, and peel off the thin, cloudy protective sheet on top (this leaves just the shocking pink-and-white vinyl sheets with a self-adhesive strip on the back). Open to page 159 and position the plastic gizmo on the page according to the directions there (the pink sheet faces you; the adhesive strip is underneath, running along the left end of the page; at the bottom of the page you should be able to read the caption, "Penn & Teller's Magic Mirror"). There's no such thing as a "Magic Mirror," of course, and if there *were* a "Magic Mirror," we wouldn't use it; it sounds cheesy. It's just camouflage. The sandwich thing is really a special kind of plastic that acts exactly like a piece of *carbon paper*, only you can use it over and over again, and you don't get black stuff on your hands.

Once the pink plastic sandwich is in place, all your physical work is done, and you're all set to use the B372 Personality Test as a cruel tool to flaunt your superiority.

Show the sucker the book, open to page 156. Explain to him that this is a psychological test. He will be the subject and you will be the experimenter. Give him a piece of paper and a ballpoint pen (stay away from felt tips!). Make sure he rests his piece of paper on the right-hand page (p. 157). Tell him to print his answers clearly on his piece of

continued on p. 122

PENN Whoa! First of all, Im not Teller. He is. Second of all, We dont charge sales tax, because were selling mostly for professional use. Its not regular retail. AGENT 1 We dont care about sales tax. I assure nothing bad is going to happen to you. Youll be paid a days wages. So: whichever one of you is Mr. Teller, just come with us. PENN Teller doesnt work solo. We work as a team. If he goes, I go, and you pay both of us. AGENT 1 Were not booking you for a show. We just need some information. PENN He wont talk to you. AGENT 1 We have people at the Pentagon who are familiar with American Sign Language. We will be able to communicate with him. PENN He doesnt know any sign language. Nothings wrong with him. He doesnt like to talk to anybody but me. If you take him alone, hell just pout. AGENT 2 Okay. We dont have all day. Both of you come on. TELLER hastily tosses a few small props into a little leather briefcase. PENN We both get paid, right? Full salaries. Each. And all expenses. AGENT 1 Yeah, yeah, yeah. Jeez! Cmon! PENN and AGENTS exit. TELLER grabs a piece of cardboard, writes on it in magic marker: GONE FOR SPECIAL COMMAND PERFORMANCE AT WHITE HOUSE. WILL RETURN 4:30. He sticks the sign on the glass panel of the front door as he leaves. DISSOLVE TO: A hall in the Pentagon. PENN and TELLER and the AGENTS are approaching a door guarded by two helmeted soldiers carrying machine guns. PENN Those guys got guns? AGENT 2 Yes. And so do we. The door opens, and the AGENTS nudge PENN and TELLER through. The AGENTS close the door behind PENN and TELLER and lock it. CUT TO: INTERIOR: THE HOLDING TANK. HALF AN HOUR LATER. A long, grim, corridor, lined with chairs. Seated in the chairs is an anomalous assortment of people: serious scientic types, Indiana Jones heroes, Sigourney Weaver astronaut-heroes, side by side with strikingly unique physical types (a beauty queen, a Zulu warrior, a classic middle-American family), and celebrities (Andy Warhol, ZZ Top, etc. Whoever is cool, recognizable, and available.) These people have all taken numbers, and are waiting to be taken into the room at the far end of the corridor. This door is ominous, an entrance, for all we know, to Hell. Over it is a red L.E.D. sign saying, Now Serving Number __. Periodically throughout this scene, the telephone intercom rings. A marine guard by the door, SERGEANT RAMBO, answers it, then calls out the number, goes to the person and leads him/her through the ominous door. At all entrances, and stationed at intervals along the corridor are helmeted military guards, heavily armed. Amenities are provided: a table with snacks and beverages provided by, say, the White House caterer. There is an atmosphere of grim threat over which a veil of genteel politeness has been unsuccessfully dropped. As PENN and TELLER enter, they see, to one side, a RECEPTIONISTs desk at which a woman is seated. PENN So here we are. Whats going on? RECEPTIONIST Who are you? PENN Hes Teller. T,e,1,1,e,r. And Im here with him because he wont talk to you without me. And the guys that brought us here said we were both getting paid your highest amount in cash with no deductions taken out, because were in show business, and we work for ourselves. RECEPTIONIST That can all be arranged. Just take a number, and the general will be with you as soon as possible. PENN We also get our expenses. And were hungry. Wed like our money for lunch now. RECEPTIONIST Well, Mr. Teller may be called into the Hearing Room soon. So, if you could just stay here, well bring your lunch. PENN We wouldnt want you wandering around and getting lost. PENN Ill have a roast beef sandwich. On white bread. With coleslaw right there on the sandwich and not on the side. Onion and Garlic potato chips. And a seltzer. My partner will have a half a chicken, done any way you like, and two chocolate Yoohoos. RECEPTIONIST While youre waiting, please help yourselves to the buffet. PENN Thank you. So whats going on here? Whadaya got us here for RECEPTIONIST Im not at liberty to discuss that. It will all be explained to you when you get into the other room. PENN I guess you dont understand. Some of our material requires advance preparation. We would like to know the situation, so we can be prepared and make a professional impression. RECEPTIONIST Im sorry: that information is classied. PENN You can tell us. We are professional magicians. We earn our living keeping secrets. RECEPTIONIST Im sure you can keep a secret, but I have to keep my job. I cant tell you. PENN Remember when David Coppereld vanished that jet? RECEPTIONIST No. PENN Did you see him vanish the Statue of Liberty. RECEPTIONIST Yes, I saw that. There was radar and everything, right? TELLER pulls a little Statue of Liberty out of his pocket. PENN You tell us whats in that other room, and well show you how Coppereld did it. We got a deal? Now youre sitting over here, right, and youre seeing the statue from this angle... TELLER starts to demonstrate. RECEPTIONIST Im not going to tell you whats in that room. PENN Okay, sister. You blew it. Were going to nd out whats in that room anyways, and youre going to die not knowing how Coppereld vanished the Statue of Liberty. RECEPTIONIST Well, Ill have to live with that, I guess. TELLER picks up the little statue to snatch it away, and knocks the RECEPTIONISTs coffee cup on the oor. It smashes. PENN and the RECEPTIONIST lean over to pick it up, PENN, ad-libbing apologies, while the RECEPTIONIST waves PENN away. Meanwhile TELLER goes through the papers on her desk. By the time she looks up again, TELLER is standing innocently with his hands behind his back... PENN You know, thats the thing about my partner. Once he rehearses something, he does it perfectly. In day to day stuff hes just very clumsy. Now, if we could borrow a quarter from you, wed like to show you a miracle we learned in New Guinea. RECEPTIONIST Im working right now. Im not allowed to watch tricks. Maybe one of the other people who are waiting would like to see your trick. PENN corrects her. PENN Illusion. PENN and TELLER walk away from the desk. PENN (to TELLER) So what did you get? TELLER hands a pile of papers to PENN. They shufe through them together. PENN So you got here lunch orders from the other room: We got a U.S. General, we got four military aides, we got a doctor... PENN points to the paper. PENN PENN looks at a different sheet from the sheaf. PENN This is a list of all the people that are in this room, and what they do for a living. Susan WeaverAstronaut... As PENN reads, TELLER looks out at the group. As PENN names each one, we cut to the probable character. PENN Dr. Randall Zwickibiochemist. Arthur Batutachief Okito tribe. Mark Chaffeecircus performer. Mark Chaffee is a midget. PENN Did we do a Shriners show with him? I dont get it. But Ill tell you one thing. Those doctors better not be getting paid more than us. And what do you got here? Her personal address book? Put our name and number under Party Entertainment and give it back to her. PENN looks at the numbered ticket. PENN Before you do that, were lucky number One, One, One, One hundred and eleven, and theyre only up to sixteen. The lighted sign above the ominous door reads Now serving number 16. PENN Ill nd out who has seventeen, and well switch the tickets. The phone rings. SERGEANT RAMBO answers it. The sign changes to Now Serving Number 17. SERGEANT RAMBO, the formidable, deadpan, heavily-armed guard speaks. SERGEANT RAMBO Number seventeen. HOLDER OF TICKET 17 Yeah, Ive been meaning to talk to someone about this. I think youve got the wrong person. Im Dr. Philip W. Millstein. And I think you want Dr. Philip N. Millstein. Hes worked with the pentagon, and we get confused all the time. Im an internist. SERGEANT RAMBO, ignoring what he has heard, takes Dr. Millstein rmly through the door, which is then locked behind him. PENN (to TELLER) Well, its too late for seventeen. Lets see if a hundred and forty has come in yet. PENN walks back to the machine that dispenses the paper number tags, just as an arriving Arab reaches to take his. PENN reaches up and plucks the number for him. PENN

Allow me! PENN looks at the number. PENN Whada we got here? Lucky number One One One. One hundred and eleven. There you go. Have a seat over there. Help yourself to the buffet. If you have any troubles whatsoever, Im sure this receptionist here will be happy to help you. PENN turns to the RECEPTIONIST. PENN You drive a hard bargain. Ill tell you the gimmick on the Statue of Liberty, and how to saw a lady in half, and all you gotta do is tell me why the Russian guy in that room is having apple pie for dessert, and our general from the U.S. of A. is eating strawberry yogurt. The RECEPTIONIST is puzzled, alarmed that PENN knows this information. She looks down at her pile of papers. TELLER picks up the styrofoam coffee cup with which the RECEPTIONIST has replaced her crockery cup, and drops it deliberately on the oor beside her desk. She looks down, incredulous, at the mess. Meanwhile TELLER replaces the papers he had stolen earlier. The RECEPTIONIST looks back at up him, and he shrugs. Meanwhile PENN has been scanning the room thoughtfully. TELLER joins him. PENN I know what these people have in common. PENN reaches into his breast pocket and extracts a pack of playing cards. TELLER, instantly understanding what PENN is up to almost simultaneously reaches into his breast pocket and extracts a duplicate deck of cards. PENN rifes through his pack, looking for a particular card. PENN They are the kind of people that give private parties. Theyre the kind of people that could use a team of close-up magicians at their next festivity. You got the business cards? TELLER nods. PENN (extracting the three of clubs from his pack and palming it) Three of clubs. TELLER nods and extracts the three of clubs from his deck, palming it. DISSOLVE TO: INTERIOR: HOLDING TANK, A FEW MINUTES LATER. PENN is in the middle of performing a card trick for DR. RANDALL ZWICKI. TELLER is absent. PENN So, you have your card clearly in your mind, and youre concentrating on it. DR. RANDALL ZWICKI I know what card I picked, but I have a lot of things on my mind. PENN So... PENN does several card ourishes. PENN DR. RANDALL ZWICKI I think the secretaries and some of the orderlies have a little get-together. Ive never attended. PENN Yeah. Those are usually awful things, those Christmas parties. But maybe you can get yourself on the entertainment committee this year. You may get something no one will want to miss. CUT TO: INTERIOR, THE HOLDING TANK. MEANWHILE, AT THE BUFFET TABLE... TELLER is making a sandwich. He inserts a face-up three of clubs under the lettuce, and puts a few toothpicks through. A heavily-armed, helmeted guard stands by, watching. TELLER is aware that he is being watched. As he is about to leave, he casually reaches out to the vegetable tray, takes a radish, and eats it. He stops chewing, as if there is something wrong with the food, and cups his hand to his mouth and coughs. A live tarantula drops out. TELLER catches it in his waiting other hand, and matter-of-factly puts it away in his briefcase. The guard, who already hates the job, hates it more. CUT TO: INTERIOR, THE HOLDING TANK. PENN AT THE FINISH OF HIS TRICK. With a ourish, PENN produces the ten of diamonds. PENN Is this your card? DR. RANDALL ZWICKI I dontl dont think so. I may have gotten confused. I dont play cards. Im not familiar with the suits. But I dont think that was my card. It was a very nice trick, though. TELLER arrives with a tray on which there is a sandwich. PENN This is my partner, Teller. Teller, this is the doc. DR. RANDALL ZWICKI stands and shakes TELLERs hand. DR. RANDALL ZWICKI Dr. Randall Zwicki, Biochemistry, Walter Read. PENN Teller! Mind your manners, offer the doc some food. DR. RANDALL ZWICKI Thank you, no. Ill get a sandwich a little later. PENN No doc, really. He isnt hungry. Have a sandwich. DR. RANDALL ZWICKI No thank you, really, Im not hungry. PENN Eat the goddam sandwich. DR. RANDALL ZWICKI is shocked at such aggressiveness. PENN Eat! DR. RANDALL ZWICKI, yielding, takes the sandwich and tentatively bites into it. He has trouble biting into it, bites harder. He continues to tear at the sandwich with his teeth until he pulls out the three of clubs. He looks at it with incredulous disgust. PENN Well! I guess its a club sandwich! PENN laughs at the joke, thinking himself a clever fellow indeed, and slaps DR. RANDALL ZWICKI on the back. PENN Now Im not claiming to be psychic, but I bet theres a business card in there for a couple magicians whod be just perfect for the Walter Read Christmas party. PENN and TELLER turn away. PENN (condentially, to TELLER) Hes on the entertainment committee. DISSOLVE TO: INTERIOR. THE HOLDING TANK. HOURS LATER. Everyone looks exhausted, beaten, depressed. Suit jackets are off, ties are loosened. Except for PENN and TELLER, who are on, bright-eyed, crisp-looking, and hard at work. TELLER has just made a pass with a magic wand around a womans hand. PENN Of course, when you put a couple of rabbits together in the dark, one plus one equals... TELLER gestures for the woman to open her hand. Many, many little foam rubber bunnies spring out. Half a dozen people watching with mild interest are mildly amused. PENN And speaking of miracles, my name is Penn Jillette, and this is my partner, Teller. We do conjuring, legerdemain, magic, sleight of hand, and a couple of real miracles. We are illusionists, and we are available for all occasions: birthday parties, bar mitzvahs, classy cocktail parties, and we can emcee on charity bills. Give em our card, Teller. TELLER plucks business cards from the air and hands them out as PENN continues... PENN So, if you need professional entertainment, give us a call. Any time. We have an answering machine. Its a funny tape; just give it a call. PENN and TELLER start to walk away from the group. TELLER, a bit hot and frazzled, loosens his tie and unbuttons the top button of his shirt. PENN Some of those guys werent American... As he speaks, PENN reaches over and buttons TELLERs shirt and tightens his tie neatly, because he knows that a professional performer must always look his best and make a good impression. PENN Ambassadors! They must be ambassadors! They throw big parties, and often. PENN and TELLER move on. DISSOLVE TO: INTERIOR. THE HOLDING TANK. HOURS LATER. Only about half the original occupants of the Holding Tank are left; the others have been taken off into the ominous door. Those who are left are weary, dissheveled, and depressed. Women are fanning themselves, and men have rolled up their shirtsleeves. The guards are sitting on their helmets. PENN and TELLER are still fresh as daisies, and in irritatingly good spirits. PENN So you have your card clearly in mind. PENN points to DR. CHARLENE NORRIS. PENN Now will you name a number? DR. CHARLENE NORRIS No. I will not name a number. I dont care about your stupid trick. PENN Illusion. DR. CHARLENE NORRIS We are being held under martial law. We are being taken into a room one by one. And the people who are leaving this room are never returning. I do not want to be entertained. I want to do something. And I cant do it alone. For all we know, we are being taken into that room one by one and killed. PENN (as if dealing with a nightclub heckler) See what happens when cousins marry? But seriously, maam, if theyre killing us one by one, why are they serving us refreshments? Thats an expensive buffet. Thats real bleu cheese. So you just calm down and name a number. DR. CHARLENE NORRIS No! DR. CHARLENE NORRIS stands up, knocks the cards out of PENNs hands, storms off, grabs a chair at the other side of the room and stands on it. Meanwhile TELLER scurries to pick up the cards, while PENN tries to keep the trick going... PENN Never mind her. (to another woman) Name a number. CUT TO: INTERIOR. HOLDING TANK. SIMULTANEOUSLY. Meanwhile, DR. CHARLENE NORRIS, standing on her chair is addressing the whole room. DR. CHARLENE NORRIS We have a right to know whats going on! We cannot be held here against our wills. There is obviously something very important going on, and we have a right to know what that is. Guards start to approach DR. CHARLENE NORRIS. DR. CHARLENE NORRIS Yes, they can paper ". . . in BIG, CLEAR letters, the way a kid would write. Take your time, and have fun the way a kid would. . . ." You don't give a hoot, of course, whether he's having fun—but you *do* want to make sure that he's writing in big, clear letters, since everything he writes on his page is being recorded on the pink sandwich underneath, where you will want to read it later.

The chucklehead will read the questions thoughtfully and answer them carefully. Tell him to pull out his piece of paper and

Take the book back. Ignore the instructions at the top of page 157. It's mumbo-jumbo. Just read the hooked fish the first of the questions on page 157. Listen closely to the answer, and pretend to study the "Simplified Cross-Reference Guide." The "Simplified Cross-Reference Guide" is useless, but the little pink plastic sandwich with the "carbon copy" of everything the cheesehead wrote *is* rather helpful. Flip through the book, pretend to consult the incomprehensible tables (pages 160–63), and tell him the answer he wrote.

Continue through all the questions, and keep turning to random pages in the book, as if the impossible labyrinth of directions we've written are cake-easy for you.

You might want to change the wording of answers a little so you're not word-for-word exact, or even miss a couple on purpose. Once you've memorized what the dolt has written, lift the top sheet of plastic and all the evidence is gone. The questions on pages 157 and 158 are just suggestions. Feel free to make up your own, ad lib. Ask your marks if they sleep with livestock. They'll answer. It's all in the name of science.

A SURE BET

(Illustrated sucker instructions in red starting on page 181.)

Get two pieces of soft, flexible rope, cord, or ribbon, about four feet long, and keep them handy. Show your "friend" the "Sure Bet" directions on page 181. Tell him you've been having trouble learning the trick, and ask him to help you. Flatter him. Tell him he has an exceptional eye for space-relations.

Follow the instructions. Everything is on the level until Step 4.

You   *Your "Friend"*

Now you are going to do a little secret move your pal won't notice. It's the move that makes the Sure Bet a Sure Humiliation. Follow the illustrations here:

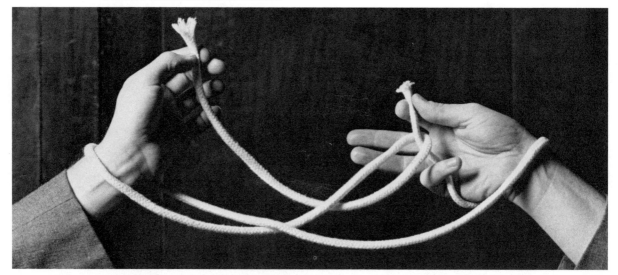

Secretly CURL YOUR LITTLE FINGER AROUND THE END OF THE ROPE just below the loop.

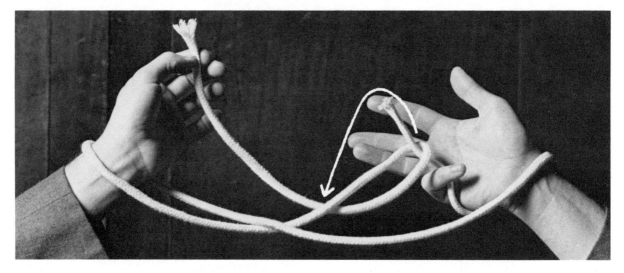

Then, under cover of the tossing movement, LET GO with the right forefinger and thumb. The loop of rope in between will slide off the end.

Immediately RE-GRIP THE END with your right thumb and forefinger. Toss the loops off your wrists, and there you'll have your
knot.

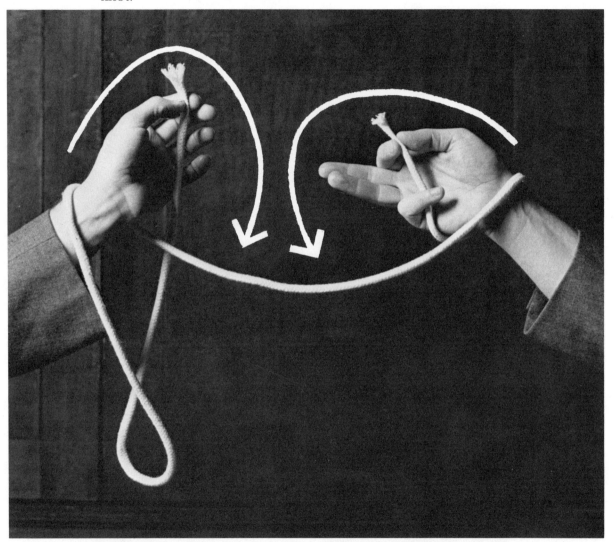

Your chum, of course, will not. His rope will either be straight
or tangled. It will not have a knot in it for the simple reason that
you *cannot tie a knot* without letting go of the ends. It is a
topological impossibility.

Look at your "friend" with pride and relief. Thank him for
helping you. Then notice his failure. Act surprised. Offer to "help."

Take him step by step through the illustrations. When he tosses the rope off and nothing comes out, act puzzled. Suggest that he may not be tossing the rope lightly enough.

When he is about to give up, suggest an experiment. Have him follow the instructions to Step 4. Tell him you think he is tossing the rope too roughly, and you want to try a test. When the victim gets to the position shown in Step 4, take the ends of the rope from his fingertips and ask him to withdraw his hands from

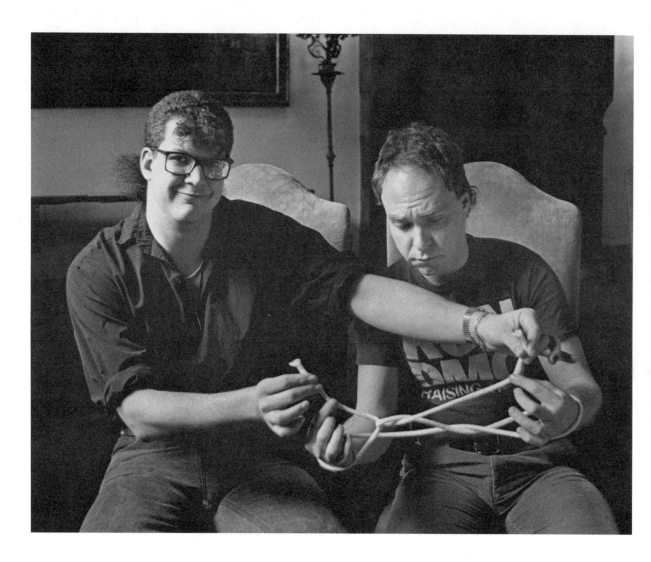

the loops ever so delicately. The knot will form. Congratulate your "friend," and enjoy his exasperation when he fails the next time.

With a properly cruel attitude, you can drive somebody crazy with this scam for weeks.

suppress any one of us individually, but if we band together, at least we have a chance. We must all hang together or we will surely all hang separately. CUT TO: INTERIOR. THE HOLDING TANK. SIMULTANEOUSLY. PENN and TELLER have been continuing the card trick in spite of the interruption... PENN Is this your card? PENN reaches over to TELLERs collar, and pulls upward. His shirt pulls out from underneath his jacket without disturbing the jacket. PENN exhibits the back of the shirt. On it, in red ink is a large drawing of the face of the Ten of Diamonds. SPECTATOR No. The small crowd, of, perhaps, a dozen, which has been halfheartedly attending to the trick, loses interest, and turns attention to DR. CHARLENE NORRIS. DR. CHARLENE NORRIS All your rights are being taken away, and youre watching a couple of empty-headed bozos doing magic tricks. The phone rings. SERGEANT RAMBO answers it. Meanwhile, PENN and TELLER, furious, march over to DR. CHARLENE NORRIS as she rages from on top of her chair. They are carrying chairs which they set up alongside hers. They climb up also. As they move, PENN corrects DR. CHARLENE NORRIS. PENN Illusions! (addressing the audience at large) Were okay. Everythings ne. (to DR. CHARLENE NORRIS) Hey, its not going to do any good to ght among ourselves. TELLER pats DR. CHARLENE NORRIS reassuringly on the back. PENN Im sure we can work this out. We gotta stick together. PENN and TELLER turn her as if to help her off the chair. As she turns, we can see a large Three of Clubs which TELLER has snuck onto her back, while he was patting it. PENN points to the card, and asks the spectator who was participating in the card trick... PENN Is this your card? DR. CHARLENE NORRIS hears the laugh and applause, realizes that something is amiss, turns around and looks around. The audience laughs more. TELLER takes the card off her back and shows it to her with a big smile. She is furious. But before she gets a chance to respond, SERGEANT RAMBO is on her, and taking her roughly and violently into the ominous door as she screams protests. PENN and TELLER chase after her, trying to free her from SERGEANT RAMBO. PENN Hey, Rambo, lets calm down. She was just heckling. We dealt with her ne. Theres no crime. Let go of hernow. SERGEANT RAMBO This has got nothing to do with you. Its her turn. GUARDS pull DR. CHARLENE NORRIS away, hurl PENN and TELLER back into the room, and slam the doors in their face. DISSOLVE TO: INTERIOR. THE HOLDING TANK. HOURS LATER. The corridor is pretty nearly emptied out. The few remaining people waiting are worn, beaten, and bear the marks of having seen PENN and TELLERs acts: One man has a Three of Clubs drawn on his back in chalk. Another is wearing a necktie which has been cut off. PENN and TELLER are sitting sullen and exhausted. TELLER is rolling a coin across the back of his hand, and PENN is shufing a deck of cards. They are sitting directly next to the entrance guarded by SERGEANT RAMBO. SERGEANT RAMBO (to TELLER) You know, Ive always wanted to learn how to do that. Think you could teach me just a basic coin trick like that? TELLER puts the coin away in his pocket and looks away from SERGEANT RAMBO. PENN Hey, sarge. You just dont rough people up for talking too loud. SERGEANT RAMBO Its just my job. Would you show me a card trick? PENN Rambo wants to see a card trick? Okay, Ill show you a card trick. PENN fans out the deck, rearranges a few cards in it, closes the fan. PENN Youre not color-blind, are you? SERGEANT RAMBO No. PENN Okay, when you see a black card, you say, Coal. When you see a red card, you say, Fire. Coldly, and with no energy or wit whatever, PENN holds up the deck towards SERGEANT RAMBOs face. On the face of the deck is a black card. One by one, PENN pulls the cards off of the face of the deck, and SERGEANT RAMBO follows the directions. SERGEANT RAMBO Coal. Coal. Coal. Fire. On the word re PENN mirthlessly springs the whole deck of cards into SERGEANT RAMBOs face. No one laughs. One of the other people in the room remarks to PENN... PERSON Watch out, Penn. Hell beat you up. PENN You dont understand, Bob. This guys a marine, a specialist. He doesnt beat up magicians. He beats up doctors. SERGEANT RAMBO (to PENN) Back off. PENN Oh, maybe I was wrong. Maybe hes a Green Beret. Maybe he can beat up magicians. SERGEANT RAMBO (sarcastically) Im sorry. Im not myself today. Im not used to dealing with the obliteration of all life on Earth on a Monday (pause. Then, sincerely) Ive ushered 231 people into that room. And 230 have gone out the back door, crying. 230 of the smartest, most knowledgable, most unique people in the world. And theyve failed. SERGEANT RAMBO reaches into PENNs upper breast pocket, pulls out the numbered paper tag, and looks at it. SERGEANT RAMBO Youre next, Mr. Wizard. Knock em dead. TELLER reaches into his pocket, brings out the coin, starts rolling it. PENN starts to pick up the cards on the oor. RAMBOS intercom phone rings. He answers, listens, hangs up. PENN and TELLER are as we left them. SERGEANT RAMBO All right, boys. Lets go. PENN and TELLER stand up. PENN tightens and straigntens TELLERs tie. PENN turns around while TELLER checks PENNs coiffure. PENN My pony tail straight? TELLER nods. SERGEANT RAMBO has unlocked the door, and is waiting. PENN and TELLER go through the door. SERGEANT RAMBO follows them and locks the door. Inside it is dark and empty. A jeep is waiting in a pool of light. The three get into the jeep, and SERGEANT RAMBO starts to drive at a steady, deliberate speed. SERGEANT RAMBO Youre about to meet some beings from another planet, boys. Real, live, extraterrestrials. These guys are aliens. And theyre like interplanetary efciency experts. See theres not that many habitable planets in the universe. Were living on one of them, and they say were redundant. They say theres nothing unique about us. See, there are no human beings anywhere else, but they say theres, like, one creature somewhere that has bones like ours. And a different one in, like, a whole different solar system that has teeth and ngernails. And maybe another one light-years away that has red blood cells. So, the way they gure it, theyre might as well destroy the human race, and re-populate earth with some species that is unique, for the good of the universe. They had checked it out completely, but they gave 72 hours for us to come up with something unique. PENN That seems fair of em. They pull to a stop. SERGEANT RAMBO Here we are. PENN (to TELLER as they get out of the jeep) Were on. SERGEANT RAMBO Break a leg. PENN Or youll break it for us. SERGEANT RAMBO smiles affectionately and drives away. PENN and TELLER are in the middle of a gigantic armory. Dominating the room is an object which resembles a giant pressure cooker. This is the pressurized atmospheric capsule in which the aliens remain to protect them. They view the activities in the Hearing Room through a narrow smoked-glass window in one side of the tank. They ask questions and deliver replies on a teletypewriter connected by a cable to the capsule. We never see or hear them directly. Elsewhere in the room we see representatives of foreign countries, scientists, state department ofcials, stenographers, and a classic cigar-smoking General. Guards with helmets stand ready with machine guns. PENN So! Which one of you is E.T.? SCIENTIST Youre Mr. Teller? PENN No. Tellers my partner right here. Im Penn. And I want to talk to the space slime thats going to destroy the human race. PENN looks at the SPACE CAPSULE. PENN Is he in there? Is he in that big pressure cooker? Hes just right in there? PENN approaches the CAPSULE and tries to see through the smoked glass. PENN addresses the GUARDS. PENN(Cont.) You guys are on our side, right? So why dont you G.I. Joes just lob a couple grenades in there, blow this mass of galactic jello back to kingdom come, and get your pictures on cereal boxes! The GENERAL is impatient. GENERAL If we kill their ambassadors, the orbiting spacecraft will destroy the human race without a hearing. PENN Maybe theyre bluffing. The GENERAL ignores him.

GENERAL Now why were these two called in? Time is running short. SCIENTIST These two werent called in. Mr. Teller, the little one, was called in. According to the people at Oxford, he is the formost authority on IndoEuropean cognates in classical languages. Nine years ago Dr. Teller left Oxford, became a magician, and stopped talking. PENN He talks to me. PENN addresses TELLER. PENN(Cont.) So, do you think the classics are going to save the world? TELLER doubts it. SCIENTIST We hoped a problem of this magnitude would bring you out of retirement. TELLER would help, if he could, but he doesnt have any ideas at the moment. PENN We dont need Indo European cognates. We dont need linguists. The human race is unique, ergo... PENN looks at TELLER, who approves of his use of the Latin. PENN TELETYPEWRITER prints. The AIDE reads the printout in a monotone. AIDE PROVE IT. PENN So...you probably covered two eyes, ve ngers, nose, a couple feet, right? How about all the emotional stuff, like Spock on Star Trek didnt have? You know, like, we cry and suffer, and save kittens and stuff...? SCIENTIST They have emotions. All our emotions. TELETYPE prints. SCIENTIST reads and explains. SCIENTIST And another 723 more that you never thought of. Including a special kind of melancholy that only accompanies potassiumrich air breathing species. PENN thinks. PENN How about the Velvet Underground? You know, The Velvet Underground? Lou Reeds band in the late sixties? Them cosmic crybabies got the Velvet Underground? TELETYPE prints. AIDE reads aloud. AIDE WE HAVE CULTURES THAT USE SOUND FOR ARTISTIC EXPRESSION. PENN I didnt say sound as artistic expression. I said The Velvets! So thats one thing you dont got. Now: you got Elvis? TELETYPE prints. AIDE reads aloud. AIDE YOU ARE TALKING ABOUT INDIVIDUALS. WE ARE TALKING ABOUT A SPECIES. I DONT THINK THIS EARTHLING UNDERSTANDS THE UNIVERSAL PICTURE. PENN screams... PENN I am talking about the universal picture. I am not talking about individuals. I am talking about Elvis Aaron Presley! Now, if you dont have Blue Hawaii, somewhere out in never never land, kindly get on your space chopper, get out of my face, out of my country, off my planet, out of the solar system, and out of my galaxy! Hows that for the universal picture, pinhead?!!! TELETYPE prints. AIDE reads aloud. AIDE I DONT THINK WE HAVE TO ANSWER THAT, GENERAL. THANK YOU, PENN & TELLER, BUT WE HAVE OTHER PEOPLE TO SEE. PENN, sad and calmed down, addresses the General. PENN Whose side are you on, soldier boy? Youre thinking too much about saving your own neck. If they destroy the human race, no one anywhere in the universe will remember Elvis. Remember when he died we all made that promise? Those space slugs arent going to remember Elvis. Or Houdini. PENN realizes what hes said, screams out... PENN Houdini! HOUDINI! HOUDINI! PENN Im sorry. I was out of line. May I ask our extraterrestrial friends one more question. GENERAL Go ahead. PENN Thank you, sir. You guys ever seen invisible thread? The GENERAL assumes this is just more raving. He wants to get on to the next interview. Coldly... GENERAL Thank you, gentlemen. He nods to the guards to remove PENN and TELLER. GENERAL Next! As PENN and TELLER turn to leave, the TELETYPE prints something out. SCIENTIST reads it. He looks up to the GENERAL. SCIENTIST General! GENERAL What is it? SCIENTIST Look! He points to the TELETYPE message. Camera dollies in to an extreme close up. The message reads; INVISIBLE THREAD? PLEASE EXPLAIN. GENERAL (O.C.) Just a minute there. They want to see the Invisible Thread. Itd better be good. CUT TO: Point of view of the Aliens.PENN and TELLER are almost out the door. The GENERALs words have stopped them in their tracks. Their backs are to the camera. They freeze for a moment. Then they turn around, PENN with a big, warm, hospitable salesmans smile on his face. As PENN speaks, PENN and TELLER approach the camera. PENN So, my friends, youve never heard of Invisible Thread. My family has kept it pretty quiet. Weve had it in my family for over 12 generations. But nothins ever been published on it, no books. It was discovered by my great, great, great, great, great grandfather. Up in Newfoundland. Theres a little silkworm up there. But its not a silkworm, its an Invisible Thread Worm. Larva of some clear winged moth or buttery or something. Its only in Newfoundlandcant live anywhere else. We have to PENN(Cont.) keep ours at the shop in the freezer for three months a year, and in the refrigerator for the other nine. And we have the only ones, outside of Newfoundland. They dont even have stuffed or pickled ones at the Smithsonian. And theyre not classied nothin. And thats why you never heard of them. All human knowledge is not put in books and on microlm. Specially the knowledge in my family. Weve kept to ourselves for thousands of years. Were a very shy people.... As PENN has spoken, the camera has slowly come in closer and closer on his face, ending with his speaking lips lling the picture. We now dissolve to a montage of vignettes of PENN and TELLER performing Invisible Thread for the ALIENS: DISSOLVE TO: P.O.V. of the ALIENS. TELLER is trying to stretch the thread out. He gets it disentangled and holds it up to the viewer. SFX: TELETYPEWRITER is printing. Off camera PENN is answering the ALIENS teletyped question. PENN(O.C.) Well, buddy, if you could see it, it wouldnt be worth a damn, now would it? DISSOLVE TO: TELLER is xing the ball of wax to the card, and setting the cards up. PENN stands by him explaining. PENN Now, being invisible, it wont hold much weight, but it will handle a card nicely. You can get a freely-selected card to the top of the deck, cant you, my space pals? SFX: TELETYPEWRITER writes. PENN leans over to look at the printout. PENN You cant? Ill teach you some time. A mana being should know how to handle a deck of cards. If Id a known you couldnt handle cards, we could have just played poker for the whole planet. Ante up my race against yours. We could use the space to spread out a little... DISSOLVE TO: TELLER tugs the thread and the top card pops up. PENN patters... PENN Is that your card? If you werent in that pressure cooker, you could pick it up and look right at it. You wouldnt see a thing, but a little glob of snot on the face. You see, he just lets go of the thread, and youll never nd it. Its a pretty thing. Its a real pretty thing. PENN and TELLER step back from the capsule. There is a beat of silence. Then, the TELETYPE prints. The SCIENTIST steps up to the TELETYPE and reads. He is stunned. He tears off the sheet and reads it. SCIENTIST They say the hearing is over. Earth is not redundant. They will leave at once from the Capitol lawn. The others in the room react with amazement. The room is lled with questions. Suddenly the TELETYPE prints again. The SCIENTIST reads the message aloud: SCIENTIST THE FOLLOWING MESSAGE IS FOR PENN & TELLERS EYES ONLY. ALL OTHERS TURN THEIR BACKS. The people in the room comply with puzzlement and irritation. Even the GENERAL grudgingly turns his back. The TELETYPE prints. As it does, the GENERAL turns his head to peek over his shoulder. TELETYPEWRITER instantly stops. The GENERAL turns his head away, and the TELETYPE resumes printing. Printout stops. TELLER tears off the typewritten sheet, folds it in half and hands it to PENN. PENN and TELLER turn to leave the room. The GENERAL nods to the guards, who block PENN and TELLERS path. GENERAL In the interest of national security, Im afraid Im going to have to take that... TELETYPEWRITER quickly prints. SCIENTIST reads the printout. SCIENTIST General, I think wed better let them go. PENN and TELLER nod. GENERAL Okay, you can keep your little secret message, but let me see some of that Invisible Thread. PENN Its $4.95 for you, General. And dont bother thanking us, or anything, for PENN(Cont.) saving the human race. Send our checks to PENN and TELLERs

Penn & Teller did their version of sawing a lady in half on Saturday Night Live, April 19, 1986. If you've got a knack for handicrafts, you'll enjoy doing this one.

HOW TO CUT AND RESTORE A SNAKE ON SATURDAY NIGHT LIVE!

1. Get a snake. We used a California king snake. (It's important to choose one with simple colorations and a pleasant personality. Do not use a viper.)

2. Examine the snake's midriff. Note the thickness. Go to a butcher, and obtain a length of sausage of equivalent diameter.

continued on p. 139

Magic Emporium. Well go back to amazing the world, and you go back to trying to blow it up. PENN and TELLER give the Vulcan hand salute to the aliens and the others in the room. PENN Live long and prosper. Klaatu barata nikto. PENN and TELLER exitamidst general astonishment. DISSOLVE TO: PENN and TELLER and the AGENTS are back in the magic shop. AGENT 1 You understand that if you say anything about this incident to anyone, the government will completely deny it. PENN And you understand that if you guys dont get those checks to us pronto, therell be hell to pay. Now, youre sure you dont need any magic props?...You know, a PENN(Cont.) few little tricks and gags to amuse your co-workers, when youre skulking around South America. AGENT 2 Dont worry. If we need any magic props, well let you know. PENN And if we ever need two guys dressed alike with guns, to follow us around, well let you know. AGENTS leave. PENN takes teletype printout from his pocket. PENN So lets see what our alien brothers in the pressure cooker had to say. PENN reads aloud. PENN DEAR PENN AND TELLER. WE KNOW A GOOD MAGICIAN NEVER REVEALS HIS SECRETS. SO WE FELT WE SHOULD KEEP THIS CONFIDENTIAL. SORRY: YOU DIDNT FOOL US FOR A MINUTE. THERE WAS NO THREAD. YOU JUST BENT THE CARD. BUT YOU DID PROVE THAT MANKIND IS NOT REDUNDANT. THERE IS NO OTHER RACE IN THE UNIVERSE THAT WOULD LIE ABOUT A THING LIKE INVISIBLE THREAD. HAVE A NICE DAY. Well, theyre crafty. Good magical minds. Next time well try the antigravity quarter, or the expanding dice. PENN takes the paper over to a wall of the shop on which are displayed autographed 8x 10 photos of famous magicians. He thumb tacks it between, say Doug Henning and David Coppereld. CUT TO: TELLER is writing on an index card. He nishes and we see a closeup of the Invisible Thread display in the case. TELLERs hands come in; he removes the card that says INVISIBLE THREAD $4.95 and replaces it with a card that says THE TRICK THAT SAVED THE WORLD $5.95. We hold on this sign and roll credits to the end. Off Camera we hear a conversation between BILLY, an 11-yearold boy and PENN. BILLY (O.C.) Hi! PENN(O.C.) Hi, Billy, what can we do ya for? Gimme seventy ve cents; Teller will get you a coke. BILLY(O.C.) Im looking for a deck of marked cards. PENN(O.C.) What trick you workinon, the Sultans Dream? BILLY (O.C.) Yeah. That, and Two Jacks and a Queen. PENN(O.C.) Teller just nished up a great batch of marked red bee-backs. You cant tell the seal was broken. $8,50 a deck... FADE TO BLACK. END ANOTHER MASTERPIECE FROM Buggs & Rudy Discount Corporation

THE END

PENN & TELLER AT THE RITZ ACT I TELLER enters from stage left. He picks up the water pitcher on the stage right prop table and pours a glass of water. PENN enters from stage left holding a large green bottle, a sheet of plastic, a hammer, and a white marker. As Penn enters the audience, TELLER crosses to the stage left prop table with the pitcher and the glass of water, and pours another glass of water. He sets the pitcher and the two water glasses on the stage left prop table, sits on the downstage right green chair and puts on a pair of inversion boots. PENN selects a VOLUNTEER from the audience and brings him up on stage. PENN Would you come up here for a moment, please? Watch your step here. Theres a lot of embarrassing things to trip over. And especially watch this dark cord here. Its a little hard to see, but if you trip over that all hell breaks loose. PENN hands magic marker to VOLUNTEER. TELLER crosses to stage right and lowers a rope with a hook on the end. PENN Would you take this magic marker and just print your first name in rather large letters right across there, please? VOLUNTEER prints name across green wine bottle PENN Okay, Stuart, see that piece of paper in there? That piece of paper kinda belongs to you now. This piece of paper gets really important with a great deal of hurry-up when the denouement of the first half happens. PENN hangs the bottle on the hook. TELLER raises the bottle to the top of the proscenium. PENN At that point, I'm going to go, like, Yo! Stuart! and I want you to scamper right up here, and bring with you this piece of plastic. And be a little careful, it may have some shards of glass in it. And also this hammer. And you probably want to put them in under your seat, don't put them on your lap cause you'll just look stupid, okay? In about 45-50 minutes, like, Yo! Stuart! then you scamper right up here. No way you can screw it up, I'm going to talk you through it. Watch your step, here. PENN hands TELLER magic marker. TELLER places it in SL prop box. STUART returns to his seat. PENN Stuart is A.O.K. cool, yknow? If the rest of you guys were as cool as Stuart, we could end the show right now, yknow?. Stuart knows certain things instinctively that the rest of you gotta be taught. That's the way I see it. PENN takes strait jacket. PENN & TELLER cross to SR steps. VOLUNTEER ties TELLER in strait jacket. PENN Come right over here, please. Just buckle him right up the back, there are four buckles there. If you can groove a little bit while your doing it, time will pass quicker for all of us. Beautifully done. What have we got here, we got a show or what? We okay? Yeah, I guess we're alright. You may be a buckler but you ain't no dancer, I'll tell you right now. Now feed his arms through the loop over there. Pull the two arms together. Just feed it right through. You've gotta pull pretty hard, but do NOT put your knee in his back, because you will hurt him permanently, okay? Meanwhile I'll do this one cause a dog shouldn't have to. You just get your kicks above the waistline, Sunshine. You can go a little further than that, its Broadway! Pull, for chrissakes! Now we're competing with Phantom. Obedience to authority, I saw the movie. Nicely done. Thanks a lot. TELLER nods his thanks to VOLUNTEER. PENN & TELLER return to stage left. TELLER lays down under the rigging. PENN hooks TELLER's feet to rigging. PENN Y'all set there, Compadre? Okay, lets party! PENN crosses to stage right green chair. He begins hoisting TELLER up. CASEY AT THE BAT. PENN Good evening. My name is Penn Jillette, this is my partner, Teller. We are Penn & Teller, and you've probably heard by now that we do magic. Now when most people think of magic they picture some greasy guy in a tux with a lot of birds, or some aging hippie shoving women into boxes. We're interested in a different kind of magic, and I'm referring, of course, to the magic of fine poetry. PENN ties the rope to the back of the green chair. PENN Wed like to open our show here this evening with a poetry reading, and I want to tell y'all right up front that I read poetry very well. And I think that even though you might be expecting something a bit more sensational out of us, that you will hang on my every word. PENN sits in chair. His left foot appears to be through a loop of black tie line. PENN And when I finish reading this poem and jump from the seat I'm seated on to take my final bow, I am sure you will be suitably impressed. PENN crosses his legs. His left foot pulls the rabbit trap out from under the trap door behind TELLER. The trap door, containing wooden spikes, crashes to the floor beneath TELLER. PENN Ernest Lawrence Thayer. The name means nothing to you. That's because Mr. Thayer was in my opinion the definition of a one-poem-poet. He only wrote one poem that became famous, but oooo, doggies did it become famous! He was a newspaperman by trade and this poem first appeared in the fourth column of the fourth page of the "San Francisco Examiner", Sunday morning, June 3, 1888. The poem is entitled Casey at the Bat. It is subtitled A Ballad of the Republic Sung in the Year 1888, and I shall be reading Casey at the Bat for you this evening in exactly one minute and forty-seven seconds, after which I will jump to my feet and take that all-important bow. Casey at the Bat. PENN starts his stopwatch. As PENN reads Casey at the Bat, TELLER struggles to free himself from the strait jacket. PENN The outlook wasn't brilliant for the Mudville nine that day; The score stood four to two with but one inning left to play. So when Cooney died at first, and Barrows did the same, A sickly silence fell upon the patrons of the game. A straggling few got up to go in deep despair. The rest Clung to that hope which springs eternal in the human breast; For they thought if only Casey could get a whack at that. They'd put even money now with Casey at the bat.But Flynn preceded Casey, as did also Jimmy Blake, The former was a lulu, the latter was a cake; So on that stricken multitude grim melancholy sat, For there seemed but little chance of Casey's getting to the bat. But Flynn let drive a single, to the wonderment of all, And Blake, the much despis-ed, tore the cover off that ball; So when the dust had lifted, and men saw what had occurred, There was Jimmy safe at second, ol' Flynn was hugging third. Then from 5,000 throats or more there rose a lusty yell; It rumbled in the valley, it rattled in the dell; It knocked upon the mountain and then recoiled across the at, For Casey, mighty Casey, was advancing to the bat. PENN checks his watch. He speeds up his recital. TELLER gives him a look of despair. He speeds up his escape attempt. PENN There was ease in Casey's manner as he stepped into his place; There was pride in Casey's bearing and a smile on Casey's face. And when, responding to the cheers, he lightly doffed his hat, No stranger in the crowd could doubt t'was Casey at the bat. Ten thousand eyes were on him as he rubbed his hands with dirt; Five thousand tongues applauded when he wiped them on his shirt. Then while the writhing pitcher ground the ball into his hip, Defiance gleamed in Casey's eye, a sneer curled Casey's lip. And now the leather-covered sphere came hurtling through the air, And Casey stood a-watching it in haughty grandeur there. Close by the sturdy batsman the ball unheeded sped. Ain't my style, said Casey. Strike one, the umpire said. From the benches , black with people, there went up a muffled roar, Like the beating of the storm-waves on a stern and distant shore. Kill him! Kill the umpire! shouted some one in the stands; And its likely they'd have killed him had not Casey raised his hand. With a smile of Christian charity great Casey's visage shown; He stilled the rising tumult; he bade the game go on; He signaled to the pitcher, and once more the spheroid flew; But Casey still ignored it, and the umpire said, Strike two. PENN checks his watch again. He speeds up even more. TELLER frantically throws the strait-jacket into the hole upstage of the spikes. PENN Fraud! cried the maddened thousands, and echo answered fraud; But one scornful look from Casey and the audience was awed. They saw his face grow stern and cold, they saw his muscles strain, And they knew that Casey wouldn't let that ball go by again. TELLER grabs the hook hanging from the ceiling. He closes the trap door using the hook. He uses the hook to unroll the carpet over the closed spikes. He throws the hook into the wastebasket by the SL traveler and reaches up to grab the bar from which he is suspended. PENN The sneer is gone from Casey's lip, his teeth are clenched in hate; He pounds with cruel violence his bat upon the plate. And now the pitcher holds the ball, and now he lets it go, And now the air is shattered by the force of Casey's Blow. Oh, somewhere in this favored land the sun is shining bright; The band is playing somewhere, and somewhere hearts are light, And somewhere men are laughing, and somewhere children shout; But there is no joy in Mudville mighty Casey has struck out. TELLER releases his feet from the bar and jumps down just as PENN jumps out of the chair, the chair flying up in the air. PENN This speech is my recital. I think its very vital. To rock. TELLER A rhyme! PENN That's right... TELLER on time! PENN Its Tricky is the title. Here we go! Thank you, thank you. I'm so glad to see there are some poetry lovers here on Broadway. PENN unties the rope from the chair as TELLER removes the inversion boots and places them backstage right. TELLER puts on his coat. PENN pulls the chair back by the stage right prop case. PENN removes his jacket and hangs it on the stage right green chair. He rolls up his shirt sleeves. A CARD TRICK. PENN We are Penn & Teller, and we are a couple of very eccentric guys who have learned how to do a few cool things. Now most of the really cool things come toward the end of the show, and that leaves our weaker material up here in the front, and I believe that the weakest thing in our entire repertoire, and indeed in anyones repertoire, is a card trick. TELLER enters carrying the Hand Stab table. PENN Now my major beef with card tricks is that card tricks seem to be to me intrinsically wimpy. TELLER slams a buck knife into the board and picks up a deck of cards. PENN Now we've got a card trick for you, and it starts really like most tricks with a card being selected. Uh, Sir, in the front row of the balcony with the mustache and the glasses? You don't have to stand up or anything, you just know who I'm talkin' to, right? Yeah. TELLER's going to rife down the deck and just yell, Yo! or Stop!, or whatever single syllable seems to be appropriate to your character. VOLUNTEER Stop. PENN Okay. Show the card around, Teller. Please make sure the balcony sees it as well. And then lose that card in the deck, would you please, Teller? TELLER executes a really bad card move. PENN laughs. PENN What, are your hands cold? That was smooth. I got here a couple of silver dollars. PENN clinks two silver dollars together. TELLER puts the cards down and holds up two pieces of adhesive tape. PENN They're not worth very much any more, but they're still opaque. Each of the silver dollars is placed on its own strip of surgical adhesive tape. Right there, and right there. (To TELLER) That move was great, man. From the balcony they saw that. You don't think so? Don't be smug about it, man. TELLER tries to give the adhesive strips to PENN. PENN Sir, did you feel that you had a free choice of that card? VOLUNTEER Absolutely. PENN Absolutely. And did you feel that you had a free choice, is now lost completely in the deck? VOLUNTEER Yes. PENN You do? I'm wearing a costume right now, so all I have in the pockets is stuff to make the tricks work, but in my street clothes upstairs, I've got probably 100 bucks, maybe a little more. Would you bet me 100 bucks right now that Teller has no idea where that card is in the deck? VOLUNTEER No way. PENN shows that the selected card is on the bottom of the deck. PENN Sir, does this surprise you very much? VOLUNTEER Not at all. PENN Not at all. So the second Teller shuffled the cards, you knew that the card wasn't lost in the deck, right? And yet when I asked you point blank, Is the card lost in the deck, you replied, Yes. And it wasn't until hard, cold cash came into it that you backed down at all, is that right? VOLUNTEER Right. PENN Yknow, a lot of people wonder why magic works, and the answer is sitting right up there in the balcony. This man is clearly not stupid. He knew the card wasn't lost in the deck, but more important than intelligence, this man here does not really give a good goddamn about our card trick or his responsibility to the rest of you. And I know what you're thinking, you're sitting way in the back, over here, and you're saying to yourself, Well, I cant see everything clearly, but I'm sure if something shifty's coming down, these people dead center are going to let us know. Right? Yeah. Don't count on him no more. And I do want to stick up for you for a second, Sir, and say it is really not a moral issue. I mean, if Teller had been chainsawing a child to death, you might very well have raised your hand, you might even have gone so far as to clear your throat. But what I'd like you to do is, we're just going to take the same card right here, Sir, and I'll just cut it about half way into the deck, then I'll give the cards a shuffle, and now that card is lost in the deck, right, Sir? Of course not, use your head. No matter how nice I pretend to be to you, and how mean I pretend to be to this man here, my first allegiance in the world is to my partner, and if he wants the card on top, the cards

3. Using food coloring, dye the sausage to match the background color in the snakeskin. Glue strips of colored paper around the sausage to match the colorations on the snake. Get someone else to do this part of the job.

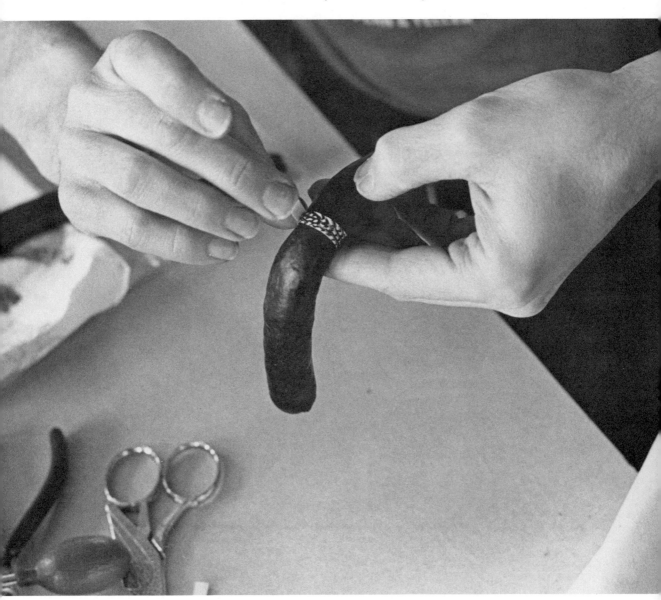

4. Buy some squirt rings. You can get them at a novelty store. Cut off the rings. Fill the squirters with stage blood.

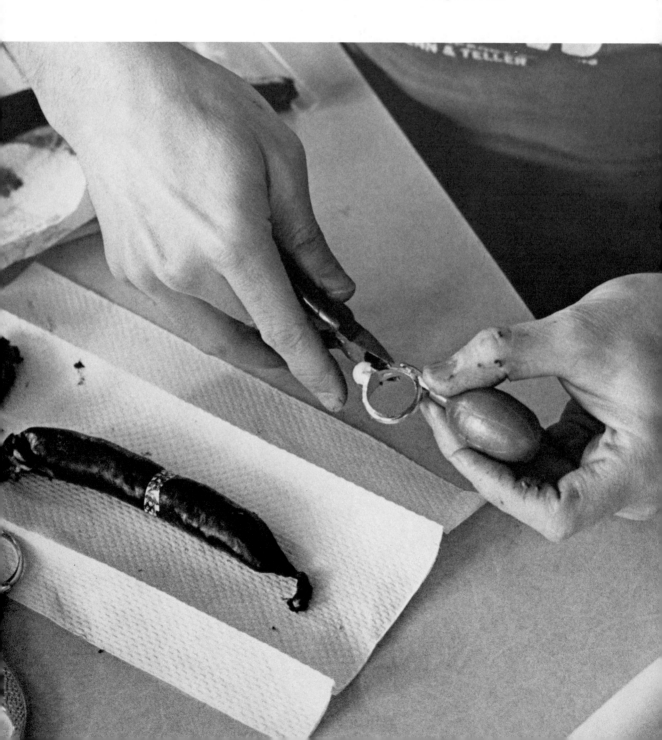

5. Cut off ten inches of sausage. Squeeze some of the in-
nards out, and jam in the squirters full of blood. Fold this
in half and hide it in your hand.

6. Get booked on *Saturday Night Live.* When they say your
name, go out onstage.

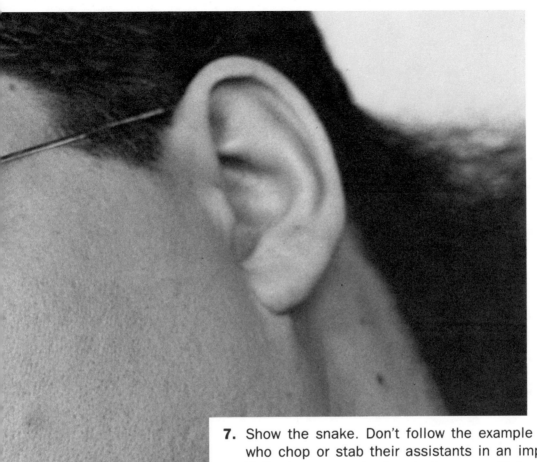

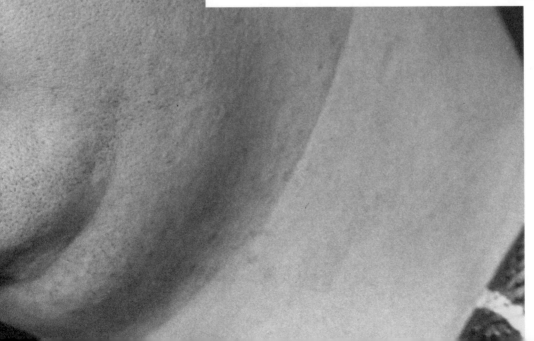

7. Show the snake. Don't follow the example of magicians who chop or stab their assistants in an impersonal way. Refer to your snake by a cute name. Make the audience care about it.

continued on p. 147

going to be on top. PENN shows that the top card is the selected card. TELLER is disgusted with PENN and losing interest in going on. PENN So since you cant trust Teller at all, we're going to do the same thing, I just want you to _ let me just give them a shuffle here just yell, I believe it was, Stop, would you please, Sir? VOLUNTEER Stop. PENN Right near the top? Okay, take a look at that card. Okay, that's the card well actually be using. Just remember that. And now I'll just do a false cut and yet another false shuffle, and the card is ostensibly lost in the deck. Okay, now, we take the opaque silver dollars on the surgical adhesive tape. One is placed over TELLER's upstage eye, one is placed over his downstage eye, and another strip is placed over the middle to stick it to his greasy little head. PENN crosses to downstage left and hands the deck of cards to a woman in the front row. PENN Excuse me, Ma'am? Can you shuffle a deck of cards? Yeah. Just take the deck and actually lose that card in the deck, would you please? PENN palms off the selected card and places it on his forehead under his glasses while the woman is looking through the deck for the card. PENN Look through it, find the card, actually lose it in the deck, would you please, Ma'am? Make sure that no one in the theatre could possibly know where that card is in the deck. Yo, Ma'am! The joke is dying. Let me explain something to you, Ma'am, okay? Now this show, like every Broadway show, is written out and rehearsed. But there are moments within this script where I am allowed to be just malicious. Now your whole sin, Ma'am, if indeed you have one, is that you're a very polite woman. So the whole time I'm talking with you, you see what you're doing? You're looking me right in the eyes. Now that's the way you should always deal with your fellow human beings. But when you're dealing with a scumball like me, keep your eyes on my hands, cause I just levered the top card off, pushed it into my palm, then I handed you the deck with the same hand. PENN levers the top card off, pushes it into his palm, and hands her the deck with the same hand. PENN Now you we're scoping out this hand. Only a putz palms with this hand, okay? Watch the move. Take the deck. She takes the deck. PENN The cards right there, obviously. Watch. Boom! PENN shows her his right hand empty. His left hand looks about as natural as the goddamn Seal Boy. PENN I show you my right hand empty. Now why do I show you my right hand empty? Because my left hand looks about as natural as the goddamn Seal Boy. I could park a Buick behind that hand, okay? So actually do, Ma'am, now really take the card back and lose it in the deck. You can shuffle them, cut them, anything you want to do. TELLER (behind Hand Stab table) Penn! PENN crosses to upstage by TELLER. TELLER grabs him and spins him around, TELLER facing upstage, PENN facing the audience. PENN What? TELLER What are you doing? PENN What are YOU doing? TELLER I'm trying to do the show. Do you think you could just shut up? PENN Heres your deck Mr. Teller. PENN , pouting, gets the deck of cards back from the woman. He places it loudly down on the table in front of TELLER, and then quietly takes it away. TELLER feels around for it. PENN Where'd they go? Where'd they go? PENN riffles it in TELLER's ear. PENN Reflexes! He then pretends to give it back to him, pulling it out of TELLER's hand until TELLER finally grabs it. TELLER is about to stab the cards. PENN Opaque silver dollars, surgical adhesive tape. He is completely blindfolded. PENN swings his hand under TELLER's nose. TELLER jumps back, startled. PENN laughs. He indicates where TELLER can peek down along his nose. As PENN rearranges the cards, TELLER stabs the knife into the table, just missing PENN's hand. He comes up with nothing on the knife. PENN That's definitely not cool, Teller. Now you're ready. Now you're set. Go! TELLER stabs again, just missing PENN's hand. He holds the knife up to reveal that he's stabbed the wrong card. PENN You got it. You got it. Is that your card, Sir, the Jack of Spades? Its really not? PENN takes the card off the knife and throws it into the audience. As he is rearranging the cards, TELLER brings his hand down, stabbing PENN directly in the back of the hand. PENN Are you even going to remember your card _ Ahhhhh! Blood flies everywhere, and runs down PENN's arm as we see the selected card impaled on the knife blade sticking out of PENN's hand. TELLER, screaming, rips the tape off of his eyes as he realizes what he's done. Their mood immediately changes back to congenial magicians. PENN Is that your card, the six of spades, the six of spades? PENN cleans up his arm with a handkerchief as he talks. TELLER shows the knife hanging off of his rear pants pocket. TELLER throws the knife back into the Hand Stab table. PENN shows that he has a small, plastic gimmick on his hand with the card taped on it, and a fake knife blade attached. PENN And the kids love it don't they? Sure they do. A little bit of good old-fashioned stigmata for your dining and dancing pleasure. Its our own Broadway mini-revival of Agnes of God for you here. This is probably the best example in the show of what Penn & Teller really stand for. This is what happens when you take a standard, wimpy piece of card magic, and add just a little bit of class to it. Now, Ma'am, you understand now that you've seen the whole bit all the way through why I had to act so rudely and so obnoxiously towards you, to not only have the audience accept the knife going through my hand, but indeed, have them praying for it. And you were such a good sport and you can call me a sentimental old fool, but damn, I'd like you to have this. PENN throws the woman his bloody handkerchief. PENN & TELLER bow, turn and shake hands, and TELLER removes the Hand Stab table as PENN brings the green chairs center stage facing each other.

CUPS AND BALLS PENN Okay, lets do some real magic. Bust it! TELLER enters from stage right with a long mirror. He sets it down on the backs of the chairs. PENN dances over and grabs three sheets of aluminum foil off of the stage right proscenium wall. PENN Woow! We're happy now! Sigfreid and Roy from hell! TELLER dances over and gets three red cups from behind the stage left proscenium wall. PENN and TELLER dance around the mirror, making foil balls and setting the cups down. When the setup is completed... PENN The Cups and Balls! PENN and TELLER do the Cups and Balls routine. PENN That theres the Cups and Balls, and I guess you guys don't realize how weird this is for us. We've been together for 13 years, and and this is our first run on Broadway, ever. TELLER cleans up Cups and Balls props while PENN talks. PENN Before this, we've always played toilets, yknow? And its weird, its different, yknow, because when we played in New York last, we played the Westside Arts, which is a way cool theatre, but the ceilings are really low, its like a church basement, so the lights are right here. And I'm a big guy, so it was kinda claustrophobic. But here, the lights are hung back there, which is great, but theres a weird byproduct of that and that's that there is light spill on you guys, and I can see, like, six or seven rows back, all the way across, the whole show. And that's really nice. It gives the show a very intimate feel and makes it very easy to perform. But during that last bit it was making me crazy. Cause there are a couple of guys right down here near the front And I don't want to point people out that during that whole bit they weren't applauding, they weren't laughing. All they were doing is nudging and pointing. And what made it really disconcerting is they were nudging and pointing at the exact instants we were sneaking the little tin foil balls under the cups. And I don't think we do that trick that badly, man. We practice it. I think the problem is, is this is the oldest trick in all of magic, I mean, there are paintings of this trick on, like, the pyramid walls, you know? Not us doing it, but two other guys, ancient astronauts, Magic Castle members or something. And theres a certain kind of person, that when they know what's going to happen in a trick, when they know the plot of a trick, its no longer a show anymore. Its a brain teaser, its a puzzle, and they just sit there trying to outsmart you. And

I don't think its good for the morale of the audience to have a couple of guys down here being really smug, and everybody else being left out. So Teller got this idea which, man, I think is the best idea either one of us ever got, and that was when we caught someone doing that kind of jive, we would just do the exact same trick. The theory behind it is really beautiful. The theory is then you would all have just seen the trick, you'd all know what to expect. You'd all know when the balls were supposed to end up underneath the little cups, you'd all be on equal footing. You could all watch it together as a brain teaser, and end up collectively smug. Now we did this a few times, and audiences seemed to enjoy it, but magicians were not thrilled. And it started with one magician and then it kept escalating until finally we hit about Def-Con 4 in the conjuring community. And if you want to prove it to yourself, pick up a copy of Genie or Linking Ring, which are two of the lesser magic magazines, and therein you will find editorials and reviews that just trash us, and are incredibly badly written. It all started about - it was at the Westside Arts, right? It had to be, like, two years ago this guy came to our show, he's a magician, and I will not say this magicians name on stage because it wouldn't be polite, and also you wouldn't recognize it, he works cruise ships, for chrissake. At the end of the show, when the show is over you guys just grab you junk and you go, you're out of here. But Teller and I, we gotta go backstage, clean up and change our clothes , you know, we're not going to wear this stuff on the street. So by the time we're leaving, you guys are ghosts. So we're walking out together, we had to meet somebody or something, and theres this one guy in the lobby like this, you know, like, a lot of attitude, like, a major 'tude on this joker. And we walk over, and this guy starts screaming right in our faces, I'm not exaggerating, screaming, and he's like an older guy, so when he screams, its just creepy, yknow. And he called us unprofessional, right? He called us immoral. And I believe that's all he'd prepared because from there on in he was ad-libbing obscenities, and we realized that all the dude was uptight about was the fact wed done the Cups and Balls twice in a row that night. The rest of the show he seemed to enjoy, although he didn't understand it. And Teller and I seem very different to you onstage, we wrote the show that way. We play up the characters to look very different. But in reality, in day-to-day life we are almost identical human beings. So the whole time this guy is screaming at us, we're thinking the exact same thought. We're thinking, if we got this guy, this mad, accidentally, how mad could we get him if we really tried? So what you're about to see has nothing to do with the show, it just proves that there is no limit to our petty vindictiveness. And it deals with breaking a few rules of magic. Now the first rule of magic is, as I said, you never do the same trick twice. So we're going to. The second rule of magic is, you never tip the gaff to the lay public _ you never tell people how a trick is being done. Well, after what that man called my partner in front of me in our theatre, I'm going to tell you exactly how this trick is being done. The third rule of magic is, you never let the audience see your secret preparation. This has to be done backstage so the audience does not know what is hidden in which pocket. PENN and TELLER load their pockets with the Cups and Balls props and simultaneously pat their pockets. PENN And the fourth rule of magic is unwritten, but I think any magician in the world would agree with me in a second, that you never, ever do the Cups and Balls with clear, plastic cups. TELLER sets out three clear, plastic cups. PENN So we're going to do the Cups and Balls again, and this time through, I don't want you to think about applauding or laughing, just get ready to do to nudge and point, as we do our version of the Cups and Balls. PENN and TELLER perform the Cups and Balls routine again, very quickly, with the clear cups. PENN We take the first ball, pretend to place it in our hand, having already placed it underneath the first cup. We take the second ball simultaneously secreting it beneath the cup, pretend to place it in our hand, and show it. We take the third and final ball, pretend to place it in our hand, pretend to show you underneath the cup, pretend to place it underneath the cup, at the same time secreting it and revealing it. Now we're all set for the second half. Three cups all loaded, three balls on top. We take the center ball, place it underneath the center cup. Take each of the side balls, really put them away, we don't need them anymore. We have three duplicates underneath the center cup. With these three balls I come over here. Now this is not juggling. What this is called is misdirection, for while you're looking over here, Teller sneaks the final ball under. Theres one more on either side, and of course, Mr. Barney Lime for our finish. That's the Cups and Balls. TELLER crosses to downstage left and picks up the wastebasket. He holds it at the stage left end of the mirror while PENN lifts the stage right end and dumps all of the Cups and Balls props into it. PENN And of course, its all done with mirrors. PENN ashes the mirror at the audience, then replaces it on the chairs. SUSPENSION PENN Now I'm going to pick someone else from the audience now. PENN enters the audience while TELLER strikes the mirror to the suspension table behind the stage right curtain. He brings out the suspension board, and places it on the chairs. He gets the wooden stool and places it downstage of the board. He sits on the board, waiting. PENN I usually pick people right up front, but I've often felt people who sit back a little bit further should be punished. (Singing) She walked in. I woke up. Never saw a pretty girl look so tough. Baby. You got that look. Don't point to other people, it looks remarkably stupid, it really does. How tall are you? VOLUNTEER 57. PENN 57? What's your name? VOLUNTEER Susan. PENN Would you come up here, please, Susan? Push your way through these people. Watch your step here. And don't worry, Susan, I'm not going to do anything to scare you at all. Boo! Joking, joking. Lacks only wit and human decency, other than that it was an almost perfect joke. Right up here. Susan, this is Teller, Teller this is Susan. She's okay, she's with me. TELLER gets off the board and opens up the blanket on the suspension board. PENN Susan, take a step up on this stool and sit down on the board facing the audience, would you please? Now Susan, theres an East Indian word fakir, f-a-k-i-r. Are you hip to that word at all? SUSAN Not at all. PENN That's the East Indian word for street performer. But that's a little bit misleading, because street performers in this country are often just five guys with a radio and a piece of cardboard. But in India, they're a whole different class of person, they're kind of a cross between a very high religious man and a talk show host, and these are the guys, Susan you know what I'm talking about they charm the snakes with the flutes, they swallow swords, eat fire now, Teller and I know quite a bit about this, and I want to tell you that all these guys are charlatans. All the stuff they do is a scam on one level or another. And all the ways they do this stuff has been published in many different books. You can go to any library and look it up. You can find out how they do all the tricks. But even with all that, I think its so charming and delightful, albeit archaic, the way Shirley MacClaine still believes in it. But they'll take knives and shove them in behind their eyes or they'll hammer nails up their nose, or they'll swallow needles, or, get this Susan, they'll lie naked on beds of spikes, or dance on hot coals, broken glass bare-footed. Do you think that kind of stuff is possible, Susan? TELLER (with his hand over his mouth) Yes I do, Penn. PENN Good. Swing your feet around and lie right back where you are, and scoot away from me a little bit. Scoot just means move, its a demonic term. TELLER takes the stool away, and wraps and ties the blanket around SUSAN. PENN Good. And give me the full weight of your head in my hands. Relax your head, and hold your hands Susan, as though you were holding the sky away, okay? That way if the sky

8. Lift the snake by its midriff, but double it over in your hand and let the loop of sausage hang out as if it were a loop of snake.

9. Hand a pair of poultry shears to a random audience member. Tell him to cut the snake. Make sure he cuts the *loop of sausage*. (Some people are funny, and will go straight for the head.)

10. Squeeze the bulbs, gently at first (for the initial ooze of blood), then forcefully, so the sausage squirts as if a blood vessel has been hit.

11. Retrieve the shears. Use them to pluck out the two pieces of sausage, as if lopping off the cut ends. Throw the ends into the audience for plenty of fun.

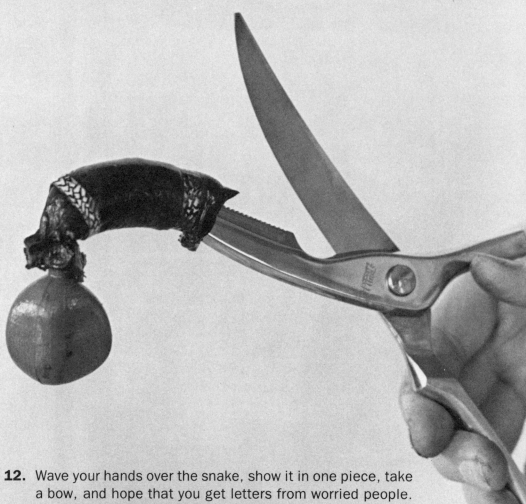

12. Wave your hands over the snake, show it in one piece, take a bow, and hope that you get letters from worried people. We got one that said, "Even if you *didn't* really hurt the snake, you put *bad ideas* into people's minds. It wasn't funny. I mean *I* knew it was a trick. But there are a lot of nuts out there who didn't. Think of what *they* might go out and do. You should be taken off the air and forced to work in an animal hospital for a few months. Then see how you feel about hurting innocent creatures." If you get letters like this, congratulate yourself on a job well done.

does happen to fall during this bit, you're the only one that's safe, okay? However, in the much more likely event of a nuclear holocaust, this particular hand position will not amount to squat, but we're gonna leave such a mysterious silhouette, okay? Now in just a moment, TELLER's going to push down on your hands. When he does, I'd like you to push back up against him, okay? TELLER pushes on the SUSAN's hands. PENN Don't win, just resist, he's a little guy, Susan. Now you feel that tension in your arms? I want you to remember that tension even when he takes his hands away, in other words keep pushing against nothing. Its kind of Zen, you might want to hum some old Grateful Dead to yourself. TELLER takes his hands away. PENN puts his hand over the SUSAN's eyes. PENN You'll probably be a little more comfortable, Susan, if you do close your eyes rather than looking directly up my nose. Now, thinking about every muscle you need to move and exactly how much you need to move each muscle, when I say lift, lift your feet three inches into the air and hold them there. TELLER holds his hand about six inches above SUSAN's feet. PENN Okay Susan? Lift. Hold, hold, hold, and relax right back down. Those aerobics are worth every penny, Susan, don't quit them. PENN lets SUSAN's head fall back gently. PENN Let your head fall right back, keep your hands in position, keep your eyes closed, please. Give me just a moment to make your hair look really bitchin'. PENN smooths her hair. He places his right hand on the SUSAN's neck, and looks at his Casio Data Bank watch. PENN I'd like you to take three deep breaths while I count them, okay? First breath, inhale, hold, exhale. Second breath a little bit slower, inhale, hold, exhale. Third breath, inhale, hold, and exhale. PENN moves around to SUSAN's feet and holds them. TELLER supports the board as PENN pulls the chair out from under her feet and places it stage left. PENN Keep breathing a little bit slower and a little bit deeper than you're used to. All you have to do is think about your breathing and that will happen almost automatically. Now, Susan, I've got your feet, do not lift them, don't lift them yet. I'm set, Teller. Go. TELLER removes the board from underneath SUSAN and places it upstage on the stage floor. He grabs a camera from the stage right prop box. PENN In just a moment Susan I'm going to ask you to lift your feet again. When you do this time there might be applause. Don't you worry about the applause. Concentrate on the weight on your hands. Keep breathing evenly and regularly. Don't hold your breath, don't hyper-ventilate, just breathe naturally. Stay with me now, Susan. Stay with me. Its going to be a little bit weird, its going to be a little bit uncomfortable, but just like before, very slowly lift your feet again. Lift your feet, Susan. PENN lets go of SUSAN's feet. She appears to be suspended in the air, hence the name of the bit. TELLER takes a Polaroid picture of the event. He puts the picture in his mouth and puts the camera back down by the stage right prop case. PENN Right there, Susan Hold, hold, HOLD, HOLD, HOLD IT SUSAN, HOLD IT. And relax, Susan, we got you. PENN grabs SUSAN's feet again. PENN Just stay in that position, Susan, we just have to remove the snakes and get all of the swords out of the way. TELLER puts the chair back, puts the board back underneath her, places the stool in front of the board, and unties the blanket. PENN Sit up, face the audience. Shut up. Chill it down. TELLER hands the photo to PENN. PENN Now, Susan, do you got any idea what happened to you? SUSAN No. PENN Cause I'll tell you, I was watching. It was krush fresh, it was megaboss. We did this experiment in teleportation. Heres a picture of you taken two minutes ago in Cleveland, Ohio. PENN hands SUSAN the photo. PENN You okay? Watch your step. That's Susan, there, Susan there. We're talking Susan, and she's there. SUSAN returns to her seat. TELLER puts the bench upside-down on the suspension board. He takes the suspension board off and puts it on the table stage right behind the curtain. He moves the green chairs back into position by the prop cases. The D.o.A. table flies in from above, and Teller guides it downstage to its resting place. PENN, in the meantime, has crossed stage right. DOMESTICATION OF ANIMALS PENN The next thing is kind of a song. Its the The Domestication of Animals, and its listed in your program as a performance art piece, but its actually much more than that. The bass guitar, suspended from wires, oats in from SR to sit in front of Penn. PENN Its a performance art period piece. And it takes place in the Pleistocene Epoch, actually the early Pleistocene, which is about 1.6-1.8 million years ago. Now that date may sound familiar to you, and that's because 1.6-1.8 million years ago is considered by most experts to be the Dawn of Man. I'll be playing the part of Man, and the song is entitled, The Domestication of Animals. TELLER, in the dark, starts squealing a balloon in the stage left microphone on the D.o.A. table. PENN diddles around on the bass, and then screams into the microphone. He starts playing the bass. PENN Okay, this is the way I got it figured. We're going to take over this planet what with our opposable thumb and our ability to perceive our own mortality and when we do we will no longer forage for food. The lights slowly come up to reveal TELLER as he finishes up squealing a balloon. PENN Now those of you that we find useful, such as the silkworm, TELLER crosses behind the table to the stage right end, and pushes a large balloon out from under a black piece of cloth. PENN the oxen, TELLER whips off the black cloth to reveal a balloon animal that looks slightly like an oxen. PENN the horse, TELLER whips another piece of black cloth off, and reveals a horse. He thumps the middle of it, and makes a galloping noise with his fingers. PENN and the honey bee, TELLER reaches under the table and brings out a large, orange bee. PENN you can live with us on these farms and you'll receive food, shelter and protection from your natural enemies. Now its no secret to any of you that we are carnivorous and those of you that we find edible such as pigs, TELLER reaches under the table and brings out a small pig. He pulls on the tail, making an oink sound. PENN cows, sheep and chickens, TELLER pulls out a chicken, and drops an egg from its backside. PENN you can live on these same farms under these same conditions, except of course when you reach adulthood you will be slaughtered TELLER cuts the beak off of the chicken, holding it between his fingers. PENN and eaten. TELLER lets go of the beak, and the head of the chicken deflates, squeaking. PENN Now we do still have some openings for pets, TELLER makes a small balloon doggie. PENN I'm talking canines, felines, certain small birds, reptiles, and sh. As a pet you will live right in the family dwelling. You will eat the family food, you will share affection with the family members, TELLER wags the dogs tail. PENN but you will of course have no vote, nor any say in any family matters. TELLER strikes a match on one of the microphones, and lights a cigar. PENN Now the vast majority of you will choose to remain in the wild. TELLER brings out the Wild Thing. PENN There are a few things I'd like to warn y'all about. First of all many of you will be hunted for sport and for food. TELLER starts popping the balloons with his cigar. PENN You will all be studied eventually in scientific experiments, TELLER examines the bee, and then rips it apart with his bare hands. He continues to plunder the animals. PENN and if you'd like to look many thousands of years in the future as our species multiplies, we will need more and more homeland for ourselves, leaving less and less wild homeland for you. This means some of the more fragile, less-adaptable species will become extinct. TELLER removes the clip from the silkworm and releases it. It gradually deflates, screaming all the way. On the last note of the song, TELLER pops a balloon in the stage left microphone. He exits USL to get rid of the cigar and remove his jacket. PENN crosses to the stage right end of the table and addresses the doggie, which is the only balloon animal left. PENN So, all things considered, if I were in your position, I would opt for domestication. PENN hits the drum machine on the D.o.A. table several times. In the blackout, TELLER guides the table back until it is hanging straight, and then it flies out. As the lights come up, PENN is standing center stage holding an apple containing 100 #6 embroidery needles. TELLER has entered the audience. EAST INDIAN NEEDLE MYSTERY. PENN I've got here an apple. And stuck into this apple are 100 size number 6 embroidery needles. Now TELLER's going into the audience to find someone to watch this from onstage. Hell need someone watching him rather closely because the objects hell be using are going to be small. They'll be these 100 needles and six feet of white thread. TELLER returns to center stage with an audience VOLUNTEER. PENN sits down in the stage left green chair. PENN TELLER's East Indian Needle Mystery. TELLER has the VOLUNTEER test one needle to see if its real. It is. He has the VOLUNTEER hold the apple, and a small jewelers case. TELLER swallows 30-35 needles. He takes another 30-35 needles, and walks down to the front of the stage. He swallows these, as well. He heads US, and takes the final 30-35 needles from the apple. The VOLUNTEER points out the final bunch of five needles on the back of the apple. TELLER takes them, grudgingly. He offers the bunch of needles to the VOLUNTEER. The VOLUNTEER, if he has a brain in his head, graciously declines. TELLER swallows them. He takes the apple and takes two bites out of it, and throws the remainder to an audience member. He invites the VOLUNTEER to examine his mouth with a pocket flashlight and dental mirror. Finding no needles, the VOLUNTEER returns to his seat. PENN hands TELLER a spool of thread. TELLER pulls off about six feet of thread and breaks it off. He throws the spool back to PENN. TELLER swallows the six feet of white thread, moves DSC, and, after suitable contortions, brings the needles up threaded. He displays the threaded needles in his outstreched hand, and clicks his heels together and bows. PENN What a guy, huh? QUOTE OF THE DAY PENN picks up a Bible from the stage left prop case. PENN This heres the Bible, and this next bit is about what happens to two men who spend too much time alone together in motel rooms. Now, Teller and I used to tour quite a bit and when I'm on the road I watch TV, its as easy as that, but Teller reads the Bible. And I don't want anybody here to be uncomfortable about us having a Gideons' Bible up here on stage. We didn't steal it nor nothing. It says right up here in the front that you want to take this Bible with you, you're welcome to, so we always do. PENN hands TELLER the Bible. PENN What happened is I'd be watching Letterman, or MTV, or whatever the hip show happened to be that night and Teller would be reading the Bible, but he's weird about it. He would open to like one page, and he would just stay there the whole evening reading those same two pages over and over again. And the next morning he'd hand me a piece of paper and on it would be written a verse from the Bible. I always presumed it was one from the night before, but I wouldn't think much of it. I'd read it over a couple of times, tape it to the rear view mirror of our ride. And as wed be driving to the next gig, I'd be looking up there and I'd be buggin'. Because that verse that he'd picked the night before would end up summing up our whole day on the road in really, really specific and very, very uncanny ways. And even though its a little bit more experimental than most of the stuff we do in the show here, I still want to give it a try. PENN takes the Bible from TELLER and enters the audience. TELLER sets SR green chair CS. He opens the DSR curtain to reveal a large chalkboard with a grid drawn on it. He writes, BOOK, CHAPTER, VERSE across the top. PENN And the first thing we need is someone rather trustworthy to watch this from onstage, which is never easy to find in our audiences here. Yeah, kid, trustworthy people hardly ever raise their hands. Let me see. What's your name Sir? VOLUNTEER Mike. TELLER writes Rev. Mike on the chalkboard under the verse heading. PENN Would you come up here, please, Mike? Just take the Bible with you. Watch your step there. Theres a chair there for you center stage. We're not going to use you for a moment or two, Mike, so kinda sit in the chair and try to look groovy, okay? Now, as you all probably know, the Bible is broken down into books, chapters and verses. Now the books of the Bible we're all familiar with, these are names like Genesis, Exodus, Thessalonians, and Habakkuk. The chapters are just regular numbered chapters like you'd have in any Jacqueline Suzanne novel. And the verses are the itty bitty teeny weeny little tiny numbers right above the words that serve to make the Bible even more incomprehensible. Now the first thing we're going to pick is a book of the Bible, and we're going to do this by using the Buggs and Rudy Discount Corporation Books of the Bible Dart Board. PENN opens the DSL curtain to reveal the Buggs & Rudy Discount Corporation Dart Board. He grabs six darts from behind the SL proscenium wall. PENN Now as you can see, all the names of the books of the Bible are up here, the Old Testament is surrounded by black, the New Testament is surrounded by red, the number of chapters underneath each book in parentheses, the center space is a free choice, and who wants to play some darts, huh? Three hands should shoot up who want to play some darts. I'm going to pick a kid in the balcony here. I'll take you in the suit coat, with the white? Yeah. The woman there? Yeah. Come on down here. Move! Yeah, you with the hair! Go! Go! C'mon! Yes, you! Push her over! Jesus, move! I need two more people to throw darts here. Yeah, the kid in the back row there. And I need one more person to chuck a dart here. I'll try to do this well-rounded here. Is there another kid? I'll take that kid there. Yeah, that's okay, yeah. Okay, now right over here. Behind this red line. And where the hell is the kid from the balcony? PENN lines up the dart-throwers. PENN And what's your name, kid? Say again? Jamie? Okay, just stand right here, Jamie. And what's your name, kid? Say again? Miles? Just stand over here in the on-deck area. And what's your name, Ma'am? Lorenza. Okay, just get behind him, Lorenza. That's a quote from the Bible, I believe. We have three Biblical names Jamie, Miles and Lorenza. Jamie, all the names of the Books of the Bible are up here, I'm sure you've got your favorite, so haul off and chuck it. Go ahead. Let it fly. Boom! Nice shot. Jamie! You're kinda right near Numbers and Second Kings. Now whichever one of those two that you pick we will go with, but if you chose the wrong one, Jamie, you're going to spend the rest of eternity in hell. Numbers or Second Kings? Numbers. You're happy with Numbers? Good, go away. JAMIE returns to his seat. TELLER writes Numbers on the chalkboard. PENN We've got Numbers there. Okay, Miles, right over here. Let 'er rip, let 'er rip. C'mon, Miles. Boom! I know exactly what Miles was thinking. I said, Who wants to throw a dart? and Miles said, Oh boy, a chance to learn a new skill in front of strangers. You can try again, Miles. Here you go, catch! Just trying to put the fear of Jesus in you, Miles. Boom! Okay, probably thinking in terms of that cluster bombing, huh? Boom! Are you happy with John, Miles? Good. Get out of my face. Miles returns to his seat. TELLER writes John on the chalkboard. PENN Okay Lorenza, let "er fly. Walk You're not going to stand where the kids were. Back up a little bit. LORENZA I cant throw either. PENN Ha, ha, ha! Throw. Boom! Looks to me like Exodus. Is that Exodus? LORENZA That is Exodus. PENN And speaking of Exodus, go away. LORENZA returns to her seat. TELLER writes Exodus on the chalkboard. PENN We have got Numbers, we've got John and we have got Exodus. PENN crosses to the audience SR. PENN Excuse me, Ma'am, would you catch this microphone, please? I'm throwing it to you. Into the microphone, what's your name? VOLUNTEER Robin. PENN Robin, if you had a choice between Numbers and Exodus, which would you choose? Into the microphone. Look at me, please. Numbers or Exodus? ROBIN Numbers. PENN Between Numbers and John? ROBIN John. PENN Let me tell you

Psychology is an important part of our work as illusionists, and we subscribe to many of that profession's periodicals. Very little of the material is directly applicable to the entertainment industry, but it's all fascinating. Teller stumbled across an experiment written up in the New England Journal of Psychobiological Sciences *that blew our minds. We are able to reprint this article thanks to the Franklin County Institute for Advanced Psychodiagnostic Study and Research in Amherst, Massachusetts, and* The New England Journal of Psychobiological Sciences. *Special thanks to Dr. Marc Garland, Dr. Camille Sweeny, Dr. Edward Gorodetsky, and especially Dr. Cindy Valk, who rewrote the following directions for our lay readers.*

B372 PERSONALITY TEST

The more science discovers about the brain, the more we learn that brain and mind are not as separate as we like to think. The physical makeup of the tissue of the brain is as important as the experiential input to the brain. Artistic taste, snap decisions, value judgments, what we like, and what we don't like, are all decided by environment, education, *and* the exact placement of the little cells and synapses that make up our four and a half pounds of wonderful thinking machine.

The following test can be rather startling. Many personality traits are interdependent simply because of where the particular memory cells reside in the brain and how they are accessed and triggered. It's remarkable how many diverse traits are interrelated. We are discovering, for instance, that how chocolate tastes to you may affect whom you like in this year's Super Bowl.

This test requires two people. One should answer the questions below and the other should check the results with the tables on the following pages. You must have two people.

B372 PERSONALITY TEST
Subject's Instructions

When you open to the test page (p. 156), IMMEDIATELY PLACE A PIECE OF BLANK PAPER OVER THE RIGHT-HAND PAGE (p. 157). The piece of paper serves two functions: (1) You will write on it, and (2) it will prevent your eyes from wandering to the Experimenter's Instructions. DO NOT LOOK at the Experimenter's Instructions; it will influence your answers and invalidate the experiment.

Now, get the room as quiet as possible. The atmosphere should be relaxed. Take your time. Read each question carefully and imagine the scene as you read it. Then print your answer on the piece of paper. Because this experiment relies in part on the left/right brain hemisphere interaction you must be sure to NUMBER YOUR ANSWERS AND PRINT THEM CLEARLY IN LARGE, BLOCK LETTERS. Once you have written an answer, do *not* change it. Also, DO *NOT* ALLOW THE EXPERIMENTER TO SEE WHAT YOU WRITE, or your results will be distorted.

Do not ask questions. Do not have anyone help you. Some of the questions are deliberately vague. The confusion, doubt, and slight discomfort you may feel is part of the test. Answer the questions honestly. There are no right or wrong answers, but you must write something for every question.

REMEMBER: THINK ABOUT YOUR ANSWER, THINK ABOUT WRITING YOUR ANSWER, NUMBER AND WRITE IT CLEARLY AND READ IT OVER SEVERAL TIMES.

155

1. You are snooping around in an abandoned workshop full of tools. You injure your hand in an accident. A tool is involved.

2. A person, your perfect sex partner, is smiling suggestively at you. You are in a public place. This person is wearing a hat. The person slowly takes the hat off and hands it to you. On the inside of the hat is written a fragment of nursery rhyme.

3. It's 20 years in the future and your closest grade school friend is a television personality. This person has changed his or her first name. The color of your friend's hair has been electronically altered.

4. You have to sit in a room and examine a fruit or vegetable for one hour. You can touch it, feel it, smell it, even destroy it, but YOU CANNOT EAT IT.

5. You see three nuns naked in a public place.

6. What is the first seven-letter word that pops into your head?

7. A friend that you haven't seen for a few months calls to tell you he or she has a new phone number. As you write down the number you realize that the area code is wrong.

8. You are riding through your home town in the passenger seat of a car. You are five years old. You see on the left side of the road, out of the corner of your eye, a sign. There is a picture on the sign.

9. You are in a small desert town. You are wearing boots. It is high noon. You notice an insect crawling across your boot. The insect has a stripe of color that you've never seen on this kind of insect.

1. What tool has hurt you?

1a. Is it your right or left hand?

2. What is the nursery rhyme?

2a. What color is the hat?

3. What is your friend's new name?

3a. What color is the hair on TV?

4. What is the fruit or vegetable?

5. Where are they?

6. Write it down.

7. What is the wrong area code? (three digits)

8. What is the picture?

8a. What is the color of the background of the sign?

9. What kind of insect is it?

9a. What is the color of the stripe?

**TO SUBJECT: Return the book to the Experimenter.
Retain the sheet of paper on which you have written your answers.
Do NOT show the Experimenter that sheet of paper.**

156

EXPERIMENTER'S INSTRUCTIONS

Do not allow the subject to read this before taking the test.

The subject has finished taking the test and is holding the answers out of your sight. Ask the questions below in your normal tone of voice. Use the answers to consult the tables below. If the answer to the question that **YOU ASK** is not covered exactly on the table, pick the answer on the chart that is closest to the one given. **DO NOT LET THE SUBJECT SEE THE TABLES YOU ARE USING** lest he or she try to change the answers to help the test along.

When you have come to the end of the table for each question, read the bottom line to your subject WORD FOR WORD. You should not leave it open to interpretation. Your subject will tell you if it is a hit or a miss. Ask the subject to simply say "Hit" or "Miss" and to give you no more information until this entire test is completed.

Ask these questions in your normal tone of voice:

Question 1 & 1a — You wake up in the middle of the night and find a tooth on the left side of your mouth is loose. You wiggle the tooth and it falls out easily. You examine the tooth and on the root is written a direction (North, South, East, or West).

1. What direction is written on the tooth?
1a. Is there blood on the tooth?

Find your reference number from (table 1a) for left or right on (table 1b). Follow the reference number on (table 1b) to the far right and bottom and use those reference numbers on (tables 1c, 1d, and 1e).

The second number refers only to the top left of the quadrant. If the blood-Yes-code is contrary to the Hammer-drill number, use the first number without letter and assume the letter is b.

Question 2 and 2a — There is a three-month old baby, a child of the friend of the family. The baby is happy and smiling. Everything about the scene is perfect, but the baby is holding something odd.

2. What is it?
2a. What color is the baby blanket?

Use the answer to the baby blanket color to reference a color number on (table 2a). The reference number can be used on (table 2b) for the color chosen for the hat. Be careful to follow the grid on primary colors all the way down the left side. For pattern answers (i.e., "stripes," "checks," "polka dots") skip to (table 15d). Once you have the reference number from (table 2b) or (table 15d) turn to (table 2c) for the nursery/baby hand chart. Note: A reference number over 25 with a vowel letter negates the first column.

Question 3 and 3a — You are in a dentist's waiting room. A friendly cat walks over and rubs against your leg. The cat has a different-colored patch of fur under its neck. The patch is a geometric shape.

3. What shape is the patch?
3a. What color is the patch?

This will use the bottom left quadrant of the color chart (table 2a) and reference to (table 2b). The patch (if not a circle) will be (table 3a) and reference to (table 3b) for the name.

Question 4 — You are being held by pirates. You have tried to escape and failed. You look out the porthole and see your friends arriving in a heavily armed ship; you are being rescued. On the deck of your friend's ship is a familiar machine. You are very glad to see this machine.

157

4. What is the machine?

First decide if the machine is "household" (table 4a), "public" (table 4b), "industrial" (table 4c), or "other" (table 4d). This will give you a reference number for (table 4e), unless machine is "not applicable," in which case go right to (table 4f) for the name. The color chart, of course, will be the same, but the upper right quadrant.

Question 5 — A person from your past that you consider an authority figure is dressed in a costume from another period of history and smoking a cigarette. You find yourself attracted to one article of the person's clothing.

5. Which article of clothing is it?
5a. What color is it?

See "Simplified Cross-Reference Guide."

Question 6 — The phone rings in the middle of the night and wakes you up. When you pick up the phone all you hear is one line from a song that was popular in your youth.

6. What is the line?

Question 7 — How many 33⅓-rpm record albums would you have if you lived in a thirty-eight-room mansion in 1973? (Please do not choose a round number.)

See "Simplified Cross-Reference Guide."

Question 8 & 8a — You are standing on the midway of an amusement park. One of the rides is on fire and burning brightly.

8. Which ride is it?
8a. How many people are on the ride?

Question 9 — You are watching a movie in a strange theater when you notice that the star of the movie is your mother dressed as an alien. The alien (your mother) has a multicolored scar that looks like a tattoo. The scar/tattoo looks like a historical figure.

9. Who does the scar/tattoo look like?
9a. What color is the scar/tattoo?

SIMPLIFIED CROSS-REFERENCE GUIDE

Question Number	Consult Tables
1	1A, 6J, 9S
2	1F, 1H, 2C, 13B
3	2A, 2B, 3A, 20X
4	4A, 4B, 7F, 4D, 4E, 16G
5	10A, 6C, 5D, 5E, 9F
6	12A–F, 1J
7	7B, 7C, 3E, 9G
8	2F, 8B, 8D, 1E
9	16A, 9K, 9M, 12D

NOTE: All tables are indexed alphabetically by series *and* page number.

Stick the groovy pink plastic sandwich thing here,
covering up these words.
Then read the secret directions
on page 119
and the Personality Test will work.

PENN & TELLER'S MAGIC MIRROR

(To be used with Penn & Teller's Magic Pliers)

TABLE 2F

	100	80	60	40	20	10
Cyclone	8L	4A	22M	2	8B	5
Ferris Wheel	30	14	2	10	12	19B
Tilt-A-Whirl	13	6	20Z	15	5U	8B
Hell Hole	23M	11P	4Z	14S	3	12U
Other	8B	8B	8B	8B	8B	8B
Funhouse	1	5	3	1	8L	4

TABLE 16G

	Black	Blue	Other	Green	Red	Orange
Bermuda Onion	8M	4B	6W	2	28	10X
Water Chestnut	14S	21	3R	4A	2	18
String Bean	10X	7	6W	21	3A	20Z
Corn on the Cob	22	4H	3B	17	8M	35
Eggplant	5B	16	23	20Z	19	1
Other	4H	4H	4H	4H	4H	4H

TABLE 8B

	> 2	> 8	> 12	> 18	> 24	> 32
Giant Swings	8B	1	10	1	19B	9
Bumper Cars	4A	30	14S	12	4	13
Other	8D	8D	8D	8D	8D	8D
Himalayas	14	8L	15	3	12U	23M
Salt & Pepper Shakers	11P	13	1	8L	5	10
Caterpillar	5	23M	8B	6W	12U	30X

TABLE 10A

	Greenish	Bluish	Redish	Blackish	Yellowish	Otherish
Overcoat	19B	23M	30X	14S	19	3
Raincoat	17	10	18	21	1S	27
Windbreaker	1S	6	3	9	2	12
Derby	15P	2	5E	26	20Z	20
Sash	24	25	22M	1S	3R	00
Other	5C	5C	5C	5C	5C	5C

TABLE 5E

	13th Century	14th Century	15th Century	16th Century	Other Century	17th Century
Laundry Mat	8	27T	20Z	2	6	5D
Phone Bank	20	6	5E	9	12	9
Slash Theater	14S	22M	10	4	10	2
Other	5F	5F	5F	5F	5F	5F
Peepshow	5C	30X	4	26	20	16
Airport	17	8	18	3R	5B	27T

TABLE 8D

	Green	Brown	Yellow	Blue	Red	Other
Station Wagon	9	2H	30X	17	5B	4
A Giant Ant	25	8	7	3	23	23N
Not Appropriate	8E	8E	8E	8E	8E	8E
A School Bus	2	2H	24	6	16	11P
Jerry Lewis	17	4	8B	19B	20	8E
The Governor	1	7	18	5A	22M	5U

TABLE 5D

	Striped	Checked	Polka Dot	Other	Plaid	Puckered
Bell Bottoms	5E	26	27	5E	00	22M
Knickers	12L	10X	5U	1S	12L	30X
Bermudas	6	2H	10X	3R	9S	13B
Other	5E	5E	5E	5E	5E	5E
Fatigues	6W	3R	19	00	1S	6
Loincloth	25	2A	26	23M	14N	5U

TABLE 12B

	Primitive	Other	Industrial	Opera	Gospel	Folk
600,001	19B	14N	9	30X	18	12L
Other	12C	12C	12C	12C	12C	12C
27	21	4A	22	6	15	8
1963	3R	6	13H	19	12B	19B
1,000,000,004	10X	12C	17	23M	22	12C
1687	6	12T	12B	4F	5U	3R

TABLE 12A

	Rock	Jazz	Chanting	Blues	Classical	Other
1707	15P	22	4F	1S	12B	30X
14	40	12B	12A	10	20	19B
898	22M	11	16	14S	2H	1S
5506	17	12T	30X	6W	15	3
98	12	00	9	23M	5	23M
Other	12B	12B	12B	12B	12B	12B

TABLE 9G

	"When the Saints Come Marching In"	"Give Me That House Music"	"You Go Back to the Top"	Cosi Fan Tutti	Other	"Love Me Tender"
202	3R	24	9	23M	7G	15
703	2	6	10X	16	4	20
808	2H	4	15	14S	7G	5U
918	8	19B	16	12T	1S	27T
Other	7G	7G	22M	1	7G	8M
214	30X	7	5X	7G	1S	5B

TABLE 1E

	Black/Black	Black/Silver	Black/Red	Black/Blue	Other	Black/Yellow
Plate of Fish	23N	3Q	14	00	16C	5Z
Mommy	10	5A	8	4	22M	30X
Snowman	22	2	6B	11P	14S	8Z
Other	8Z	4	8Z	3Q	8Z	19
Lawn Mower	1D	9	3	7	7	4
Lake	12	13	21	15	20Z	3R

TABLE 1J

	Birthdays	Volcano	Toast	Jack in the Box	Goosebumps	Other
Genetic	11	2	4	2	5U	12
Cowlick	2	3	5	9	13	8M
Belcher	7	00	23	18	2	12
Literal	15P	8M	12L	22M	10	9
Between	1	19	6	15P	17	5B
Another	4	1S	7	3R	3	18

TABLE 7B

	Rock/Violence	Other	Rock/Love	Rock/Protest	Rock/Journey	Rock/Groovy
Relative	5	4	1Z	8X	20	12
Friend	6	10	2	12T	13	18
Lover	12L	20	9	00	4	2
Employer	8W	7D	15	11	2H	14
Teacher	1	7D	3	16	3Q	5
Not Appropriate	7D	7D	7D	19D	12F	17

TABLE 12C

	Vibes	Guitar	Piano	Recorder	Other	Tuba
> 412	6	8	24	00	23M	14S
> 6504	5	12F	13H	5	12F	15
> 1	14S	16	8	12F	3Q	15P
< 2	19B	7	12T	4	2	19B
Not Appropriate	12F	12F	12F	12F	12F	12F
< 7777	16B	11	10	22	11	1S

TABLE 7C

	Jazz/Cool	Jazz/Hot	Jazz/Driving	Other	Jazz/Dixie	Jazz/Up-Tempo
Joe	3	00	9	7D	18	21
Don	1S	27T	22M	7D	1Z	12U
Sally	6W	6	11	2	3	24
Other	23M	2H	4	7D	7D	14
Stranger	1	7D	1	7D	7D	30
Bob	16	2	3	15P	16	5B

TABLE 12F

	Hot Dog	Pipe	Penis	Eclair	Not Appropriate	Rigatoni
Without	17	3R	14S	15	4	14S
Trigger	10X	2	5	20Z	6W	19B
Western	18	8M	15	19	11	5U
Another	12G	12G	12G	12G	12G	12G
Nowhere	14	10	12T	1S	20X	22M
Oblique	17	11	15P	3	12L	23M

TABLE 3E

	Grandma	Sister	Stepbrother	Pet	Cousin	Other
Pop	10	5	18	3	1S	7D
Other	6W	2	10	6	30T	7D
Rhythm & Blues	22M	14	12T	7D	7	7D
Reggae	12V	27T	20	10W	15	7D
Opera	4	25	23M	9	6	7D
House	5U	5	3	1	19B	7D

TABLE 20X

	Auburn	Chestnut	Frosted	Raven Black	Bleach Blond	Other
Cindy	17	00	10	4	13	20Z
Cammie	24	2	7	2	12	19
Julie	5	12	9	17	3Q	5
Eva	13B	15	6J	1A	15	6
Joy	16	20	28	15A	4	14N
Other	14N	30	16	18	2	8

TABLE 16A

	Green	Orange	Other	Yellow	White	Beige
Other	9B	9B	9B	9B	9B	9B
Elvis	12	1L	16	4Z	20	6
Joan of Arc	2	14	3A	18	5C	22
Jesus Christ	5X	9P	13	8	11W	7
Paul Revere	5	1	10	24	15	25
Jack Kennedy	2	23	22	20X	2H	30X

TABLE 9K

	Red	Blue	Ivory	Black	Brown	Pink
Harry Houdini	4	9P	4Z	6	250	10
Caesar	1	23	1L	5C	6	9B
Lorne Green	12	2H	7	20	1L	25
Harriet Tubman	5X	5	20X	15	8	22
Other	9C	9CX	9C	9C	9C	9C
Batman	23M	22	1S	24	30X	7

TABLE 9M

	Gold	Silver	Navy Blue	Emerald	Violet	Other
Spider	19B	10	15P	12U	23M	2
Fly	20	3	8M	13X	4	5B
Ant	4F	12	27T	6W	8A	6W
Praying Mantis	14	21	11	5B	5A	7C
Other	9D	9D	9D	9D	9D	9D
Roach	3	22M	13	2	15	1

TABLE 12D

	Purple	Black	Mint Green	Midnight Blue	Salmon	Plum
Daddy Longlegs	25	7A	20	23	7B	9
Other	9E	9E	9E	9E	9E	9E

ON SABBATICAL

If you're going to appreciate how significant Saturday, December 2, 1987, was to me, you'll have to picture my life at the time.

I was Herschel Derrickson, teacher of Latin and classical culture at a public school in Trenton, New Jersey. I was fifty-eight. I was large and stayed fit by lifting weights. I wore glasses. I was bald, but not ashamed of it. I had a wife, Bina, born in India, and two children, Warren, then in college, and Betsy, a senior in high school and a star tennis player.

When you have kids, it's easy to forget yourself. Bina and I had invented a way to remember. We called it a sabbatical. Every Saturday one of us would take the day off, away from home, spouse, kids, and job. We alternated, so we each got two Saturdays per month off.

When it was Bina's turn (second and fourth Saturday of the month) she often spent the entire day going from one movie theater to the next, seeing as many as five films in a day.

On my sabbatical days I liked to get up one hour late (at seven-forty), shower, dress, and take a train to New York. I would have breakfast at Mary Elizabeth's Tea Room on Thirty-seventh Street, unwholesome, cholesterol-laden scrambled eggs on a slice of Virginia ham, with coffee, cinnamon roll, and more coffee. Then, feeling a little lively from the caffeine I would hop a subway downtown to Isaac Mendoza's Ann Street Bookstore.

I loved Mendoza's, one of the last of the dusty, rummage-around-and-discover-a-jewel bookshops in the city. And when the quiet man in jeans unlocked the door to the stairway leading to the upper two floors, I always felt like a robber breaking into Tut's tomb.

So. There I was on the second floor hallway of Mendoza's, on a bitingly cold Saturday in early December. I had taken off my hat and coat, and was standing by the deep-set, grimy window at the end of the children's section.

I like buying used books for the kids. I like the way they smell. And I prefer older editions, especially the ones I had myself as a kid. It depresses me to think of youngsters reading a Hardy Boys adventure in which nobody jumps on the running board of a roadster.

I was looking for Christmas presents for my nephews and had just found an edition of *Treasure Island* that attracted me with a cover illustration of a smiling Long John Silver leaning on a shovel over a horrified man buried up to his neck in sand. I turned the book over in my hand and flipped to the flyleaf to check the price: $4. And there also I saw an inscription—in adult handwriting—which read:

> *To the young Master Teller,*
> *from Aunt Millie*
> *Christmas 1958*

Perfect, I thought. It will be a Christmas present again, this time to Charley from Uncle Herschel. I knew my nephew would like it. He's thirteen, and his favorite bedside reading is *The Big Book of Famous Tortures*. I set the book beside my overcoat on the ledge of the deep-set window.

I scanned the shelves again. This time I found a black paperback with *Spooky Magic* in ghostly lettering. I opened it. It was a book of magic tricks, illustrated with drawings of a small boy wearing 1950s school clothes and floating a playing card with a piece of black thread. My younger nephew, Nicholas, would like this one. He was almost eleven and, having learned the trick behind Santa Claus, was forever trying to prove himself wise by tricking his elders.

I looked inside to check the price. A buck. A previous owner's name was scratched out at the top of the page, and underneath was

Teller
the magician

in a child's attempt at old-English script. I picked up *Treasure Island* and compared. It *was* the same name. Curious as to whether more books might be from the same library, I checked the flyleaves of half a dozen others. None of them was; only the two books that I had chosen. They lay by my overcoat, glowing in a spotlight of sun that forced itself through the soot-encrusted window.

I moved on to the occult section. I am not a believer in the occult, but I've noticed I can often find books on the Loch Ness monster among the crank sciences, and the Loch Ness monster fascinates me. It is a myth, pure and simple, the product of yellow journalism in the 1930s. But I loved the idea of a Scottish plesiosaur hiding for centuries at the bottom of a black pool. And I enjoyed the stories of daffy amateur monster hunters skulking around the shores, trying to prove the great Orm's existence with snapshots of logs floating by castles at dusk.

There were no books about Nessie, but a two-volume set called *Mediums of the Nineteenth Century* drew my attention. I found myself pulling Volume Two from the shelf.

Why had I picked it up? The cover was dull and textbook-ugly. Being called *Mediums of the Nineteenth Century,* it was no doubt full of credulous rubbish and ravings about "magnetic influences" and "fields of spiritual force."

But as I held it, the book fell open to a passage describing how a crooked spirit medium had secretly obtained his information by taking carbon-paper impressions under the blotter of the desk on which his clients wrote their questions for the spirits. I was intrigued. I flipped to the flyleaf: 2 vols. $2.

The price was certainly right. The two volumes of *Mediums* joined *Spooky* and Long John Silver with the shovel, and I carried them all downstairs. As I walked up to the cash register I heard the lock of the stairway door click shut behind me.

"Well, Martin, I guess that's it for me today. Any deals?" Often the cashier, whose name I had learned on previous sabbaticals, would round off my total and forget the tax. I always enjoyed that, less for the sake of the money than for the pleasure of being treated like one of the family.

"All our books are deals, sir," he answered with a tired smile.

"Yes, I guess they are. I'm just getting greedy. By the way, how is your friend the limo driver?"

"Philip?" Martin looked uneasy. "How do you know him?"

"You told me all about him, how he had to drive Lauren Bacall, how she hit him with a bottle of champagne and cut the bridge of his nose."

He looked hard at me, trying to remember. "I told you that? That's very odd. I'm a gabber sometimes, but—when did I tell you that?"

"A month or two ago. Saturday. You remember me, don't you? I'm here every other Saturday. I always pay by check. Books are tax deductible for teachers, you know."

"Sorry. I thought you looked familiar. I just couldn't place you. I must have some wire in my head disconnected today. Here, let me get these totaled up."

Mendoza's had no cash register, just a drawer for money, and a note pad on which they calculated the bill in pencil. Martin opened Volume One of *Mediums of the Nineteenth Century* to check the price. There, inside the cover of the volume I hadn't examined upstairs, was an inscription:

To Teller

How much would you charge to haunt a house?
Rosey

Halloween 1975

"Look at this," I said. "All three books I got today were once owned by the same person. I guess you must have bought them all from one estate, right?"

Martin looked down at the name in the inscription, then quickly back up at me. "I guess we must have." A strange smile passed over his face. "What did you say your name was?"

"Herschel Derrickson."

"Hmmm." He looked down at the books, added the rest of the prices. "That will be seven plus tax."

"Fine. I'll just . . ." I reached for my checkbook, then realized it was in my overcoat, and I'd left my overcoat upstairs.

continued on p. 170

about a force I was using on you that worked perfectly. And that is, the one that I held until the last you were more likely to pick. The reason being that the other two could be eliminated twice, in two different rounds, and also you heard that one last, so it was fresh in your mind. With all that information in your head, do you want to stay with your choice of Numbers, or do you want to change your mind? ROBIN I'll stay with John. PENN John. You won that round. Now, you are picking John by the book of the Bible and not by the person that threw? You aren't picking John because you thought Miles was the cutest or something like that, are you? ROBIN Right. PENN You're picking by the book of the Bible? ROBIN Right. PENN Okay, Robin, this is all fun and games to you, all right? In about four and a half minutes there ain't gonna be no more fun in this room. I'm gonna come right back here and I'm gonna point right in your face and I'm gonna ask you fairly rudely if you had a totally free choice. At that point, for the dramatic movement of the show, I need an unequivocal, unhesitating yes from you. If you are not prepared to give that, in other words if you do not believe you had a totally free choice, don't do me any favors, don't second- guess me, all I care about is you having a totally free choice. Is that John, or do you want to change your mind? ROBIN John. PENN And you had a totally free choice? ROBIN Mm- hmm. PENN You're positive? TELLER stars John on the chalkboard. PENN Turn to John, would you please, Mike? Its in the New Testament, theres an index in the front, no reason on earth to embarrass yourself. Now John, as we all know, has in it 21 chapters and we're going to choose one of the 21 chapters and we're going to do this... PENN grabs the wading pool from off SL. PENN by using a child's inflatable craps table and a couple of fuzzy dice. Get outta my way, I'm going to hell. PENN heads up the SL stairs to the SL box seats. TELLER tosses the wading pool out into the front, SL seats. PENN Now if we throw one die well get a number between one and six, two dice between two and twelve, three dice between three and eighteen, four dice between four and twenty- four. One, two, three, or four, how may dice shall we throw, Kid? KID Two. PENN Two. Okay, would you stand up here, please Ma'am. What's your name? VOLUNTEER Cherie. TELLER writes Cherie's name on the chalkboard. PENN Cherie? Right up here Cherie. CHERIE stands up by the box railing. PENN Would you examine these dice, Cherie, and make sure theres nothing unusual about them. Come right up here. They're not misspotted or loaded in any way? They seem okay to you, Cherie? CHERIE Yeah, they're fine. PENN Yeah, like you're a goddamn fuzzy dice expert, right? PENN has people in the orchestra hold the wading pool over the seats. PENN Now, Cherie, just throw these right down here one at a time. Boom! Call it out, Sir. Four? And one more, Cherie, right down there. And a three. Which makes seven, of course. TELLER writes the numbers down on the chalkboard and adds them up. He crosses SL and behind the middle red curtain. PENN Now, Cherie, I'm going to give you a choice. If you think that seven is a random number, and random number is defined during this show as just a number that I didn't know in advance. If you think I sincerely did not know that was going to be a seven, well stay with that, no reason to change it. If you think I might have finagled it or fudged it to make it come out to seven, you can throw this last die again, and add that number to it. Do you want to stay where you are or throw once more, which do you believe is more random, Cherie? CHERIE I'll stay where I am. PENN Stay where you are? You're sure? Had you thrown just once more, Cherie, you would have won this... TELLER enters from stage left with a TV box on a hand truck. He wheels the box around the volunteer sitting on stage, and then returns it to off SL. He then crosses SR to the chalkboard. PENN Sony 27 color portable Trinitron television with wireless remote. Goddamn damn damn damn damn! I tried to tell you, Cherie. I said it louder. We've been doing this bit for over four years, and no one has won the goddamn television. But don't you worry, Cherie, its just an empty box cause just like Doug Henning we deal with illusion. TELLER adds the numbers up. PENN You can sit down there, Cherie. CHERIE sits down. PENN takes climbs down the SL ladder from the box to the stage. PENN Turn to chapter seven in John, Mike. And when you get to John seven, Mike, would you tell me how many verses there are, please? The verses are the little numbers. Like, 50 or 55, I imagine. Probably a little quicker to look at the last one than it is to count them. 53, okay. Now, Mike, I like to think of all art, but especially the Penn and Teller show as a microcosm for our lives here on this planet. The way Shakespeare expressed this was to hold the mirror up to nature. Now we've been doing our damndest to accomplish that, first of all with the darts being thrown, we had a combination of fate Now fate is always there. We didn't have to add that in, we already had fate we also had skill, and in Lorenza's case, maybe a wee bit of chance, I wasn't sure. We were led to believe by Cherie it was totally chance. But once in a lifetime, or dare I say it, Mike, once in a century, a man comes along who is completely unfettered by chance or by skill or by fate. Heres a man who just sees what he wants and unbridled, reaches out and grabs it. Now Jimmy Swaggart claimed to be this man, but I'm willing to bet its really Mike. PENN climbs down the ladder from the box to the stage. PENN I want you to look down here at 53 of these verses in John, Chapter 7, and I want you to choose any one your little heart desires. But wait, hear me out, Mike. I don't care how you pick, man. If you've got a favorite verse in John, chapter 7, by all means, consider it. If you've got a favorite concept, favorite place on the page, even a favorite number is fine, but however you pick, I want to hear a number from you when you finally choose, and there are three rules I'd like you to follow. They're simple, Mike. First rule: do not make up your mind for sure until I snap my fingers again. I need an open mind from you until then. Second rule: do not change your mind. And the third rule is, Mike, the whole time you're looking down here, trying to concentrate with these hot lights on you and people staring at you, I'm gonna be messing with you. Okay, Mike? PENN kneels down beside MIKE. PENN Lets look down here together, shall we? Now you're going to have to read this aloud in front of what is laughingly referred to as your peer group, so I suggest you pick a short one, and also stay away from the hard words, neither one of us wants to have to say Meglanites up here on stage, okay? Lets see what we got here. Oh, we've got Sodom and Gomorrah, if you want to pander to the home team. The oxen shall stall. I hate when that happens, don't you? And while you're looking down here, Mike, I want to talk to you guys. I want to talk to you guys about my main man Mike. I call Mike my main man not only because its really alliterative, but also because Mike has the toughest job of any human being we call up here from the audience. Oh yeah, Susan, you floated in the air, you big cry baby, we told you what to do. We held your goddamn hand for chrissake. Not Mike, man. Mike is cut loose. Little dome of anarchy over him. He's a wild man, so bug off. Look at them Mike. Look at em, look at em, look at em. They're all ambivalent towards you. Cause half of each of these people sincerely want you to screw us up, and you want to do what's right, don't you, Mike? Sure you do. Let me borrow this for a second. PENN takes the Bible and goes to a person in the front row. PENN If you were Mike, which is one of the few things I still believe in this crazy godless universe, is that you aren't Mike, but if you were Mike, would you have any idea which one of these verses in Chapter 7 of John I'd want you to pick? Does it say in yellow highlighter, Pick 4, Mike, or I'll rip your face off. Is it underlined, starred, is it checked, is there any sort of hint at all, writing in the margins? Get down on your knees and thank God you weren't born like Mike. PENN returns the Bible to Mike. PENN Up here on stage, cut loose, sailing without a compass. Now we don't know very much about Mike. Mike could already have a favorite number he always uses. Mike could have a apartment number lower than 53.

Mike could already have a favorite verse in this chapter. He could have vanity license plates that say John 7, 12, we don't know. But he's picking one verse and one verse only. The one verse that he believes will best sum up this evenings performance. He's looking down there, he's concentrating. He's picking that one verse. We have chosen John, Chapter 7, verse... PENN claps his hands and then snaps his fingers. MIKE 46. PENN Say again? MIKE 46. TELLER writes this number on the chalkboard. PENN Verse forty- six. Well, how did we get here? PENN and TELLER, ala David Byrne, hit their respective foreheads and do the Same as it ever was gesture from the Talking Heads video. PENN First of all, who threw the dart into John? That was Miles. Where you at, Miles? Miles, you over here, Miles? Where you at, Miles? Yeah, Miles, stand up right where you are, would you please, Miles? Come down here into the aisle, would you please? Now, Miles, a weird thing is going to happen, Miles, man. Now some of the people, Miles, who are into the magic of the show are going to stay staring right up here at the stage. They're going to stay glued right to Teller. But some of the rest of the people who are following the plot of the show are going to look at you. Now anyone that looks at you, Miles, you stare right back at them. See that guy there? Stare him down, man. Over there, stare them down, stare em down. Look deep into their eyes. The eyes are the window to your soul, Miles. Let them look deep in your eyes. Deep in his eyes. I want to see a polite show of hands. How many people here believe that this man, Miles, is a professional but very young- looking, dart - thrower who comes in every night, chucks a dart into John then sits down? Show of hands, please? Beautifully done, Miles, you were worth every penny. You can sit down. How many people in the balcony believe there is nothing on this board except John over and over again and spelled differently? Robin, was I trying to get you to pick John? Into the microphone.   ROBIN No. PENN Did I say it louder? Did I say Do you want Exodus or John? Did I make John seem more attractive to you, thusly, like, hey, Robin, do you want John? Do you think if you had picked another one, like, oh lets say Exodus or Numbers, I would have kept bullying, badgering, confusing you 'til you changed your mind to John, then cut the game right there? Only one question matters Robin. Did you think at the time. I don't give a damn about now, I live in the past, I always have.   Did you think at the time, that you had a totally free choice?   ROBIN Yes. PENN Good! You're going to love the next election, Robin. Could I have the microphone back, please? What I want to know is, who is this audience really believes we were able to build electromagnets into fuzzy dice? PENN picks up a fuzzy die. PENN I don't think so. PENN kicks the wading pool across the stage and throws the dice against the SL curtain PENN We cant even find our car. Now we come to my man Mike. PENN approaches whomever is with MIKE. PENN Are you here with Mike tonight? Go ahead, deny him three times, are you here with Mike tonight? Has Mike been acting a little bit weird lately, a little bit nervous, a little bit uptight? Phone ring around the house, you pick it up, its like mmmmmmm. He picks it up, its like Pick forty- six, Mike! Newspapers, magazines, Falcon and the Snowman kinda stuff. Things around the house you cant explain. Mike has money, he has cars, he has hookers running amuck? Have you ever seen Mike sit onstage with such a condescending smile towards a professional entertainer before? WHOMEVER IS WITH MIKE No. (Or Yes. Or Often. Or whatever.) PENN Thank you. PENN returns to the stage. PENN Bust it, Mike. Read it for me, man. Read it for me, please. You've got a microphone right there. Into the microphone. MIKE The officers answered, Never a man spake like this man. PENN Now take about, I don't know, 15 minutes and kind of apply that to your personal life would you please? You don't have to do that, Mike. Oh, Mike, man, wow, wow! Its been a great day for you. Cause not only did you pick a swell verse, which is going to get you a lot of applause when you sit down, but also I covered for the hookers so you're golden. Thanks an awful lot, and do watch your step, theres going to be a crossfade. Mike returns to his seat. TELLER puts green chair back next to the stage right prop case. PENN Mike. Mike! Saint John, Chapter 7, Verse 46. The officers answered, Never a man spake like this man. Ahhhhhh! PENN falls to the ground as if hit by a diamond bullet. He jerks and rolls around screaming. TELLER experiences shivers up his spine. PENN Wow! Teller, did you just get that Damascus thing? Its like a diamond bullet. I'm looking down here at a verse supposedly picked at random, and I'm saying to myself, Goddammit! Out of the whole Bible, what could sum up the Penn and Teller show this Friday night better than John, Chapter 7, Verse 46, about the officers answering, and this is the kind of uncanny miracle that happened to us on the road every day. PENN slams the Bible shut and tosses it to TELLER, who puts it on the SL green chair. PENN Yo! Stuart, scamper time. C'mon, Stuart. Bring your stuff with you right up here, Stuart. Come on, Stuart. Nice New York scamper, no L.A. avocado scamper. STUART comes up onto the stage carrying the plastic sheet and hammer. PENN drops the hammer on the floor and takes the plastic. He gives one end to STUART and has him stand SR. PENN holds the other end and stands SL. PENN Right up here. Now, Stuart, before the show really started I asked you to come up here and sign that bottle, right? In a symbolic, weird sort of way, I kinda gave the piece of paper in the bottle there to you. And you've been looking up here during the boring parts of the show, and saying to everyone around you, Yo! That's my paper up there, right? You're feeling righteous, right Stuart? I want to ask you a couple of fairly paranoid questions, Stuart, but before I do, I want to make you a promise and that is, Stuart, I want to promise you that I'm not going to insult your intelligence up here on stage by expecting you to pretend to believe in things that I myself don't believe in. What I mean is, Stuart, I'm not going to give you any of that hippie garbage, about the cosmic plain, and powers greater than us, and the great beyond, cause Stuart, man, I don't believe in nothing. I think that Jeanne Dixon and all the astrologers, and Kreskin and Uri Geller and all the psychics and the faith-healers and the fire walkers and the tarot readers and the trance-channelers, they are all, every one of them, just liars. And they're lying to themselves and/or everybody else. Every single reputable test of the paranormal has come out zero, zip, zilch, it don't happen, man. If you want to use some common sense, ask yourself, if somebody, anybody, could predict the future, if they could read minds, even the smallest percentage over chance, wouldn't these people end up working for the government or the Stock Exchange or hang out in Atlantic City? They would not be bending spoons and doing two- bit shows in Times Square, right? Heres the paranoid part, Stuart. Is it your birthday today? STUART Its not. PENN Its not? STUART No. PENN Anniversary of any sort? What I'm getting at Stuart, is there any reason that one of your wacky, wild, zippy, zany friends - and I know you got em, Stuart - any reason one of them friends would have hired 952 unemployed, Equity, Broadway actors to sit in these seats, and act like they were watching a show just to blow your mind, freak you out, mess with that gray matter? Is it possible you're the only one here that bought a ticket and everyone else is cast? Bigger cast than Cats or Les Mis? No wonder we're always sold out, its one ticket, Stuart, its one ticket. Nothing seemed weird to you at all, huh? Every show you go to, women named Susan walk up on stage and oat? You didn't notice that Mike was a groove machine from stem to stern? Stuart, what the hell were you thinking when the whole audience would laugh in unison at jokes that just weren't funny? Use your head, Stuart, Robins been on The Love Boat more than four times. Imagine, if you will, a man named simply Stuart, one name like Aristotle or Prince. Comes into a Broadway theatre, only to enter the twilight zone. TELLER smashes the bottle with the hammer. PENN

169

"Sorry. Would you unlock the upstairs again? I'm afraid I've left my overcoat on the second floor."

"Your *overcoat*?" Martin looked amused. "Certainly, Mr. Derrickson." He took the keys from behind the counter, walked with me to the door and unlocked it.

I ran upstairs and looked on the ledge of the deep-set window by the children's section. No coat. I checked by the occult books. Still no coat.

I hurried back down. "Has anybody been upstairs since I came down?"

Martin was peering into an open *New York Times.* He lowered his newspaper and grinned at me knowingly. "No, sir. Not that I noticed."

"Damn. I think somebody stole my overcoat. Are you sure you haven't seen it? A mid-thigh thing, brown leather, with a red hunting hat stuck in the sleeve?"

He suppressed a laugh. "An overcoat and a hunting hat, Mr. Derrickson?"

"What? It's not a joke. My wallet and my checkbook are in it."

He winked at me. "Oh, I'm sure it will reappear. Let's forget the tax and make that seven dollars even."

I had met crazy people and callous people in Manhattan before, but this was really too much. Didn't he realize how much inconvenience this was going to cause me? I reached into my trousers pocket, and, relieved to find all my cash still there, took out a ten-dollar bill and flung it on the counter.

He made change and put the books into a brown paper bag.

"There you are. Sorry about the Disappearing Coat Trick. Good thing it's not *snowing* outside, eh?" He burst out laughing.

Speechless, I picked up the change and the bag and started out of the shop.

"Thank you, Mr. . . . Derrickson!" he called after me between spasms of laughter. "Have a good matinee!"

The first thing I noticed after I slammed the door behind me was the temperature change. It had warmed from a bitter eighteen degrees to what must have been well over sixty. The gray, overcast sky was a bright blue, and it seemed for all the world like spring.

Well. That was more like it. I didn't *need* the stupid coat. I'd miss that hat, though. They didn't make them like that anymore. A red, plaid hunting hat, like Elmer Fudd's.

And yet . . .

The weather was so glorious, it was hard to stay angry. Why waste this day? The credit cards were insured, and I had a pocket full of cash. Good, I thought. Mustn't let a little commonplace robbery ruin my sabbatical. I bought a newspaper.

"Have a good matinee!" he had said. Well, perhaps I *would*. I'd take a train to the theater district and choose a show from the newspaper as I rode. Humming to myself, I crossed City Hall park and descended into the subway station.

As I turned from the token booth I stopped short.

I was staring at a poster for a Broadway show. It was a six-foot-tall photograph of two men in matching gray business suits: a large bespectacled fellow with an extravagant forelock and a smaller pale man with round, boneless cheeks, pointed chin, large eyes, receding sandy hair, and a smirk.

The copy on the poster read:

NOW ON BROADWAY!
at the RITZ THEATER

TUESDAY—SUNDAY at 8:00 • SATURDAY & SUNDAY at 3:00

There it was, that name again, as if it were following me.

I am not a superstitious person. I don't believe in synchronicity, fate, karma, or any of the other unverifiable hypotheses of order of the universe. It was a coincidence, a startling one, yes, but nonetheless a product of chance in nature.

Still, how could I decline a six-foot-tall invitation?

I sat down in the subway train and opened the newspaper to find the address of the Ritz Theater. The train stopped dead. I looked up. A teenage boy and girl sitting across the aisle were staring at me. I stared back. They looked away. The train started up. I looked down at the paper again. The Ritz, I read, was on Forty-eighth Street, west of Broadway.

"Excuse me." The girl of the teenage couple was calling to me across the aisle. "Could you tell me what time it is?"

"A little after two."

"Thank you," she said, and started to giggle.

Presently we came to my stop, Times Square. As I stepped out the door of the train I could hear the girl talking to her friend. "There! I told you I could make him talk." I glanced back as the train pulled away.

The teenagers were still watching me.

I looked at my watch. It was two-thirty. I was standing in front of the Ritz Theater. No doubt the man whose name was following me around was already backstage, preparing.

I had gathered from the pictures and reviews in front of the theater that he was the small one with the receding sandy hair. I would try to get backstage and meet him. I would show him the books and tell him about the coincidences. The reviews had said that he rarely spoke. But if it turned out that these *were* his books, and I was bringing back a bit of his past, I imagined he'd talk to *me*. He might even give me a free ticket to see his show.

One picture in the display particularly caught my eye. In this one my man was imprisoned and apparently drowning in a glass tank full of water, while his tall partner stood by smiling like Long John Silver.

There must have been something suspicious about the way I was staring at that picture, deep in thought, clutching my brown bag, because I noticed a little boy from the box-office line pointing to me and whispering to his father.

I knocked at the stage door. A burly red-haired man opened the door and said jovially, "We don't want any! Hahaha! Come on in. He's here, Vinnie."

Vinnie, a smallish fellow in his fifties with tinted glasses and a Don Quixote beard, turned away from a black-and-white TV, on which he was watching football. "Well, look who made it! Hey, it *must* be spring, right? He ain't wearing his hat!"

I thought of my lost Elmer Fudd hat.

"How about a doughnut?" A round Irish face with a broad smile poked a box full of doughnuts over my shoulder. It seemed a little strange to be offered food by total strangers, but these people seemed so cordial. I took a jelly.

"Thank you very much. Say, do you think it might be possible to see Mr. Teller for a minute?"

"Vat you vant wit heem?" Vinnie did an impersonation of Peter Lorre. "I *svear* he deedn't do eet, meester. Ve got vitnesses."

Irish with the doughnuts grinned and said in a big voice, "Absolutely. We was there the whole time, officer."

"No, seriously, I have some books I think may interest him."

"Oh, a bookie!" said Irish. "Imagine, Vinnie! A bookie you ain't met!" He laughed.

Vinnie put his arm around me. "We are honored to have you with us, sir. Any bookie of Teller's is a bookie of mine. Help yourself. Go right up the stairs to Dressing Room Two. If you need me, I'll be drawing your bath, sir," he said, holding up the end of a green garden hose. As I started up the stairs, he began to sing, "Fly me to the moon . . ."

At the top of the stairs was a seedy parlor, painted Day-Glo magenta with blue accents, like the inside of a giant heart. There was a couch, an overstuffed chair, a refrigerator, and a small kitchen table with an electric kettle, assorted mugs, and a bowl full of foil-wrapped bags of various kinds of tea. I helped myself to a cup of Earl Grey.

The door of Dressing Room One was open, and I could hear a raspy, forceful voice from inside. "I don't want to be too hard-ass about this, but Teller and I really hate working where they serve liquor. No. We never even played the comedy clubs. I know that, but we *hate* improv."

The door of Dressing Room Two had a red plastic plaque stuck on it, inscribed THE OTHER ONE. It was locked. "Damn," I muttered, taking out my keys, and juggling tea, doughnut, and bag of books. I unlocked the door, kicked the wooden wedge in place to hold it open, and sat down at the makeup table, next to a rack of gray suits.

"Half hour, please. The call is half hour," said a woman's voice over the loudspeaker system.

I looked over at the gray suit hanging freshly pressed on the rack, then turned to the mirror and fluffed my receding sandy hair. A cockroach ran across the tabletop and disappeared into a crack.

I took a large bite out of the doughnut, then thought of the books in the bag from Mendoza's. No. Better to wait. My fingers were all covered with jelly and powdered sugar.

There would be plenty of time to look at the books later.

THE PERCEPTION TEST

(Answer Page)

How many times did *you* spot the **s** on the box in the back cover? The correct answer? It shows up **six** times. Most people overlook either the s in quotation marks or the one at the end of "does."

Now score yourself:

YOU COUNTED	YOUR SCORE
six	Eagle eye
five	20-20
four or less	Get a white cane.

How many
times does
the letter
"s" show
up in this
sentence?

Now Stuart, Teller earns his living doing sleights with these hands you see in front of you here. TELLER takes the corner of the plastic from STUART. PENN I earn my living doing sleights with these hands here. So if you're not a brain surgeon, Stuart, would you reach into the broken glass, and pull out that piece of paper that's in there? Ha! Just kidding Stuart. PENN and TELLER drop the plastic on the stage. PENN And Stuart, would you open it up and in your best, loud, clear Sunday school voice, would you read everything that is written on it, and then turn it toward the audience so that the masses may gawk. Read it out nice and loudly now. STUART he officers answered, Never a man spake like this man. Goodness, gracious, great balls of fire! STUART turns the paper so the audience can see it. PENN You shake my nerves and you rattle my brain! (To STUART) You may keep that. (To audience) That's Stuart there! STUART returns to his seat. PENN You knew we were messing with you! (Singing) Well- ah- well- ah well, the little things that you say and do. Make me want to be with Jews. Now it takes about 15 minutes for the posse backstage to set up the weird half of the show, and during that time there are soft drinks for sale right over here, and also its probably still raining out, but if you want to go outside, at least stretch your legs, get a breath of fresh air. But if you do have a breath of fresh air, please make sure you have a cigarette to keep that yin and yang kind of balance. Well see you back here in about 15 minutes, and most important — rave on.— END OF ACT I. ACT II PENN goes back SR from the audience to put on his jacket. He enters from SR. A CARD TRICK PENN Welcome back. All of the tricks we do in the show are what's called stage magic. But theres another kind of magic called close-up magic, which is magic done for up to 10 people at a time. And all the real breakthroughs in sleight-of-hand technology seem to take place in close-up. And when magicians are getting together to show off for one another, what's called in the trade finger-flinging, they almost always work in the close-up form. And because theres such way cool, wicked decent stuff happening in close-up, we want to do thing for you. And because it is close-up, I need a couple of people from the audience to watch this from onstage. Let me just see who we got here. Ma'am, what's your name? Would you come up here please, Jeanne? Yeah, right up here, please. Now I'm going to show you something you probably already know, but I'll just run it by you again. Its how to use a stopwatch, Jeanne. Right up here. VOLUNTEER comes on stage. PENN Now, Jeanne, as you can see this button here is marked, Start/Stop. When you hit that button, move your thumb away, these numbers go up by themselves. The numbers, of course, represent seconds. I need a readout from you every 30 seconds. So when it hits 30 seconds, you'd go 30 seconds, at 1 minute you'd go, 1 minute, at 1 minute 30 you'd go, 1 minute 30, and you'll have plenty of time to figure out the rest of the numbers. And, Jeanne, heres a microphone, and please don't be afraid of it, okay? Bring it right up to your lips, and say the numbers right into the end of it, very, very loudly. I will be talking and you have to try and get over me, and I'm fairly loud. Theres your microphone, theres your stopwatch, and I'll tell you when to start it. And theres a timekeeper box for you here. PENN leads JEANNE to box downstage left. PENN And if you stay in this box, Jeanne, the lights will stay focused on your face, and you won't have shadows across there. You'll look much better, okay? PENN crosses to SR. PENN Okay, now I need someone else here. Yeah, how about you, Sir, what's your name? VOLUNTEER Bill. PENN Could you come up here, please, Bill? Right over here, Bill. I'm going to do a card trick for Bill, and most times when magicians do card tricks, and we're no exception to this, I'm going to cop to it, they'll start with an open box. And the reason we start with an open box of cards, like on TV, is not because of convenience, but because once the cards are out of the box, we can gimmick the deck. We can stack it, we can mark it, and theres probably a couple dozen other things you've never heard of, like corner- shorting, and crimping, and so on. So when magicians do card tricks for one another, they almost always start with a sealed deck of playing cards, like I'll be using for Bill. Now, Bill, those two lights that are focused on Jeanne, there are people back as far as those lights, for whom this is a very small prop. So to give those people something to look at, Bill, would you go over and grab that scuba tank, and don't try to lift it, its stupidly heavy, and drag it over to right about here, would you Bill? Yeah, right over here. Rather slowly, Bill. And, Jeanne, you better watch your ass for a second. As BILL drags the scuba tank SR, MARC pushes a water tank with TELLER inside CS. TELLER is breathing through a regulator attached to the scuba tank. PENN Right over here, Bill. Great. Wonderful, wonderful. Now like I said, to make it a little more interesting visually, my partner, Teller, is going to be holding his breath for the entire card trick. Now god forbid we should make anyone anxious, Teller is not holding his breath now. As you can see by the hose going in and the bubbles coming up, Teller is breathing relatively comfortably through this scuba regulator, and won't actually stop breathing until the card trick proper begins. Now, Bill, if you would, would you grab that lock off of the key, leave him with the key, but grab the lock, pull it off the key, and feed it through the hasp, and lock it securely, locking him securely in his underwater coffin, okay? Thank- you, Bill. Now this aquatic phone booth was built especially for Teller. As you can see, the bars come below the surface of the water to stop him from floating to the top, or forcing his nose or mouth to the top to breathe that glorious air that we all too often take for granted. Now Teller is holding the key to this lock right here, and, indeed, quite literally to his life, in his upstretched left hand, and has sworn on his honor as a gentleman, that he will not relinquish this key until these supremely skilled hands find the card selected by Bill. Now for those of you who are trivia nuts, the worlds record for holding ones breath, on purpose, is 5 minutes and 35 seconds, and is held like so many other records in this business, by the great Harry Houdini. Now, Houdini was breathing regular air. If you hyperventilate with pure oxygen, you can go a tad longer, but it is extremely dangerous. Now if 5 minutes and 35 seconds does not seem particularly long to you, I challenge you to hold your breath along with Teller - stay in your seats - but take a deep breath, and hold it, when I start the card trick, until I find the card. Now, Jeanne, I have not forgotten you. What I'd like you to do is stare right at TELLER's lips, and the second that regulator comes out of his mouth, stopping his breathing, hit that button on the right. And right after you hit it, would you glance down at it and make sure that its functioning properly, that the numbers are going up, and so on. And when you get to 30 seconds, start your readout, and remember, Jeanne, the louder, the better. We want it very, veryloud, if you could. Watch his lips closely and be ready. Now, Bill, would you grab this hose here, and very gently wrench the regulator out of TELLER's lips, would you please? BILL pulls the regulator out of TELLER's mouth. PENN There we go! Okay. And Bill would you do me a favor and just take the regulator and the tank and drag it over to the lovely and talented Marc Garland, our Director of Covert Activities, as featured in the New Yorker Magazine. Everything working fine, Jeanne? JEANNE Yes. PENN And as soon as you get back here, Bill, well start the trick. BILL takes the tank and regulator stage left to MARC. MARC stalls BILL for a bit. MARC strikes the tank and regulator, while BILL returns to stage left. TELLER signals him to hurry along. PENN Right over here, Bill. Now, Bill, when magicians are doing tricks with a supposedly sealed deck - 30 seconds! - Right. Nice and loud and out to them. Real loud. That was a good first time, though - they will slit the bottom, pull out the deck, gimmick it, put it back in and Scotch Tape it back up again. Is there any Scotch Tape on there, Bill? BILL Uh, no. PENN Okay, would you please remove just the shrink wrap, don't break the seal, yet. Remove the shrink wrap and then examine the seal that's on there. Just throw the shrink wrap on the floor there. Now these seals are guarded about as closely as currency or stamps by the U.S. Playing Card company, because the seal is important to the integrity of the gambling industry. JEANNE One minute! PENN Has that seal been tampered with at all? Okay, would you please open that? One minute are we at? Yeah, nice and loudly. Break the seal with this buttery knife, would you, Bill? Okay, would you reach in and remove the deck of cards, throw the box on the floor. You'll find an advertising card on the face, two jokers on the back, remove them both and throw them on the floor. The jokers on the back, too. And please, Bill, shuffle the cards thoroughly and take your time unless you have a thread of human decency anywhere in your body. How we doing here? JEANNE Fine. PENN Okay. I didn't mean fine, actually, I wanted the time. What's that? JEANNE 1 minute 30. PENN I wasn't inquiring about your health. And, Bill, you all set? BILL Yep. PENN Now this is the first time I've touched this deck from a sealed pack, and what I'm going to do is I'm just going to fan them out, no monkey business, just fan them out, and I want you to pick a card. Make sure you have a free choice, if you want to change your mind go ahead, but take one card only. Don't let me see it, please, be very careful. And then wait until I'm turned around and then show the card to the audience. And show it to the balcony as well. PENN turns his back. TELLER turns in the water tank and hides his face. PENN He's showing the card around, Teller! JEANNE 2 minutes! PENN 2 minutes, Teller, 2 minutes! When you're done showing that card around, Bill, would you please take this marker, open it, take the cap off, and sign your name on the face of the card. Not on the back, on the face. The face is the side of the card that's different from all the others. The side with the spots and pips and values. Sign it large, but so it could not be duplicated or forged in any way. When you've signed the card, please give me the pen back with the cap on if you would. Okay, and show your signature on the card to the audience and the balcony, please. Okay? JEANNE 2 minutes 30. PENN Y'all set there, Bill? Back over here, Bill. Don't let me see the card. Now you haven't crimped it or anything have you? Its very easy to find a crimped card in a new deck. BILL No. PENN Okay lets place it right back in the deck. I will shuffle it in. Now I will find that card chosen by you from a sealed deck. What are we at, Jeanne? JEANNE 2:45. PENN 2:45, Teller, and we be jammin'. I have not asked you your last name yet, Bill. What is your last name? BILL Panzer. PENN Panzer? And do you go by Bill or William most of the time? BILL Bill. PENN Bill. Do you use a middle initial? BILL Not really. JEANNE 3 minutes. PENN Not really. Okay. Bill Panzer. Hold your hand out, would you please, Bill? PENN counts cards into BILL's hand as PENN spells his name aloud. PENN B-I-L-L. Panzer. P-A-N-Z-E-R. Bill Panzers card. PENN Did you sign it with Bill or Panzer? BILL Excuse me? PENN Did you sign it with Bill? Did you sign the card with Bill? BILL Yeah. Its the wrong card. PENN Ooh. No problem. Ha! JEANNE 3:30. PENN 3:30. Okay. B-I-L-L- P-A-N-Z-E-R Bill Panzers card right there. Again, its the wrong card. PENN Is that youre card? BILL No. PENN Now, when you wrote on the card, it did come out on it, right? BILL Yeah. PENN Now I don't seem very worried, Bill. And the reason is that before the show even started, I put a card in my left- hand suit jacket pocket. But to make it a little more interesting, I put the card in an envelope. PENN reaches into his pocket and suspiciously pulls out an envelope. It looks like he's putting a card in it and sealing it. PENN Has that envelope been tampered with in any way? BILL No, its sealed. JEANNE 4 minutes. PENN Theres no slit - 4 minutes, good. PENN has BILL hold the envelope up to the light. PENN You see theres a card in there, right Bill? Would you read what it says on the envelope, please. Loudly. BILL Friday, June 12th, 1987, 5:37 pm. PENN Which, if you believe what you read, is before the show even started. What are we at, Jeanne? JEANNE 4:15. PENN 4:15. Now, Bill, what I want you to do, this I want you to do is to rip the top off this envelope, remove the card carefully, verify that it is the proper suit, and the proper value, and your name on it, its not a forgery. When you're sure its your card, remember, you have the punchline, not me, so loudly say, Yes, Penn, that's my card, and then show it out to the audience, would you please? Wait until I tell you. What're we at? What're we at? JEANNE 4:27. PENN 4:27. Okay, go, go. JEANNE 4:30. PENN goes over to the tank, and gets ready to take the key from TELLER and release him. BILL That's it, Penn... That's not it. PENN That's not it? PENN and TELLER exchange looks. PENN crosses back to BILL and takes the envelope. He checks to make sure there isn't another card inside. He checks his pocket. He has screwed up the trick. JEANNE 5 minutes. PENN Thank you! I just palmed off the wrong card, that's all. PENN realizes he better let TELLER out. PENN Teller? PENN goes over to the water tank and tries to get the key from TELLER. PENN I, ah, I cant find the card, Teller. I lost it in the shuffle. Just give me the key, Teller. TELLER pulls the key down into the tank so PENN cant reach it. PENN Teller! Its not your fault. Don't be a jerk. Teller, give me the key! Teller! Give me the - Teller! Teller! Give me the - Teller! Teller! Give me the key! Teller! Give me the key! Don't be a jerk, man! TELLER points back at BILL, indicating that PENN should find the card. PENN returns to BILL and starts counting off cards. PENN B-I-L-L P-A-N-Z-E-R. Goddamnit! Wrong card. JEANNE 5:30. PENN 5:30? (To himself, but everyone can hear) 1- Mississippi, 2- Mississippi, 3- Mississippi, 4- Mississippi, 5- Mississippi. (Turning to TELLER) Congratulations, Teller, you broke the record. B-I-L-L P-A-N-Z-E-R. Jesus. How old are you, Bill? BILL 31. PENN 31, huh? Add the 3 and the 1 together, that gives 4. 1-2-3-4. Its still the wrong card. TELLER, having changed his mind, is trying to get PENN's attention to let him out of the tank. PENN 1-2-3-4. Dammit! JEANNE 6:00. PENN Thanks. Ah, was it a red card or a black card that you had? BILL Black. PENN Black. B-L-A-C-K. Its the wrong card. TELLER throws the key at PENN's head. He is starting to drown. PENN Bill, its on the floor, help me out here, Bill, would you, please? PENN and BILL begin looking through all of the cards on the floor. TELLER is thrashing and drowning. PENN (on the floor) Did you see a card? Did the cards land here? Yeah. Its somewhere on the floor, Bill. It was a number card, is that right? TELLER is dead in the water. JEANNE 6:30. PENN 6 minutes 30? Grab the key and let him out. Let him out, Bill, I'll find the card. Let him out, let him out. The keys right there. Did it come back this far, any of them? BILL tries to unlock the padlock. The key doesn't work. PENN Just let him out, Bill. Hell be out just let him out, okay, Bill? We're okay now, just let him out, Bill. Its a copy, jiggle it, for chrissakes, Bill. Jiggle it! Jiggle the goddamn key! BILL Its the wrong key! PENN What're we at, Jeanne? What're we at? JEANNE 6 minutes, 48 seconds. PENN 6:48? Yeah. Screw it, Bill, he's brain-dead. PENN comes back onstage and tries the key in the lock. Its just the wrong goddamn key. PENN That's just the wrong goddamn key, Bill. JEANNE 7:00. PENN Bill, theres a rule in circus, that whenever someone's doing a dangerous stunt, they're ultimately responsible for their own rigging. So although the roustabouts may set up the high- wire, its always the walker himself that checks the turnbuckles the final time. So it was clearly TELLER's responsibility to make sure this was the right key. And I don't think theres really a... JEANNE 7:30. PENN Thanks. ...theres really a court in the world that would blame you for this, Bill. Even though you locked him in and took his air hose. PENN brings BILL with him DSC, and bows his head reverently. PENN I was 5 years old in 1960, when a man from Hibbing, Minnesota changed his name from Zimmerman to Dylan, and went on to change a decade. In my youth it seemed like the people in this country were more concerned with truth, honesty, and justice, than just the money of the 50s. When I graduated from high school in 73, the pendulum had swung back to creature comforts and climbing the corporate ladder. Its now 1988, I am 33 years old, and I would like to think that one man has ushered in the dawning

BEING MORALLY OPPOSED TO THE WALKMAN CARRIES WITH IT CERTAIN RESPONSIBILITIES

by

PENN JILLETTE

I was leaving my business manager's office. The elevator arrived right away and I got on to find there was another passenger. She was black, she had a beautiful smile, her headphones blended with her hair, and she was listening to some pop love song on her Walkman. It was loud, but I couldn't make it out. Maybe I'd never heard it before, but it was a love song. I smiled, slipped on my super-cool candy-red headphones, and turned the Clash's *London Calling* way up.

We had ridden together for several floors when we were joined by one of those bicycle delivery guys. He had a little hat, the tight black bicycle pants with the reinforced crotch; he was Hispanic and had the little tiny headphones that fit right in the ear so you can only see a couple little spots of blue and some wires coming out of the ears. He looked at us, wrote something on a manila envelope, put it in his backpack, and turned up his music. I have no way of knowing what he was listening to, because "Revolution Rock" was filling my head. But whatever it was he was enjoying it. We swayed our heads together in different rhythms.

The three of us rode a few more floors, then were joined by a businesswoman type. She had on one of those female biz suits, and her hair and makeup were soft and natural. I think she ran every morning or at least took a dance class. Through the light tint of her glasses, I saw her look at each of us and roll her eyes up. Then she started shaking her head like we weren't going to notice. My fellow passengers didn't notice, but I slipped my headphones down around my neck and said, "It must sound like Charles Ives out here, huh? Is it too loud for you?"

She gave me this little condescending smile through her tastefully lipsticked mouth and said, "You people just cut yourselves off from everybody, don't you? I mean, it's really bad enough that no one even makes eye contact anymore, but you people just walk around in your own little worlds. We're a culture of very lonely people. It's sad. It's really very sad."

Since the other two people in the elevator were still in their own respective little worlds, I appointed myself spokesperson for us three lonely people. "You were really dying for human contact here, weren't you? Huh? You walked on this elevator and said to yourself, 'Oh, Jiminy Cricket! I really wanted to talk to this delivery boy, this receptionist, and this big ugly son of a bitch with a square head. But, alas, they've cut themselves off from my personal contact. I guess I can't have any meaningful dialogue with them. Darn!' You don't give a yuppie-tweed-fuck about the three of us! You just need something sensitive and humanitarian to talk about over your fuckin' power lunch. . . . I'll make a deal with you—we'll take our headphones off and we'll listen to you, but you better have something to say. And when you ask him what kind of bike he has and he tells you, you better really care. And you better keep us entertained . . . do a little fuckin' dance if you have to! When each of us walked onto the elevator we smiled at one another and you just rolled your fuckin' eyes. So, you want personal contact? Shoot!"

So, this was another elevator ride in the big city during which I didn't fall in love, make a friend, or even set myself up to get laid. But I do enjoy the Clash.

A SURE BET

Most people assume it's impossible to tie a simple overhand knot without letting go of the ends of a piece of rope. Bet your friend that you can do it.

The fact is, of course, that it *is* impossible. But if you follow the instructions and diagrams below, and HANDLE THE ROPE VERY LIGHTLY, you can create the illusion of a knot, take your friend's money, and he'll be none the wiser.

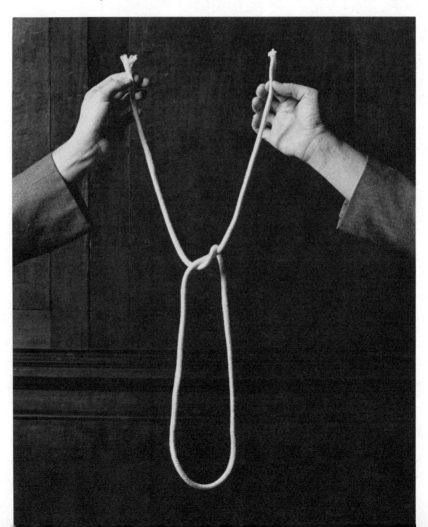

1. Hold a piece of rope about four feet long between the thumb and forefinger of each hand. At *no* time release your hold on the ends. Bring your right hand inside your left wrist, . . .

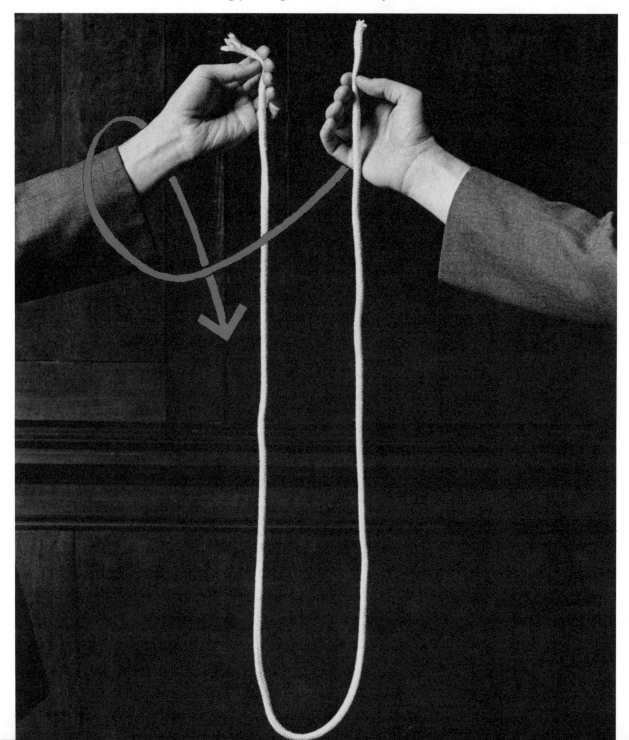

2. And pull about a foot of the rope out over this wrist and down behind. *continued on p. 186*

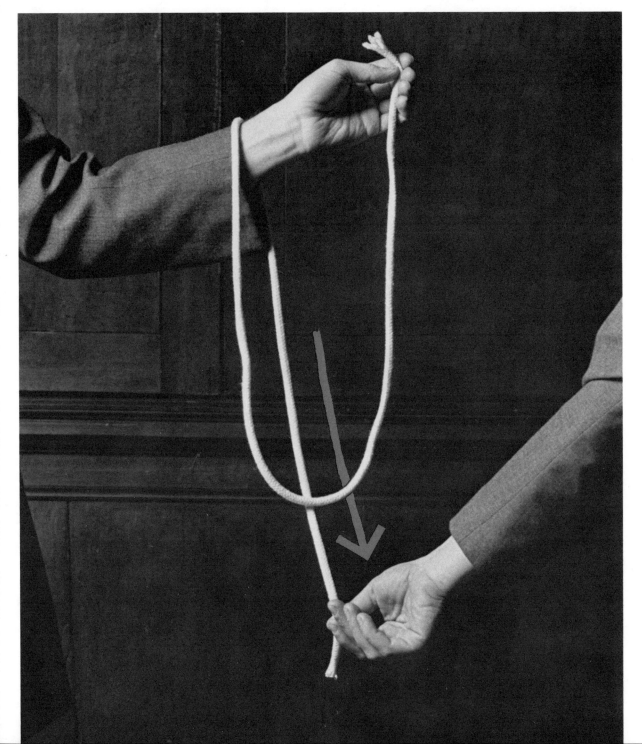

of the new Age of Aquarius, by being willing to die for a principle he believed in, albeit an insignificant card trick. I would like to publicly dedicate my entire solo run on Broadway, to be entitled, simply, Penn, to the memory of this great man. Lets gaze once again on the face of the one true hero of our generation. PENN crosses to the water tank. He begins to turn TELLER around by his upstreched left hand. PENN Ladies and Gentlemen, my ex- partner, Teller. TELLER is facing front now, and everyone can see that the chosen card is on TELLER's face mask. PENN And is that your card, Bill? Is that your card right there, Bill? Thanks so much, you can sit down now. You can keep the key, it doesn't t, anyway. BILL returns to his seat. PENN Thank you. That's his card there! Nine of clubs. And, uh, yeah. Thanks, Jeanne. You did a good job, Jeanne. And watch your step here, we've already had enough tragedy for one night. JEANNE returns to her seat. PENN shrugs his shoulders. He knocks on the front of the tank with the stopwatch. TELLER is dead. PENN picks up a couple of cards and looks at the front row. PENN Did he splash you guys? He did it on purpose, you know. Right to the end he was a mean little bastard. PENN throws a card at the balcony. MARC enters and starts to wheel off the tank with the dead TELLER. PENN Hi, Marc. Is there another key backstage so you could let him out? MARC I'll check. MARC wheels off the tank with TELLER's water-logged corpse. PENN starts singing and playing with the stopwatch. MARC returns to the stage with a push-broom, sweeps up fallen cards, and water. Just as he is about to sweep the debris off SR... PENN Oh, Marc, did you find the key and let him out? MARC reaches into his pocket and pulls out a key. He hands it to PENN. MARC Oh. Is that it? MARC sweeps the debris off SR. As he is about to cross SL... PENN Marc, I cant tell just by looking at it. Would you go back and check it and let him out if its the right key? MARC Okay. MARC crosses SL with the key and exits. PENN stands there looking off after him. After a moment...PENN Nope. MOFO THE PSYCHIC GORILLA MOFO entrance music plays. Loudly. The upstage curtains part, and MOFO rolls straight downstage. The lights slowly come up, revealing him in his total splendor. MOFO (ON TAPE THROUGH SPEAKER ON MOFO UNIT) Good afternoon and welcome to the show. I am Mofo the Psychic Gorilla. You've seen me on national television and read about me in the Guinness Book of World Records. Ten years ago I was a savage beast in the wilds of deepest, darkest Africa. Harvard medical team captured me for use in a biological experiment. First they severed my head, then they performed an operation designed to increase my intelligence and give me the gift of speech. However, my animal sixth sense remained intact allowing me to read minds. PENN, dressed in a bush jacket and safari hat, enters from stage right, flourishes a deck of cards, and shuffles them. He then enters the audience. MOFO (ON TAPE) My colleague Penn is now entering the audience carrying a perfectly ordinary pack of playing cards such as those you might use in your own home. Show the cards to the people, Penn. PENN I just did that Mofo. MOFO (ON TAPE) And give them a little shuffle. PENN I did that, also, you're so psychic, you monkey-face. MOFO (ON TAPE) And now, Penn, select a subject for the first test. PENN steps to the lip of the stage and points at a person. MOFO (ON TAPE) Nice choice Penn. Allow that person to look at all the faces of all the cards, make a clear, conscious selection, and withdraw that card from the pack. Unbeknownst to the audience, THE TAPE is now over, and TELLER is providing MOFO's voice from a microphone backstage as he gets dressed. MOFO (FROM BACKSTAGE) Concentrate on the card please. Mofo sees a black card, is that correct?PENN Yeah- ha, Mofo, that's righty, righty right.MOFO (FROM BACKSTAGE) A spade. Is that correct? PENN Yup, yup, yup, yup, yes. MOFO (FROM BACKSTAGE) The five of spades, is Mofo correct? Thank you very much. I'm Mofo, the Psychic Gorilla. You know, Penn, when I lived in Africa, I used to play cards with the natives. PENN Oh, Zulus? MOFO No, Penn, I usually won. PENN (Laughs heartily) Oh, back off, he's just gorilla. MOFO (FROM BACKSTAGE) Select a second subject now, Penn. PENN moves to the left side of the stage and points at another person. MOFO (FROM BACKSTAGE) Nice choice Penn. Allow that person to look at the faces of all the cards, make a clear, conscious selection, and withdraw that card from the pack. Concentrate on the card please and answer my questions yourself this time in a loud, clear voice straight into the microphone. Mofo sees a black card. Is that correct? VOLUNTEER Yup.MOFO (FROM BACKSTAGE) A club, is that correct? VOLUNTEER Yup. MOFO (FROM BACKSTAGE) The seven of clubs. Is Mofo correct? VOLUNTEER Yup. MOFO (FROM BACKSTAGE) Thank you very much. I'm Mofo the Psychic Gorilla. You know, a lot of people ask me how I do this little miracle. Well, actually, its very simple. First, I imagine myself in your position. A MOVIE SCREEN with a tripod flies in, and a carousel projector starts to project slides on it. The first shows MOFO, seated among the audience members. MOFO (FROM BACKSTAGE) I ask Penn to select a subject. THE SLIDE changes to show PENN selecting MOFO. MOFO (FROM BACKSTAGE) Nice choice, Penn. Allow that person to look at... THE SLIDE changes to show MOFO contemplating a fan of cards. MOFO (FROM BACKSTAGE) ...all the faces of all the cards, make a clear, conscious selection, and withdraw that card from the pack. THE SLIDE changes to show MOFO holding the card in his mouth. MOFO (FROM BACKSTAGE) Concentrate on the card please... The SLIDE shows MOFOS eyes. MOFO (FROM BACKSTAGE) ... and answer my questions in a loud clear voice. Mofo sees... As MOFO speaks, there is a sequence of slides: RED BLACK MOFO (from Backstage) A ... DIAMOND RING CLUB SANDWICH OPEN HEART SURGERY SHOVEL (SPADE). MOFO (from Backstage) A ...BLANK FLYING ACE. MOFO (If its not the Ace) Not the Ace... TWINS (TWO) THREE MARX BROTHERS FOUR MARX BROTHERS FIVE MARX BROTHERS SIX...PACK OF JOLT COLA CHICAGO SEVEN EIGHT BALL NINE POSTER OF NINE TEN BO DEREK (TEN) JACK KLUGMAN QUEEN ELIZABETH I ELVIS (the KING). PENN VALUE of SUIT. That's what it is Mofo. Right there. Right now, MOFO (FROM BACKSTAGE) Thank you very much. I'm Mofo the Psychic Gorilla. SLIDE SCREEN GOES BLACK. MOFO (FROM BACKSTAGE) Now folks, I don't want to insult your intelligence by expecting you to believe that a beheaded, talking gorilla can actually read minds. Of course not. Its a trick. The cards are marked. Show the markings to the people Penn. PENN Okay, Mofo. PENN shows the back of random playing cards, squinting at them. BACKSTAGE, MEANWHILE, TELLER SNEAKS ON STAGE AND HIDES BEHIND MOFO. PENN This heres the ace of diamonds. Mofo added a dot right there with White Out. This here is the two of diamonds. He took one of the dots out over here using Red Out. And using a very clever combination of White Out, Red Out and a teeny- weeny stencil, he actually changed the sex of this angel on this bicycle here. By now, TELLER is in position behind MOFO, and provides MOFO's voice from here until the end of the bit by speaking into the microphone attached to the MOFO unit itself. MOFO Some markings are larger than others. PENN shows a card with 2 of spades written in large magic marker on the back. PENN Theres a good- sized one for you right there. Its just a joke. MOFO But Mofo can read even the tiniest markings at vast distances. Select a subject now, Penn, at a vast distance from the stage. PENN runs up to the balcony. SLIDE OF PARIS. MOFO Too far, Penn. SLIDE OF A PAGODA. MOFO I seem to losing contact. SLIDE OF KANGAROO CROSSING. MOFO Where are you, Penn? We see a SLIDE OF PENN'S POINTING HAND. PENN Right here, Mofo! MOFO Oh, there you are Penn. I see you've already selected a subject. We see a SLIDE OF PENN'S HAND POINTING TO TELLER'S FACE. MOFO Nice choice Penn. Allow that person to look at all the faces of all the cards, make a clear, conscious selection and withdraw that card from the pack. THE SLIDE CHANGES TO SHOW TELLER SELECTING A CARD. MOFO Concentrate on the card, please, and answer my questions in a loud clear voice. THE SLIDE CHANGES TO SHOW ONLY TELLERS EYES. MOFO Mofo sees. Penn, show the person how to hold the card so that Mofo can see the tiny markings from the stage. TELLER peeks out over the top of MOFO. MOFO Mofo is experiencing some technical difficulties. Could someone adjust Mofo please? TELLER comes out SR from behind MOFO, and turns MOFO's head slightly. The microphone that TELLER is holding feeds back loudly through MOFO's amplifier. TELLER strains to see the selected card. He then returns to his position behind MOFO. One might suspect that TELLER is the voice of MOFO. MOFO There, that's better. Mofo sees the (NAME OF CARD) is that correct? SCREEN GOES BLACK PENN (NAME OF CARD) that's what it is Mofo. Right there, right now. MOFO Thank you very much. I'm Mofo the Psychic Gorilla. Oh, Teller, Teller, since you happen to be so near by, why don't you come out on stage where you can see a little better? TELLER brings out a chair from SL behind MOFO. MOFO I know how much you enjoy watching good magic. TELLER sits down stage left of MOFO. MOFO That's it Teller, just sit back and take it easy. TELLER sticks a cigarette into his mouth MOFO You deserve a break after that underwater tour-de-force. PENN brings a VOLUNTEER up on stage and places him between MOFO and TELLER. PENN You're going to do as Shakespeare said and hold the mirror as if it were up to Mofo. PENN hands a hand mirror to the VOLUNTEER. PENN Stand right here next to the sh and the five million volt generator. Good. You're going to bounce Mofo's eyes up into the box, not literally, of course. There you go, Mofo. PENN turns MOFO's head stage left towards the VOLUNTEER. PENN Shell be your mirror, reflect what you are. MOFO Nice choice, Penn. PENN arranges the mirror in the VOLUNTEER's hand so that MOFO can look into it for a trick over- the- shoulder shot. PENN And remember, kid, no matter how fashions change, this angle of incidence will still equal the angle of reflection, okay? Knock em dead, kid. PENN drops the safari hat on the VOLUNTEER's head, covering their face, and climbs up the ladder to the stage right box to have a card selected by someone. PENN Hi, Honey, I'm home! MOFO Good afternoon, kid, what's your name? KID (NAME). MOFO Once again? KID (NAME). MOFO (NAME)? Absolutely correct! Thank you very much. I'm Mofo, the Psychic Gorilla. TELLER turns stage left, just like MOFO. MOFO Alright, Penn, select a subject. Allow that person to look at all the faces of all the cards, make a clear, conscious selection and withdraw that card from the pack. PENN does so. PENN Okay, (VOLUNTEERS NAME), now take the hat and put it so you can use your eyes a little bit. (VOLUNTEERS NAME)? Yeah. Okay. Now, line the mirror up between me and Mofo. Raise it up a little bit higher. Raise your hand up. Raise your whole - yeah, good, good, good. And tilt it toward - ah - back toward me just a tad. Back toward me. I'm the one out here. Keep it up there, okay? All that matters, (VOLUNTEERS NAME) is that you believe its important. That's perfect right there. MOFO This time, Mofo gazes into (VOLUNTEERS NAME)'s mirror. TELLER takes a purse mirror in a compact from his jacket pocket, and holds it up to read the reflection of the card over his shoulder (like a trick shot in a marksmanship exhibition). MOFO ...to see the reflection of the tiny markings on the.. (NAME OF CARD). Is that correct? PENN The (NAME OF CARD) that's what it is, Mofo. MOFO Thank you very much. I'm Mofo the Psychic Gorilla. MARC enters from SR and stops DSR as MOFO speaks to him. MOFO Oh, good afternoon, Marc Garland, Director of Covert Activities. MARC Hello, Mofo. MOFO Marc, I see you're wearing an attractive T-shirt. MARC Thank- you, Mofo. MOFO Where did you get such a chic chemise? MARC At the concession stand in the lobby, Mofo. MOFO Wouldn't they make terrific gifts for all occasions? MARC What a great idea. PENN (to audience member) C'mon, I've had enough, and I'm sure you have, too. I'll buy you dinner. MOFO And now for my final and most difficult feat, Penn has selected a young lady from the audience to accompany him out the emergency exit, A SLIDE, SHOWING PENN and a mannequin leaving the theatre by an emergency exit. MOFO across 48th street ... SLIDE OF PENN AND MANNEQUIN IN STREET MOFO And into Hakata, the Japanese restaurant across the street. MOFO ..the Japanese Broadway bistro, featuring ten traditional noodle soups from the land of the Rising Sun. The slide changes to show a diner at HAKATA. MOFO Health- conscious Americans enjoy the low- cholesterol cuisine created by Hakata's chef, Tsukasa Endo. The slide shows Tsukasa Endo. MOFO Yes, always first-class ingredients and taste at Hakata... The slide shows a bowl of soup and Hakata's hours. MOFO ...The Japanese Broadway bistro featuring ten traditional noodle soups from the land of the Rising Sun. All right, Marc, align your mirror with (VOLUNTEERS NAME)s. MARC Okay, (VOLUNTEERS NAME)? We're going to bounce Mofo's eyes all the way out the door, hang on one second. MARC yells out the rear door. MARC Yo, Jim, you all set out here? All right! Jim, the House Manager, is standing at the door with his hand mirror. We're going to bounce the reflection of the card all the way back to Mofo. Its going to be great. Could you raise your arm up a little bit (VOLUNTEERS NAME)? Raise your arm a little bit higher, no, raise it up, yeah. Now turn the mirror out towards me, yeah, not that far, (VOLUNTEERS NAME). Back towards Mofo a little bit. No, ah, a little bit back towards Mofo, (VOLUNTEERS NAME). Hold it right there, (VOLUNTEERS NAME), that's PERFECT! MOFO I now have a direct line of sight from (VOLUNTEERS NAME)s mirror to Marc Garlands mirror... SLIDE SHOWS MARC GARLAND MOFO to the mirror held by Jim, the house manager, SLIDE SHOWS THE HOUSE MANAGER MOFO to the mirror hanging from the truck and guarded by one of New Yorks nest, SLIDE SHOWS TRUCK AND COP MOFO And finally to, Hakata, the Japanese Broadway Bistro, featuring ten traditional noodle soups from the land of the rising Sun. SLIDE SHOWS HAKATA AD. MOFO Alright, Marc, have the card selected. MARC Select the card! JIM Select the card! MOFO Now have her concentrate. MARC Concentrate! JIM Concentrate! MOFO The young lady, now enjoying one of ten traditional noodle soups, has selected the six of clubs, the six of clubs. Alright, Marc, call her back. MARC Bring her back! JIM Bring her back! MOFO Well, (VOLUNTEERS NAME), Mofo psychically detects that your arm is growing tired, so you can now return the hat and the mirror to me. Put the hat right on my head, I'm the furry one to your right. Just lean over the five-million volt generator, that's it. And set the mirror down anywhere there. Face the audience and take a bow, would you please? And return to your seat. Well done, (VOLUNTEERS NAME). (VOLUNTEERS NAME) returns to her seat. MARC returns from the audience and exits offstage right. PENN and his VOLUNTEER come onstage, PENN holding a large soup bowl. PENN positions her downstage right, gives her the soup, and stands US of her and holds the wireless microphone up for her. PENN Mofo, this is Donna. Donna, Mofo. MOFO Good afternoon, Donna. DONNA Hi. MOFO Donna, when you left the theatre just moment. Donna, when you're addressing me, be sure you look at me and pay no attention to the man in the gray suit, okay? When you left the theatre just moments ago, Donna, where did you go? DONNA We went to the restaurant, Mofo. MOFO By restaurant, Donna, are you alluding to Hakata, the Japanese Broadway Bistro featuring ten traditional noodle soups from the land of the rising Sun? Nice choice, Donna. And while you were there, did you select a playing card? DONNA Yes I did, Mofo. MOFO And when you selected that card, which you are now clutching against your bosom, did you show that card to Penn? DONNA No, I didn't. MOFO Did you show it to any of the other health- conscious Americans?

3. Push the end in your right hand in through the left-hand division of the loop, and back out through the right-hand division.

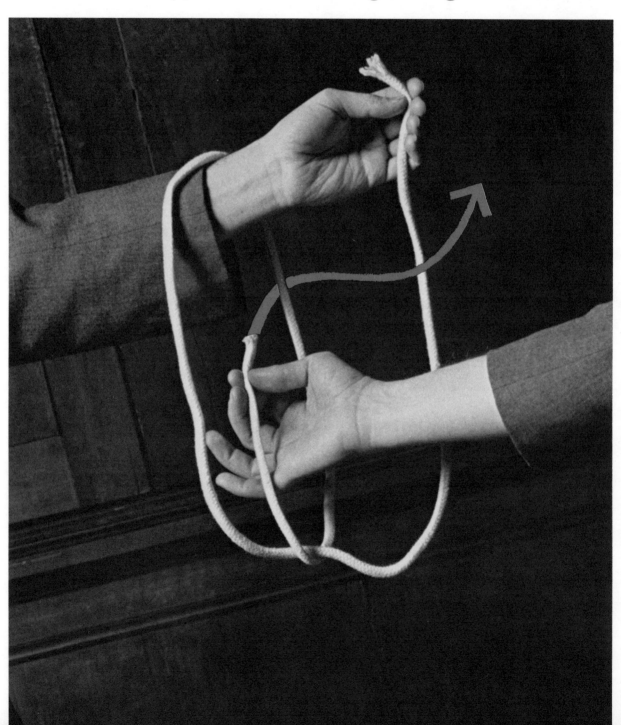

4. Move your hands apart and adjust the loops to look like this:

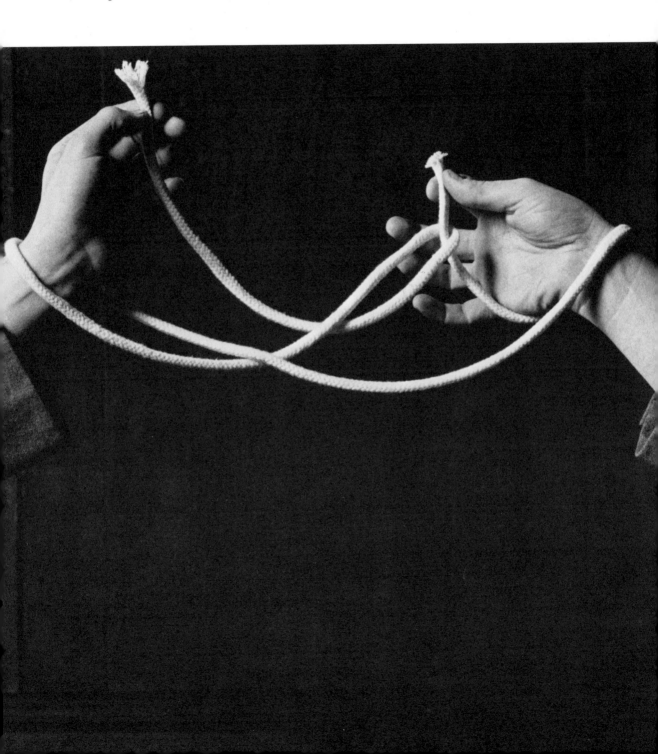

5. **LIGHTLY** toss the rope off your wrists.

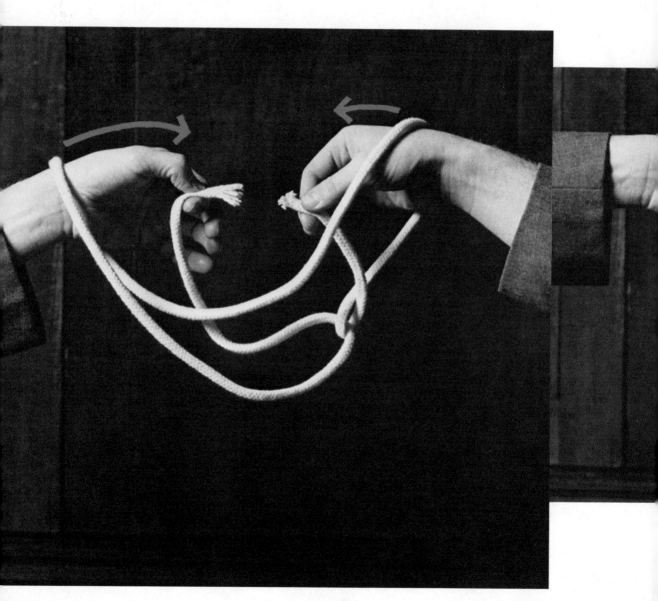

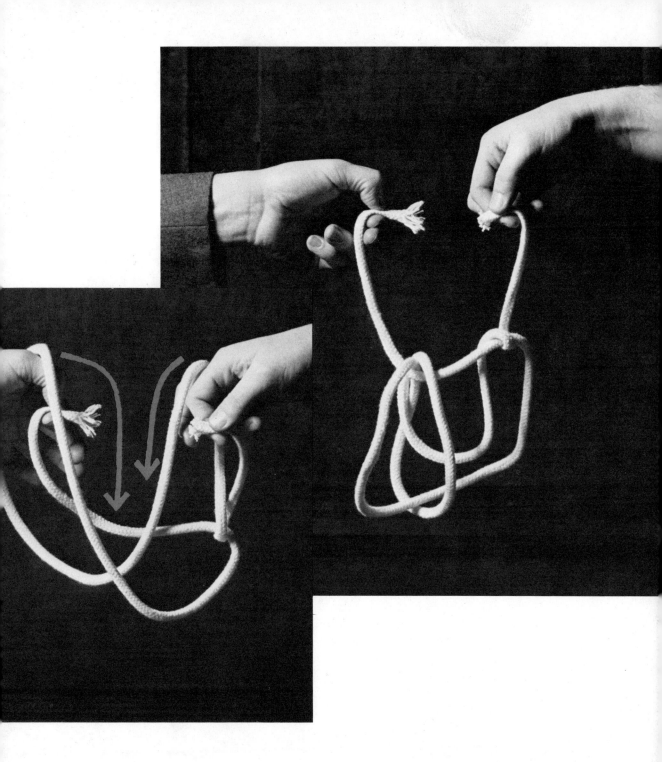

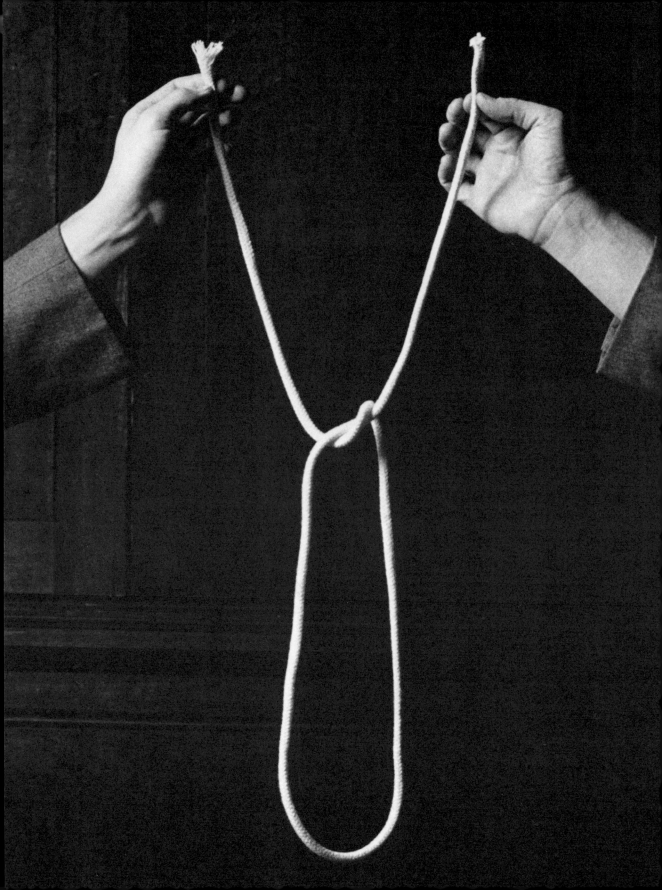

6. There's your "knot."

It can be untied like a regular overhand knot, and not one in fifty people will be able to tell the difference, so you'll be able to collect your bet with impunity.

Once you have the knack, you can even challenge your victim to follow you. Bet your victim double or nothing that he can't do it no matter how closely he watches you. The method is so intricate that nobody will ever catch on just from watching.

There *is* something of a knack involved in learning to tie the illusion-knot. Just follow the diagrams, and remember to handle the rope VERY LIGHTLY.

DONNA No I didn't. MOFO Donna, who in the whole wide world knows which card you selected? DONNA Only me. MOFO Only you, and Mofo, the Psychic Gorilla! For Donna, while you were at Hakata, the Japanese Broadway Bistro featuring ten traditional noodle soups from the land of the rising Sun, Mofo said you had selected the six of clubs. Please show the audience the card that you selected. DONNA shows the card to the audience. It is the correct card. MOFO The six of clubs. Thank you very much. I'm Mofo, the Psychic Gorilla. SLIDE GOES TO BLACK AND SCREEN FLIES OUT. DONNA returns to her seat with the soup. PENN takes the card from the DONNA and exits stage right. TELLER crosses to behind MOFO, leaving the chair in place. MOFO Animal lovers, please take note: Mofo receives no salary whatsoever for his performances here, but subsists entirely on your generosity in purchasing those souvenir t- shirts in the lobby after the show. Thank you and good afternoon from Mofo, the Psychic Gorilla. MOFO moves straight upstage until out of the light. As the MUSIC fades, PENN is singing. PENN I took that girl, home to my place. I was watching every move on her face. She's alright now, she's alright now. Ho! Ho! HOW WE MET? PENN I was dreamin' when I wrote this, forgive me if it goes astray. But I swear I had a feeling, I felt that it was judgment day. PENN and TELLER are seated side by side center stage. TELLER is wearing sunglasses. PENN, legs crossed, is hitting his boot and singing. PENN Seemed it, Mama. The sky was all purple, there were people. PENN notices TELLER next to him and stops singing. PENN Ha-ha-ha-ha! I'm sorry, man. Did that ever happen to you, man, where you're singing and you're rocking and all of a sudden you notice theres a stranger right next to you? It happens to me a lot. Also happens to them guys who were them Walkman headphones a lot too, you know. But I don't wear headphones. I don't need em. Cause I may sound like a lousy singer to you, man, but I sound great in my head a lot of post- production up there. So, you like Prince? I was just singing an old song by Prince. You hip to Prince? Yeah, he had that movie out called, Sign O'the Times. I've thought about that movie alot, and as close as I can figure, man, like, that O, like, it must stand for of. TELLER does not react to any of this. PENN So you've got something like really seriously wrong with you, right? I guess you just don't want to talk to me. If you don't want to talk to me, that's cool. I'll just go back to singing. Its not a threat, I'm just telling you. PENN screams directly in TELLER's ear. PENN Get your motor running. Head out on the high. Ha! ha! ha! I'm sorry, man. I do that every time, man, y'know. Every time I'm trying to impress somebody, maybe make a friend, I end up screaming right in that persons face. I'm not rude, I just, I get these ideas and I push too hard. I want too badly to be liked, that's my problem. You look like you got your problems too, huh? That's okay man, I gotta split. I've had enough of this. I'm outta here. PENN stands up to leave. PENN and TELLER are handcuffed together. PENN Ha! ha! ha! ha! This is great, this is terrific. What is this? Is this, like, one of them gorilla- grams, I mean, someone pays you like 60 bucks and their friend ends up cuffed to a creep? Cause is ain't my birthday, ain't my anniversary, nothing man, so you just handcuffed yourself to a random stranger. Who's bigger than you. We gotta talk. PENN sits down again. He taps TELLER on the shoulder until he gets his attention. He signals elaborately as he speaks. PENN We...are...handcuffed...together. Yeah, I know what you mean. I was shocked at first, too, but I want to get out of these things. I go to certain kinds of parties, and wed look stupid standing side by side. TELLER turns away. PENN grabs his chin and turns TELLER back to him. PENN Sorry, man, I don't mean to grab somebody who's obviously afflicted, but I want to get out of these handcuffs and you aren't exhibiting very much leadership potential. PENN points offstage left. PENN So, I noticed theres a phone booth right over there. Well just go to the phone booth TELLER pulls PENN's tie out from under his vest and jacket. PENN We're handcuffed together and it ends there, okay? Theres a phone booth right over there. Well just go to the phone booth and just call the police, okay, police? They'd send over a cop car, patrol car, cherry topper. I don't know if you've ever looked in the trunk of a patrol car, but they got tool kits in there, and they probably got a hack saw, might even got bolt cutters PENN stands to head offstage left. TELLER doesn't move, and pulls back against the cuffs. PENN Just head over there - Ouch! Let me give you a really simple equation, okay? Metal into flesh equals pain. Its the principle behind bullets, alright? Now, c'mon, lets go to the phone. C'mon. It'll be fun. PENN pats his leg and whistles as if calling a dog. Then PENN pulls TELLER out of the chair by the handcuffs. PENN What did you learn from that experiment, huh? You stood up, apparently against your will without me even touching you, because we are handcuffed together, schmuck! And we're going to that phone if I have to drag you on your goddamned face, now come on. TELLER starts jerking and pulling on the cuffs, circling PENN. PENN What're you doing? Don't be buggin', man, I got a hundred pounds on you. Okay, just chill out. TELLER swings at PENN. PENN blocks the punch and grabs TELLER by the throat. PENN I was waiting for that, I was waiting for that. You're a dead man. You got that? And furthermore, you're dead ass is going to that phone, your dead ass. Cause you played me for a chump, man, and I ain't no goddamn... TELLER collapses in PENN's arms, apparently passed out. PENN Oh, Jesus, God. I got you. Breathe. You're okay. Breathe. You're cool, you're cool. TELLER puts PENN's tie in his mouth and pulls back. PENN, avoiding being choked, grabs the back of TELLER's head and hugs him to his chest. TELLER runs his hand up PENN's arm, as if embracing him. PENN realizes they are no longer handcuffed together, and pushes him away. PENN exits stage left. TELLER sits back down. He pulls the handcuffs out of an inside pocket. Puts one end on his wrist. Places his hand behind the chair and crosses his legs. SHADOWS A rose stands center stage, with its shadow cast on a white screen behind it. TELLER enters stage right with a knife. He crosses to stage center. He reaches up and puts the point of the knife against the paper, next to the shadow of a leaf. He cuts the shadow of the leaf. The corresponding leaf on the flower falls. He crosses stage left. He cuts the shadow of another leaf. The leaf falls. He cuts the shadow of the rose petals. One by one, the petals fall. One last petal remains. TELLER shoves the knife into the paper, and the last petal falls. TELLER looks at what he's done, and casually runs his fingers along the edge of the knife. He pricks his thumb with the knife. His finger does not bleed. Holding his hand up so it casts a shadow on the screen, the shadow of the thumb bleeds down the screen. TELLER places his hand in the blood, and it runs down the screen from under his hand. As he turns and looks out at the audience in shock, he smears the blood down the screen as we fade to black. PENN is center stage in the dark. PENN Everything Teller and I do in this show comes from a love that we share of the American side show, the freak show. PENN lights a candle, and he is seated on a stool center stage. PENN Now the real name for the freak show is the Ten-in-One Show, and its called the Ten-in-One Show because you get ten acts under one tent for one admission price. When I was a kid I used to go to The Franklin County Fair, that's where the carnival came near my home town, and that fair would be in town about ten days every year, and every one of those ten days I'd go to the fair and every day at the fair, I'd wind up at the Ten- in- One Show. And I loved the freak show. I loved it because you'd pay your 75 cents and you were allowed to go into a tent with people who were entirely different from you and then you could just stare at them. And I loved the freaks, but I especially loved the self- made freaks, the fire eater, the sword swal- lower, the tattooed people, because they had made an extra decision to be there, and I can remember standing in that tent watching that fire eater and I swear my whole life was there, it meant everything to me. And my friends would go with me to the Ten- in- One, but my friends were different, cause they took the whole show as some sort of weird challenge, and all through this fire eaters perfect act, my friends would be talking, and they'd be saying stuff like, Oh, I know how he does that, Penn, he just coats his mouth with something. They would try to convince me there was some sort of something you could smear in your mouth, then go suck on a soldering iron, and it wasn't going to hurt you, right? And its not just kids, its also adults, and its usually a man, and its most often a man who's with some woman he's trying desperately, and often pathetically, to impress. And you'll hear this guy who just thinks he has to pretend to know everything, you know? So he's saying stuff like, Oh, don't worry about him honey, he's just using cold fire. Or Needles. Now the reason that Teller and I are working together today, is that about 13 years ago I saw Teller on stage in Jersey, alone and silently eating those needles. When I watched him up on that stage I got the same feeling in my guts that I used to get watching the fire eater as a kid, and I knew we had to work together, and we have been ever since. Now, I go in the lobby during intermission, I talk to folks and I hang out, I go outside. But the whole time I'm talking, I also try to listen, and I've learned a lot from eavesdropping on you guys for all these years. And one of the things I've learned is that theres a certain kind of person that comes to our show, and they may like the show, but they don't get it. And these are the people that cannot accept mystery. Now I want to try to make this clear to you, because I may mean the opposite of what you think. By not accepting mystery, I am not talking about scientists, and I am not talking about skeptics. Cause I'm a skeptic, and I've always felt that skeptics love the mystery, and that's why they don't want to believe in anything. They don't want to have any faith. They either want to have it scientifically proven over and over again, so it cant be denied and it works, or they want to leave it alone. That's it, they're okay with that. The kind of people that cant accept mystery are the kind of people that, when theres a mystery there, they just believe the first thing they're told for their whole life, or they pretend to have an open mind, which means they believe anything that sounds good. Or they'll make up something that makes sense to them and they'll just believe it. Just anything that will shut the mystery out of their heads and stop them from thinking. Because a wrong answer is better than mystery. And I'll hear people doing this even with things as trivial as the Needles. I'll hear guys in the lobby with these real authoritative voices gathering little crowds of people going, Oh, yeah, Needles, yeah, I figured that one out, sure, he's got a little pocket in the back of his throat, its a skin graft from his leg, he just throws them right back in there. Or my favorite one, and I actually heard this, I did not make this up. Some stuff I just make up, but this I heard. There was a guy in L.A., who was talking about candy needles. Now I don't know where this guy ever heard of candy needles, but I assume he figured they're manufactured around Halloween time, as treats for the neighborhood children. I don't know. Anyways, about 20 years have passed, and those kids that I grew up with, I guess they're all still living in Greenfield, Massachusetts, and I turned out to be a fire eater, and the ironic thing I found out, is theres no trick. Not to this. To everything else in the show theres a trick, don't let anybody tell you differently. Susan floating in the air, she wasn't hypnotized, there's no balance point. If you want to try that at home, get a couple of chairs, clear your mind, study Yoga, you'll break your ass. It's a gimmick, it's a lie, it's a cheat, it's a swindle! But this is a stunt, and there's no such thing as cold fire. And if you still believe there is such a thing, and you think I'm be using it, wait 'til I get it lit, you raise your hand, I'll stick it in your eye, prove it to you. TELLER enters from stage left with the fire-eating props. PENN Now TELLER's coming out here with a fireproof camping fuel container. In it is lighter fluid, it's Ronson brand, and he's dipping the torches in. TELLER hands PENN a torch. PENN The torches are cotton, sewn tightly around a threaded, metal rod that's then screwed into a wooden handle. Its not the cotton that burns, its the fuel that burns and the way fire-eating works is this. You've got moisture throughout your mouth, and all that moisture has got to evaporate from any given part of your mouth, before that part will burn. So you learn how to handle the burning vapors, then you gotta make it look good. Now if you've got a lot of saliva in your mouth and that's at least where I try to keep most of mine, you rub your lips right along the cotton and pull that vapor off. Now the vapors still burning, but if you breath in a little bit, the audience cant see it, so you got a beautiful surprise there. Then you just wait 'til the time is right and just let it ow, like it was magic smoke. When you want to put the fire out, theres a move for that, too, and its the move that gives it the name fire- eating. Now, you're not actually eating the flame, but I guess they figured that Oral Fire Extinguishing didn't sound that butch. When you feel your mouth drying out, you close your lips tightly, that cuts out most of the oxygen and (snaps fingers) the fire goes out. Now when I was being taught this, I got burned every time I tried it, and I still get burned occasionally, but the burns you get from fire eating are for the most part extremely minor. They're the kind of burns you get, you know what I'm talking about, when you eat a pizza too fast, and that cheese is gonna snag you, or you gulp some hot coffee. Now I'm not trying to snow you no more I'm not talking no mind over matter jive. Theres no such thing, it just hurts like holy hell. But its not dangerous. The dangerous thing is something lay people don't even think about, and that is every time you do this act, no matter how carefully or how well, you swallow about a teaspoon of the lighter fluid, and that stuff is poisonous, that's why they go to all that trouble to write Harmful or Fatal if Swallowed on every can, and the effect is, to a certain degree, cumulative. Now I say a certain degree, I do eight shows a week, I'm a big guy, its a limited run, that doesn't affect me. Carnies, the real boys, they'll do up to 50 shows a day, and in as little as two or three years that stuff'll build up in their liver and they'll get sick enough, they actually have to take time off and do another line of work in the carnie while that liver regenerates, which, thankfully, it will do. Now I take the time to explain all of this to you in such detail because I think its more fascinating to think of someone poisoning themselves to death slowly on stage than merely burning themselves, and after all, we're here to entertain you. I really tell you this cause this is the last bit in the show, and when you leave here tonight and you're thinking about our show, as I hope you will be, I don't want you to be thinking about how we did it. I want you to be thinking about why. So sit back and relax, I'm going to burn myself. TELLER lights the torch. PENN This move right here and this move right here are called stalling. Now I realize you guys have been sitting in these seats a long time, but if you can just bear with us another moment, wed like to look out at you guys. Cause theres an obvious but still unique quality of live theatre, and that is that while we're doing the show, you're right here in the room with us. And that means we can see you. And if light happens to fall on one of your faces and we catch your eye, well, well look right in your eyes. And well do a small part of the show, couple lines, for you, and I mean, for you alone, you, staring right in your face, only you. And when we do that, and we've picked you, and you know its you, cause you can just feel it, we're not paying any attention to you at all. We're trying to get the laughs, make the tricks work. We cant worry about you individually. So what I'm saying 'convolutely' is that right now is the place in the show we can look at you and we can really pay a little bit of attention. And its really important. And I used to feel that importance should be made explicit, so I would do these little speeches about community and the speeches were superficial and they were contrived, and I really believed them, so they were embarrassing. So now I'm trying to learn to just shut up and look at you. TELLER's got it down. And if you're the kind of person

THE HOUDINI SPIRIT MESSAGE

by

TELLER

I

Bess opened a tearoom after Houdini died. She needed company. She had been married thirty-two years. People knew her only as the widow of her husband. She sat with customers, all down-and-out showbiz cronies, and reminisced about the old days.

Weeping in her tea, she'd show her friend how Harry had inscribed inside her ring the words of "Rosabelle," the song she sang when they first shared a bill on Coney Island, where they fell in love:

Rosabelle, sweet Rosabelle,
I love you more than I can tell.
Over me you cast a spell.
I love you my sweet Rosabelle.

Her friend would smile and ask her for a loan. The tearoom failed.

Bess became an author, wrote a screenplay based on Harry's life. It never sold. She tried becoming what she'd lost—"The Greatest Lady Wizard"—failed and sold her documents and recollections for publication in *Houdini, His Life Story*. The book, made from her notes, included tables of the code that she and Harry used in vaudeville mind reading.

To the press, Houdini was still news, which meant that Bess now answered questions for him. "Did Houdini think there was a life beyond the grave?"

"He hoped there was, but would not let himself believe until he heard his mother's voice speak through a spirit medium the word 'forgive'—that was her *dying* word, you know. He never heard.

"He was afraid that if he died before me, crooked mediums would come and take advantage of my grief, deceive me with their tricks and make me say things that would discredit Harry's work exposing fraud and superstition. So he made a plan that whoever died first would try to reach the other in a code, a system we both knew so well by heart that even death would not make us forget. The medium who brings ten words from Harry will win ten thousand dollars as reward."

Bess made this statement to the *Brooklyn Eagle*, March 27, 1927.

II

In February 1928, the pastor of the First Spiritualist Church of New York, the Reverend Arthur Ford, became entranced by his celestial guide.

He said Cecilia Weiss, Houdini's mother, was present, saying, "All this later life my Harry sought to hear from me a certain word I spoke before I died, 'forgive'—that was the word—his wife Bess knew it, no one else. Contact her. See if what I say is true."

They sent the message on to Bess. She was impressed. "This is the first time," Bess wrote in reply, "that any spirit message had appearance of the truth. Had Houdini heard that word, it would have changed, I think, the whole course of his life. Strange in the message that she called him Harry, not Ehrich as she called him all his life. But, of course, she has that heavy German accent. It really is a trivial mistake."

III

In December 1928, Bess came down with influenza, badly. On New Year's Day she tumbled down a flight of stairs and hurt her back. Delirious, she cried, "Harry, dear, why don't you come back to me from the other side?" She reached her arms out, as though grasping him, and said, "I knew you would come back to me, my dear!" Then she blacked out.

As she lay ill on her couch, two members of Ford's congregation came, bearing a message which they said had come one word at a time through Reverend Ford. It took, they said, ten seances and several months before the ten-word message was complete: "Rosabelle, answer, tell, pray, answer, look, tell, answer, answer, tell."

They saw a look of shock, asked if the words made sense to her. They did. The two advised her to arrange for Reverend Ford to come and hold a seance in her home.

Two days later, Bess was lying on the sofa, a bandage on her head, as Arthur Ford, sitting blindfolded with a handkerchief, went into a trance. As witnesses looked on he spoke the words he'd written in the note, "Rosabelle, answer, tell, pray, answer, look, tell, answer, answer, tell," in a strange voice which he said was Houdini's.

He asked her whether what he said made sense to her. She said it did. Then he went on: "Thank you, sweetheart. Now take off your ring and tell the witnesses what 'Rosabelle' means." Then softly Bess began to sing,

> *Rosabelle, sweet Rosabelle,*
> *I love you more than I can tell.*
> *Over me you cast a spell.*
> *I love you my sweet Rosabelle.*

The Houdini voice explained what this song meant to Bess and Harry, then went on: The strange words of the message were the cues from the Houdinis' vaudeville mind reading. Each word or pair of words stood for a letter of the alphabet. They spelled "believe."

Almost gloating now, the voice explained: "Rosabelle, sweet Rosabelle, BELIEVE! Spare no time or money to undo the attitude of doubt I had on earth. Teach the truth to those who've lost the faith, my sweetheart. Tell the world there is no death."

And that is what Bess did. Next day the headline—"Widow, Ill, Communes with Houdini"—showed up all around the world. And on that January 9, Bess made a statement to the *New York World*. She said, "I did not know what words Harry would use. Of course I knew that it would be in code, but, when he said 'believe,' I was surprised."

IV

What could have made Bess act the way she did? How could she be surprised to hear from Ford things she had told the press in interviews or given to be published in a book? What made her think the word "believe" was more than something Reverend Ford had just made up to make a point and publicize himself?

Was she unbalanced? After three decades in Houdini's shadow, was the light too much? Her health was always "fragile." What did "fragile" mean? They say she loved champagne. And in the latter years, when "health" prevented her from working in the show with Harry, they say she often sat backstage and sipped.

There was a darker possibility. When the insurance money started to run low, and she had sold Houdini's props, had Ford offered Bess publicity and profits from a lecture tour they'd make to "spread the good word" of life after death?

That's what the press thought, not surprisingly. Almost overnight the headlines changed: "Houdini Message a Big Hoax!" they said. Investigative journalists obtained a copy of the letter Ford had sent two days before the seance, in which he claimed to have received the "code words" from his "guide." This, they said, was evidence that Bess and Ford had hatched the plot together. Ford was accused of fraud and brought to trial by his own congregation. He was not convicted, but the cloud of doubt remained.

Bess never spoke to Reverend Ford again. She disavowed the message: "I was ill, both physically and mentally. Such was my eagerness that mediums were able to prey upon my mind, make me believe, and say things that would bring my husband shame."

V

Bess kept a candle burning for ten years in her apartment by a picture of Houdini. And each year on Halloween she took that candle to a seance, hopeful.

In October 1936, high on the famous Knickerbocker Hotel roof in Hollywood, she tried one final time. No handcuffs opened, and no trumpet spoke. No message wrote itself upon the slate. No table rose. No tambourine stood up and danced.

Bess made a little speech: "I do not think that Harry will come back to me or anyone. I think the dead don't speak. I now regretfully turn out the light. This is the end, Harry," she said. "Good night!" And she blew the candle out.

that needs to sum things up, all you need to know now is that you're in our tent, so its okay, and the side show ain't dead. That's for damn sure. PENN does a few moves, and ends with both torches being put out. PENN No, no, no. Not yet, creeps. That was just the upper palate. I'd still like to burn my tongue. Now I realize this is a legitimate, Broadway theatre, kind of a swanky, Jackie Mason-type joint, and you might not have been expecting this kind of hurricane-hell-driver jive out of us. And I just want to tell you if that half a knife blade that hooks over my middle finger with the load compartment that drips out the red paint, or Teller putting the needles in his mouth, or being underwater, or that last thing took you by surprise and up- tightened you a little bit, this next thing will probably make you puke your guts out. PENN does a tongue- transfer. Someone in the audience invariably moans. PENN What the hell are you complaining about? PENN retains a flame in his mouth. TELLER lights a cigarette from the flame. PENN puts out the last torch. TELLER hands PENN a cigarette. PENN lights it from the candle. PENN and TELLER are just in candlelight. PENN I've got a couple of announcements to make. First of all, I hope New Yorkers are hip enough to realize how many people it takes to put on a show like this, but theres a lot of people thanked in your program, and they all deserve it. I want to thank Cathy, our Stage Manager, and her whole posse throughout the theatre that really make the show go on. I want to thank Richard, Tom, and Steve our producers, Artie our Director, Cindy our manager. And Marc Garland, who's my best buddy from high school, and Marc's been with us since way before the beginning. You don't even get to see him except for like a minute during Mofo, and the water tank, but he's really important. He handles all the props. He actually makes all the balloon animals, so at least he has something to fall back on. And he also stacks all our decks of cards, which is more important than you've hopefully realized. We've been extended, obviously, or you'd be watching a different show. But we're going to close here March 20th, then we really have to leave and do our movie, Penn & Teller Get Killed. We're hoping its not a documentary. And wed like some people in here the next month, so if you liked the show at all, and got an extra minute and could yap about it to your friends, wed sure appreciate it. I notice theres quite a few kids here tonight. Kids, I don't want to insult you. I don't think you're stupid, but I've got to say this so try to forgive me in advance, and that is to say the stuff we do here on stage is very dangerous, you shouldn't try any of it and you shouldn't even smoke cigarettes unless you want to look cool. My name is Penn Jillette. This is my partner, Teller. Thanks. TELLER blows out the candle. PENN and TELLER stand and bow. They switch sides and bow again. They exit up the aisles of the theatre and out the front door, where they sell T-shirts, videos, records, hats, posters, etc.

THE END

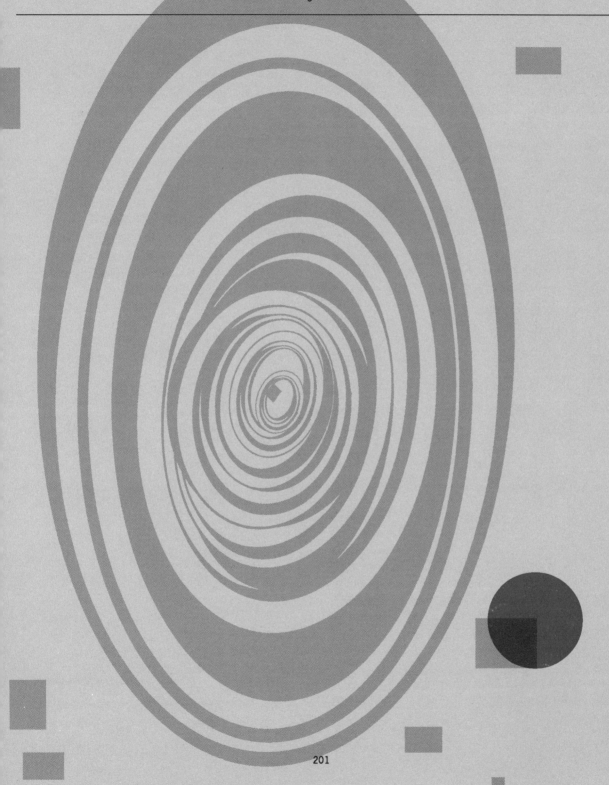

PLUGS

1. For information about joining a secret society of pranksters, misfits, and Penn & Teller fans, send a self-addressed, stamped envelope to:

    > TELLER & PENN
    > Box 1196
    > New York, NY 10185-0010

    The same envelope will get you, whether you want it or not, the lowdown on how to get your own copy of Penn & Teller's video version of *Cruel Tricks for Dear Friends*, a tape that enables you to use your video recorder as a tool for playing seven all-new, mean-spirited practical jokes on your unsuspecting guests.

2. Got a modem? Call MOFO EX MACHINA, the bitchin'est BBS in the jungle. Just call 212-764-3834, hit ENTER twice, and type the password MOFO (300 or 1200 baud, 8 bits, 1 stop, no parity).

PENN & TELLER THANK

(in absolutely no order)

Dave Brody, for making roaches and snakes pose; Marc Garland, for wrangling the props; Annette Kirszrot, for sculpting the scleral shells; Le Madeleine (bistro, bar, and garden restaurant), for the loan of its existential, *entre deux guerres* courtyard; T. Gene Hatcher, for artistic editing on Teller's stories; Frank Zappa's "Freak Out," for getting Penn to read Kafka; Lou Reed's song titles, for introducing Penn, and consequently Teller, to Delmore Schwartz's work; Eddie Gorodetsky, for being a truly funny man and for suggesting the book's title; Joe Teller, for inspiration on the front cover lettering; James Randi, for exemplary morality and magic; Camille Sweeney, for making the incomprehensible charts; Cindy Valk, for making sure P & T look good; two moms, two dads, and six other relatives for lending their names to fictional authors and characters; D. G. Rosenbaum for inspiring two separate characters in two separate stories; all the talented and ingenious posse at Villard, especially Dennis Dwyer, the Henry Ford of swindlers, who figured out how to mass-produce gimmicked books, and Leta Evanthes, for orchestrating the production; Tony Loew, for his elegant portraits of awful things; Bob Bull, for adding the inside of his head to the inside of our heads and smearing it beautifully on the pages; Danny Cassano, for having dinner with Penn; Peter Gethers, our boss, for being ballsy, patient, and imaginative; Esther Newberg, for holding on to the serial rights.

ABOUT THE AUTHORS

1948   Teller

1955   Penn Jillette

1975–81   "Asparagus Valley Cultural Society" (Philadelphia, San Francisco)

1981–84   "Penn & Teller" (Baltimore, Minneapolis, Los Angeles) PBS-TV special, two Emmys and International Golden Rose Award

1985–87   Off-Broadway, Westside Arts, Obie Award, *Late Night with David Letterman, NBC's Saturday Night Live,* Houdini Special, Emmys, MTV, "Comic Relief," "Invisible Thread"

1987–89   Broadway, home video (*Cruel Tricks for Dear Friends*) using video recorder for pranks; writing, shooting, and release of *Penn & Teller Get Killed,* an Arthur Penn film; this book.